$\dfrac{x \times x}{\ddot{\smile}}$

THE
TURMERIC
TRAIL

ALSO BY RAGHAVAN IYER

Betty Crocker's® Indian Home Cooking

Raghavan Iyer

THE TURMERIC TRAIL

Recipes and Memories
from an Indian Childhood

St. Martin's Press
New York

www.stmartins.com

Black-and-white photography in text courtesy of Raghavan Iyer, except for *Raghavan Iyer with his Amma and sister Lali* (page 241) by Tom Berthiaume.

Color insert food photography copyright © 2002 by Mette Nielsen. Photography assisted by Kevin Hedden. Food styling by Robin Krause.

Book design by Kathryn Parise
Map by Virginia Norey

LIBRARY OF CONGRESS CATALOGING-IN-PUBLICATION DATA
Iyer, Raghavan.
The turmeric trail : recipes and memories from an Indian childhood / Raghavan Iyer.—1st ed.
p. cm.
Includes bibliographical references and index.
ISBN 0-312-27682-6
1. Cookery, India. I. Title.

TX724.5.I4 I94 2002
641.5954—dc21

2001057898

First Edition: June 2002

10 9 8 7 6 5 4 3 2 1

This book I dedicate to the departed souls of
my grandmother, Akka,
her son and my father, Appa,
and my business partner and friend, Nancy Herman.

I am truly blessed with three mothers:
Amma, who gave birth to me;
Lali, my physician sister who delivered me
and is responsible for many of my successes;
and Mom (Esther Erickson), who gave me a place in her heart
in a foreign land called the United States.
I offer this book to you all with utmost respect and gratitude.

❧ CONTENTS

✾ ACKNOWLEDGMENTS

The recipe for a book's success is peppered with jaggery-sweet love and tamarind-sour heartache. Simmer the two with heated passion and you get *The Turmeric Trail: Recipes and Memories from an Indian Childhood*.

Begin by collecting in a large memory bank valuable stories, both happy and sad, and a battalion of six siblings: Lali, Vishu, Shankar, Mathangi, Bhaskar, and Ravi. Mix in their wives, husband, and children for added richness.

Mull over the idea of putting them together in a cookbook spiced with memoirs and vignettes. Bring in Jane Dystel, tenacious, compassionate, and one of America's most well-respected literary agents, who will work with you to shape a proposal that is worth bidding on.

Lavishly sprinkle into the mix a kindhearted and very talented editor, Marian Lizzi from St. Martin's Press, a well-entrenched publishing house in Manhattan (called Bombay of the West by us Mumbaiites).

Start the oftentimes lonely process of testing recipes in your home kitchen. Test and retest them to make sure they actually work! Rely on friends like Ann Nelson and Rebecca Dalton (especially for her endless retesting of the idlis recipe to get it just right) when you need an outsider's educated viewpoint.

Fold in a group of close male friends consisting of Jiten Gori, Molu (aka

R. J. Singh), Benny Martin, Ryan Willis, and Dr. Jeff Mandel (a physician in this group can be very helpful), whom you can rely on to follow (for the most part) your directions on making the recipes during numerous Boys' Night sessions (enough fodder for a new book).

Rely on the expert advice of close friends like Mary Small and Beth Dooley, who are true "word wizards."

If need be, consult daily with your close friends Paulette Mitchell and Mary Evans, colleagues in this cookbook world who can commiserate with you when things don't go right but also can levitate the fermented writing process with juicy tidbits of gossip.

But above all, have a loving, comforting, and warmhearted partner of nineteen years like Terry Erickson who can be there for you every step of the way.

When the book is close to completion, to lovingly agitate the now-calm environment, bring in two-year-old Robert, who will come into your life as your newly adopted son and bring you unknown joy laced with a heavy dose of utter chaos.

Now gently fold in talented food photographers Mette Nielsen and Kevin Hedden and food stylist Robin Krause, respected for their unending passion and art.

Sprinkle into the blend gifted Mara Lurie, production editor at St. Martin's Press, and Julie Mente, editorial assistant, to bind the project together. Place all of these elements into a preheated printing press and watch the well-designed pages come together to make a spicy, sweet, tart, hot, and nutty book.

PREFACE:
Akka's Journey

My turmeric trail of memories is spiced with the strength and sadness of my family's story. At the heart of it all is Alamelu, my grandmother whom we called Akka, born in 1897 in the priestly community of Chidambaram in southeastern India once upon a time. . . .

Alamelu kicked the old, stonewashed, and frayed saree off her tiny body, which was already swathed in a nine-yard saree. It was a hot night and her sleep was far from peaceful. Even the thin saree that acted as a sheet was unbearably heavy. She sat up with her short legs stretched in front of her; her protruding belly made it difficult to see her diminutive toes. She stared around the tiny room with exposed drab gray stone walls, wiping the pearls of sweat off her brow. She lifted herself off the chattayee with great difficulty, the flimsy hand-woven mat fashioned from thin bamboo offering no cushioning from the concrete floor. Her husband, Sunderasan, was still asleep, his piglike snoring making his hairy stomach shake in synchronous harmony. She waddled over to the back of the house and out the door to the outhouse, which was really a three-walled roofless edifice. The ice-cold water that she poured over her dark, thick hair shook off all sleep from her pint-sized but pregnant frame as it seeped through the many layers of her well-worn saree. She reached under her coffin-heavy fabric and scrubbed herself clean with abrasive coconut husk dipped in a paste of red soil and water. She draped a clean saree over her wet one as she peeled away the soaked layers, careful never to expose her swollen nakedness.

She walked barefoot over to the well, and lifted a brass stockpot tethered to a rope. She dropped it into the well and heard the familiar thud as it made contact with the water's surface. Gently maneuvering the rope, she dunked the pot into the clear water and bent over to pull up the rope and pot. Her reflection stared back at her, crystal clear against the early morning's dusky rays. She looked much older than her fifteen years, her face harried with the harshness of the daily grind.

She carried the water back against her hip and entered the kitchen filled with the aromas of roasted mustard seed and red chilies that still hung in the air from last night. She walked over to the opposite corner from the kitchen and lit the oil lamp that illuminated the small statues of Nataraja and his lingam, then poured a teaspoonful of holy water from the silver udruni over his phallic symbol of fertility. She reached for the box of kunkuvam and, with forefinger and thumb, pinched a generous amount of the red powder and applied it to the parting in her hair. She dipped her ring finger into the snake-shaped container and shaped the familiar bindi on her forehead between her eyes, a round and painful reminder of her marriage to Him. She knelt down with great difficulty in front of Nataraja and bent over to kiss the floor while touching the deity's feet for blessings on her way down.

She crawled across the floor on all fours toward the kitchen, unable to stand up as the sharp pain tore through her insides. When the labor wave subsided, she prodded the pile of wood that she had set a match to before she went outside to bathe. She blew gently into the warm heap to fan the flames that rose above a square of four large red bricks. She placed the pot of water she carried from the well atop the bricks to boil so there would be hot water for her husband and mother-in-law for bathing.

She saw Him stir from his sleep and her fingers shook with anxious dread, afraid that the water would not be hot enough to warm his body, fearful of the eye-tearing sharp tug on her hair she had to endure so often by her mother-in-law's okra-rough hands because her child body, pregnant for the first time, was not swift enough to do the chores.

She felt the water, warm and comforting, just like her Amma's maternal love that she craved. Her wedding day seemed so long ago, twenty-four hours after her eighth birthday. She was dressed up in a bright red pavadai laced with gold-green silk threads. Her hands and feet smeared with freshly ground paste made from turmeric root and rinsed in milk shined golden yellow, enhancing her soft tamarind-brown skin, offering the neighboring women a golden backdrop to the green mango-colored mehendi, lacy henna patterns they drew with dried twigs.

On her wedding day, she heard the heart-thumping mridangam drum keeping beat with the baleful piercing emanating from the nadaswaram (a long horn). She felt important, as this was her moment. Her Amma, Kamakshi, had informed her, between uncontrollable sobs, that in spite of her misgivings, she was being married off to her cousin Sunderasan, succumbing to her husband's demands that were greased with financial promises. Sunderasan was after all *the* vakhil gumasta (law clerk) to the only lawyer in town. A gumasta who wielded more power than the lawyer himself, a man who permitted legal access only to those whom he could benefit from, a man whose face showed the scars from being afflicted with smallpox as a young boy, a man fifteen years older than the child bride of eight.

At the ceremony, he stood gangly thin across from her with the gold mangalsutram (an amulet worn by married women) dangling from a turmeric-stained rope. She sat on her father's lap, head bent, staring at her soon-to-be-husband's gnarled, taro-root feet, waiting for the lasso rope to descend over her head and around her flimsy neck. The Sanskrit shlokas (sacred verses) of the vaadiya (Brahmin priest) hummed in her ears and she placed her right hand in her husband's as he led her in a circle around Agni, the god of fire, a god ignited with dried dung cakes smoldering in shame surrounded by fertile coconuts in husks that were rubbed with ground turmeric, and baby bananas poked with sandalwood incense sticks that glowed on betel nut leaves. The saptapadi (seven steps)* ended after the seventh round—and so did her childhood innocence.

She stayed in her birth home for another two years, now the property of Sunderasan, learning from her amma the dutiful chores that would be expected of her as a wife. She watched as Kamakshi roasted yellow split peas, red chilies, and coriander seed along with other whole spices in a lightly greased skillet over a wood-fueled fire. She became skilled at grinding the soaked rice and udhtham paruppu (urad dal) separately in a kaloral, a giant, heavy-stoned mortar and pestle that she cupped her thighs around, her arms aching with the incessant hard work. Preparing idlis, dosais, sevai, and kozhakuttais became second nature, dumplings and crepes that she could now whip up with programmed speed.

One morning, around Alamelu's tenth year of life, Kamakshi shook her

*The saptapadi is a symbolic walk around the fire seven times. (Sometimes it's seven steps.)

awake from deep sleep. Her body ached and she felt a sticky wetness between her dough-soft thighs. Somehow Amma knew what had happened as she led her to the outhouse and bathed her gently, feeding her bananas in sugared milk, explaining the arrival of bloodstained womanhood. Kamakshi's heart sank. The time had come for her daughter to wear a nine-yard saree, a single piece of fabric that would suffocate her childhood and force it to come up for air as a mature ten-year-old woman who now belonged to her husband and his family.

Alamelu was led into her husband's house to assume a wifely role that would prove to be painfully pitiful, riddled with merciless beatings, verbal abuse, and total control over her body. The following day her chores began, the responsibility of making all the meals burdened her frail shoulders while her mother-in-law scrutinized her every move, perched on the swing bench that hung from the room's high ceiling. Food was abundant in her husband's house, but Alamelu soon found out that hers would be rationed. She prepared robust flavored pigeon peas with pumpkin and coconut-smothered rice to accompany a root vegetable stew with chilies and fresh karhi leaves, and served them all piping hot on lotus leaves, hand threaded in multiples of three to fashion a dinner plate. When they were done eating, her mother-in law, Dharmambal, doled out small portions of the meal in the medium-holed wicker moram, dustpan-shaped, normally used for winnowing rice and wheat, as Alamelu learned to eat carefully without losing any of the grains through the holes.

For three days each month, as was customary among women, Alamelu could not come into contact with anyone. She lived next to the outhouse in a shack, mercifully grateful for the quiet solitude the loss of her eggs offered her. And then one month she missed her forced imprisonment. Soon her hunger increased, but the rationed portions of shaadum, sambhar, and water-thin buttermilk remained constant, as her tiny belly swelled with alarming speed. The water over the fire threatened to boil over, and she was jolted back into reality from her past as the baby kicked its legs in its limited home within her. She smiled for the first time since she left her Amma's house, and with tender compassion she rubbed her belly, comforting her soon-to-arrive firstborn, her son, my father.

Three more sons were born to Alamelu in between the daily doses of tight slaps and hurtful words. Her firstborn doted on her, bearing equal physical abuse from a useless father and spiteful grandmother. Soon all four sons became exposed to the ravages of smallpox, with the two middle ones, within months, succumbing to the illness. Alamelu's revulsion for her husband and mother-in-law fueled her to protect her two remaining sons. She needed physical strength to nurture herself and her children's growing bodies, fortitude she gathered by skimming off the cream that floated to the top each morning she boiled milk in a jodhtalay, a brass drum that rested on the wood-fueled fire, stirring it constantly to prevent the milk from scorching. The coffee that she brewed each morning by roasting and grinding the beans for Him and his mother was taboo to her and the children. She quickly learned to pilfer handfuls of the more accessible coriander seed when she was not being watched, wrapping it in her saree pullow. She roasted the seed, dark and nutty, and pounded it. She placed the grounds in the digakshin and poured hot water over it. She thinned the dark brew that filtered into the lower container with additional hot water as she and her two sons sipped it, the liquid making its way through their bodies, providing them with a secret, coffee-like comfort.

As her oldest son Ramachandran grew, so did his penchant for reading and writing. The world unveiled itself to him through books read in the light of a small oil lamp, the light oftentimes pinched dark by his grandmother, who thought it a waste of valuable oil. He found refuge at the home of the only doctor in town, a kind man who provided him with ample light and solace blended with the paternal affection that he craved. Once he graduated from high school, and when he realized he would never be given the opportunity to further his educational hopes and dreams, he fled to the large city of Bombay with two rupees and the clothing on his back, leaving his mother and brother behind to continue bearing the abuse until the day he could afford to send for them, away from the town of Chidambaram.

This was what Alamelu waited for, the day when she collected her youngest son, and in the still of the night slipped out of her penitentiary with a tattered saree around her body, no jewelry, no bindi, devoid of any reminders of her wedded status. They walked by Chidambaram's stone-carved, sprawling temple built as a tribute to Nataraja, the dancing reincarnation of Shiva, the destroyer of evil. She remembered the Tuesdays, once a month, when she was forced to smear her face, hands, and feet with turmeric paste, gathering in her yellowed arms mango leaves, coconuts, and baby bananas as she circled one hundred times Nataraja's larger-than-life golden statue whose left leg was raised over the right in his Ananda Tandam pose, the blissful dance to destroy sin, all for the eternal hope of maintaining her suhagini status, a married state that judged her worth in that Brahmin-kissed town.

The bustling metropolis of Bombay and the one-room studio apartment was now home to her and her two sons. Ramachandran, the oldest, had secured a job with the Indian Navy and soon married Gangabai, a wheat-skinned beauty who "decided his choice" among many marriage proposals.

Their children came, and Alamelu cherished them all with unconditional love, never once raising her voice or hand toward them during occasions of childhood discipline, painful reminders of her own humiliation squelched within her belly, which was now draped by colorful sarees her son provided.

In 1958, her oldest grandson was being readied for his poonal, a thread ceremony that heralded his foray into the Brahmin's world of adulthood amid great fanfare and religiosity. There was a knock on the door and He stood at the doorstep, frail and ugly, hoping to make peace with lost family and grandchildren's comforting attention. Alamelu's eyes turned the shade of overly toasted coriander seed, her years of misery now reflected back from His pock-filled face with sickening brutality. He spent a few days in that one-room apartment, as she busied herself with her grandson's poonal arrangements. She never spoke to Him and maintained adequate distance. He returned to Chidambaram once the poonal ceremonies were over, defeated, his presence never acknowledged by the wife and children he had treated so cruelly. He died in 1959, burning alone on his ghee-laden funeral pyre.

Ramachandran and Gangabai for one last time produced a son in 1961, a chubby boy whose birth brought great joy to the Iyer household. The father took great pride in seeing his eldest daughter, now a doctor, bring his youngest child into the sultry world. Alamelu held me close to her ample bosom, kissing my full cheeks, her eyes brimming with tears of joy laced with sorrow because I was the unfortunate one, the first child born to my father after my grandfather's death reincarnated for the sole purpose of rectifying her dead husband's hateful existence. I was her favorite, one who could never do any wrong because I was unknowingly roped into her burning past.

Alamelu, whom we all called Akka—older sister, a name we picked up from our great-aunt—spent the rest of her life with us. She seasoned her stews, vegetables, noodles, and our lives with her fortitude, independent spirit, and unabashed opinions, which she had finally learned to share out loud after years of quiet servitude.

As you turn these pages, hold my hand along my turmeric-brick road, yellowed with ageless stories, perfumed with spicy aromas, and peppered with succulent dishes. Savor it all!

Akka

THE
TURMERIC
TRAIL

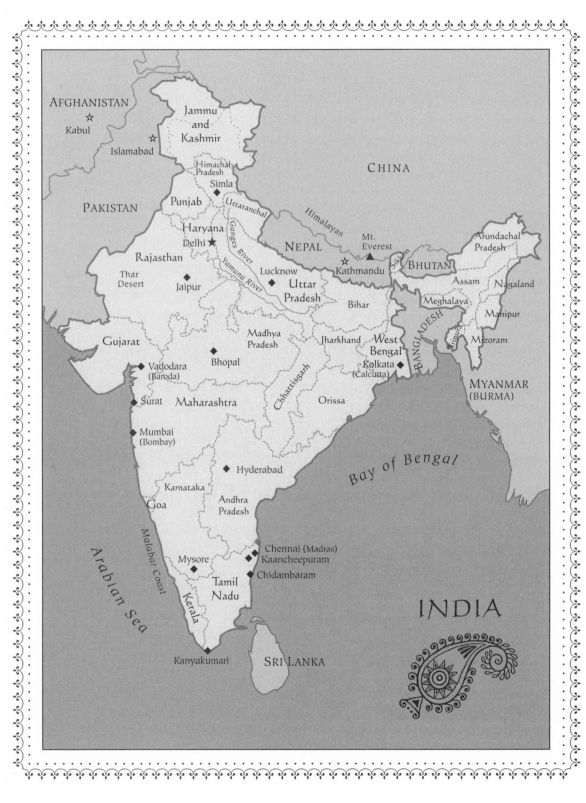

INTRODUCTION:
Indian Cooking, North and South

I consider myself very lucky to have been born and raised in a large, bustling metropolis like Mumbai (Bombay). This western port city is home to many of India's millions, and the Brahmin, southern Indian heritage of my family roots comingle harmoniously with multiregional heritages of other inhabitants.

During my early years I thrived on typical Tamilian foods that reflected southern India's reliance on rice, lentils, coconut, chilies, and black mustard seed. Idlis (steamed cakes), dosais (lacy crepes), sambhar (spicy stews), and rasam (spiced tamarind broth) were staples in my Amma's kitchen. The roasted, nutty, and spicy flavors of the south peppered our foods, which were reflective of our community's priestly teachings. Meats, fish, poultry, and eggs were forbidden from our home, but milk, yogurt, and butter, considered gifts from the holy cow, coated our lacto-vegetarian palates.

As I grew older, especially during my early school years, I became aware of the richness of foods from my friends' cultures, their heritages painting a different culinary picture than mine. This was just the beginning of my induction into a world that now encompassed such diverse spices and flavorings as cloves, cinnamon, garlic, fenugreek leaves, and mango powder—all crucial to classic north Indian fare. Visits to northern Indian restaurants and my friends' homes in Mumbai introduced me to hot, buttery naans (clay-oven breads), creamy spinach sauces studded with paneer (homemade cheese), and aromatic pulaos (delicately spiced basmati rice). The startling differences in their usage of herbs, spices, and legumes compared to south India's were an eye opener.

Closer to home, I fell in love with my city's street foods the moment I sampled them. They were taboo, especially during Mumbai's virulent monsoons. But on occasion when my medic sister's admonitions were ignored, I discovered the unusual combination of ingredients in dishes like Sev Batata Pooris (page 21), Ragada Patties (page 24), and Paav Bhaaji (page 36) that made me crave them time and again. Soon I was thrown into the allure of unripe mango, crispy garbanzo-bean-flour noodles, hot chilies, and cilantro chutney mellowed with tart and sweet tamarind date chutney. I found comfort in Falooda (page 42), Mumbai's signature beverage of rose-flavored milk, ice cream, and soft vermicelli, and Pista-Baadam Paal (page 44), steamed milk perfumed with pistachios, almonds, and sugar. These were foods that originated in the pans, woks, and bowls of street vendors, and were rarely found in our home kitchens. Their proper place was on Mumbai's beaches and street corners, made by non-Brahmins (as my grandmother Akka often reminded me) to appease a large segment of the population that did not have wives, mothers, and sisters who could cook for them. But of course they appealed to my rebellious senses and also to the millions of family-blessed workers who needed that "extra energy boost" between teatime and a late dinner hour. Yes, indeed, there was a difference between street foods and home foods, but I loved them both equally, showering each with my unconditional love and attention as a father would his two offspring. So I've included recipes for street foods and home foods in this book, as well as specialties from the north and south of India.

Herbs, Spices, and Legumes
In the Indian Pantry

Spices, herbs, and legumes form the backbone of Indian cuisine. This mini-glossary will provide you with a thumbnail description of the ones I have used along the Turmeric Trail.

A NOTE ABOUT SPICES

Because we extract multiple flavors from the seed of any given spice, whole spices play a very prominent role in Indian cooking. Whenever possible, purchase spices in small quantities in their seed form. When recipes call for ground spices, grind the seed in either a coffee grinder (reserved for spices only) or with a mortar and pestle, just before adding it to the recipe. With this method the inherent oils in the spice are released with optimum aroma and flavor.

Store the spices in an airtight jar at room temperature. That convenient shelf above the stove is not a good idea, as the moisture and heat will ruin them very quickly. Refrigeration is also not recommended, because the dampness will alter the spices' qualities and flavors.

I use spices as a painter uses his or her palette of colors: to create subtleties in texture, appearance and, in this case, flavor. Because each spice has a unique taste, true substitutions never exist. Oftentimes I recommend not including a spice if it is unavailable, but other times I urge you to use an alternative that may not necessarily showcase the dish's classic flavors but nonetheless is a satisfying rendition of the original. My one piece of advice, when it comes to spices, is this: Never be afraid of them. Once you get to know them through every possible sense, let your imagination lead you to explore them like never before.

A Note About Legumes (Lentils, Beans, and Peas)

My students and readers are always amazed when I unveil India's wide world of legumes. Sixty varieties of beans, peas, and lentils make up the legume family in India. Quite a few of the common dry varieties are available in natural food stores and large supermarkets. You will need to make a trip to your nearest Indian grocery store or even visit the Web sites recommended at the end of this book, for some of the harder to find varieties.

Dal is a term used generically to mean any lentil-based dish. It also is used to differentiate between a whole lentil and one that has been split and hulled (the skin removed). Whole black lentils are called sabud urad, but the split and hulled ones are referred to as urad dal. Every household in India, whether vegetarian or nonvegetarian, serves a dal of one kind or the other at every meal. It is an inexpensive way of eating, and its nutritional value is exceptional.

Dried legumes are always sorted for stones and other foreign objects before use. They are usually shipped in large gunnysacks, and dust particles are a natural attraction to them. It is still common practice for women to sit on the floor during quiet afternoons, when they are "resting" between preparing meals and other household chores, with a large platter full of grains, sorting them for illegal aliens. In recipes that call for rinsing, place the legumes in a bowl and cover with water. With your fingers, gently wash the grains for ten to twenty seconds, then drain. Repeat five or six times until the water in the bowl is clear.

Dried beans, whole lentils, and peas require soaking for a few hours prior to cooking. This expedites their cooking times. Discard the soaking liquid and cook the legumes in fresh water because some of the carbon dioxide–forming sugar leaches into the soaking liquid. This is one of the reasons that spices like turmeric, gingerroot, asafetida, and bishop's-weed, considered helpful in the digestion of legumes, are added to many preparations that contain them.

Legumes are best stored in a cool, dry spot outside the refrigerator. They have a very long shelf life, but if you are concerned about attracting bugs, by all means refrigerate or even freeze them.

HERBS, SPICES, AND LEGUMES USED IN MY GRANDMOTHER AND MOTHER'S KITCHEN

Asafetida (peringayam/hing): This is a very strong-smelling spice derived from a fennel-like plant. The hardened sap, dark chocolate in color, is sold in brick form in Indian grocery stores. Purists buy the chunky version and grate it as needed. The powdered version (which may contain traces of ground turmeric for color) is more widely available in natural food stores. Hing is used in small quantities to alleviate the discomfort from digesting legumes. The aroma does not offer any clue to the onion-garlic flavor of this spice. Store it tightly wrapped or in a glass jar to prevent its aroma permeating its storage area.

Black mustard seed (kadagu/rai): This variety is slightly stronger than the more commonly available yellow kind, the source of ground mustard used in American kitchens. Some of the seeds are dark brown. South Indian cooks pop them in hot oil, like popcorn, to extract an unusually sweet and nutty flavor that is crucial to this region's foods. Mustard oil, which is extracted from the seed, is highly pungent and flavors almost every dish in eastern India, especially in the cuisine of West Bengal (Calcutta being its most prominent city).

Black peppercorns (molaghu/kala mir): The world's best peppercorns are grown in Malabar in southern India. Their potent flavors and pungent aromas provide crucial subtleties to blends from this region.

Black-eyed peas (lobhia): These tiny, comma-shaped, off-white legumes with a black dot in the belly center are widely available in supermarkets, dried, frozen, or in cans. See Shundal (page 104) for cooking instructions.

Cardamom (yelaika/elaichi): Green cardamom pods are widely used in Indian desserts. The seeds are often removed from the pods before use. (The pods are discarded.) They are highly aromatic and menthol-like and are considered a powerful digestive and breath freshener. (When sun-bleached, they turn white, though their flavor remains the same.) Black cardamom pods resemble shriveled prunes and have a very smoky flavor. They are never used in desserts but do flavor many north Indian savory recipes.

Chili peppers, dried (red) and fresh (green) (shepa and pacche molagha/lal aur hara mirchi): Members of the capsicum family, the chilies used in India are the Thai (small and thin like the eyes of a bird) or cayenne (long and curvaceous) variety. The thickness of a pepper is a benchmark of its spiciness—the thinner ones are more potent than thick ones. The chemical capsaicin, harbored in the pepper's vein, is a major source of pleasure for endorphin-rush seekers. If you remove the pepper's vein and seeds, the heat level is reduced, but this is never done in Indian kitchens. Contrasting chilies with ingredients like bread, rice, or yogurt or other dairy products reduces their sharpness and provides crucial balance in many recipes. Ground red pepper is derived from sun-dried red cayenne chilies.

Cilantro (kothamalli/taza dhania): The leaves of this strong-smelling and flavorful plant of the parsley family, bearing close resemblance to Italian parsley, are also known as Chinese parsley or coriander leaves. It is widely available in supermarkets across the country. Sold in flat-leafed bunches, cilantro can be stored for a week in the refrigerator. When you purchase a bunch, trim off and discard the bottom two inches and rinse under cold water. Transfer the leaves to a salad spinner and spin the moisture out completely. If you don't have a spinner, place the washed leaves in a few layers of paper towels, fold the towels into a roll, and gently squeeze to absorb the moisture. Transfer the washed leaves to a zip-lock bag and seal shut by squeezing the air completely out of the bag.

Coconut (thénga/nariyal): South Indian cooking without coconut is like a motherless child: empty, discomforting, and very sad! Coconuts (and there are many varieties) are used to represent marital harmony, fertility, and even the souls of departed loved ones. Their abrasive husks are often saved for scrubbing pots and pans, and also make their way into the shower as a washcloth. The thick white meat is used for daily cooking. Choose one that has dry eyes (the three indentations on the end of the coconut that is attached to the palm tree). Shake the coconut to hear its water slosh around. If you hear silence, chances are the meat inside is rotten. Rinse the shell under water. Hold the coconut in one hand, and with a hammer or meat pounder, gently but firmly tap the coconut around its midsection. As soon as the shell cracks open, the water inside will gush out (so make sure you have a small bowl to catch the sweet off-white liquid). With a sharp paring knife, score the meat in large pieces. Gently pry out the pieces from the shell with a firm butter knife. Peel off the thin dark brown skin and place the meat in a food processor. Pulse it into small shreds. A medium coconut will yield about 2 to 3 cups of shredded meat. You can freeze the unused portion for 2 months. Asian grocery stores stock freshly shredded coconut meat in their freezers.

Dried, unsweetened shredded coconut (sometimes sold as powder) is also available in supermarkets and natural food stores. One half cup of dried, unsweetened is comparable to 1 cup of freshly shredded. I often soak ¾ cup of dried, unsweetened coconut in ¼ cup of warm milk for that freshly shredded taste. If you are desperate, purchase sweetened shredded coconut and soak it in hot water, then drain. Repeat three or four times to get rid of as much sugar as possible. In India, we use a coconut grater (a barbaric-looking implement) to get the meat from the shell without any hassles. The emptied shell is often used as a scoop for various tasks.

Coriander seed (kotamalli varai/dhania): When cilantro is allowed to seed, it produces tiny, yellowish-brown seeds that smell slightly citric. Their flavor does not resemble, in any way, that of cilantro.

Cumin seed (jeerai/zeera): They have a deep "earthy" flavor, robust and slightly citrusy. I use the common, grayish-brown cumin, similar in appearance to caraway. The seeds are nutty and highly aromatic. This variety is well known in the United States because of its use in Mexican cooking.

Fenugreek seed (mendhium/méthi): These dark brown seeds from the highly perfumed plant have a complex, bitter flavor. The leaves of the plant are used extensively in foods of northern India.

Gingerroot (inji/adrak): This gnarly looking bulbous root is widely available in all supermarkets. Choose ones that are firm to the touch. Snap off a piece and store it in the refrigerator for up to three weeks. If the skin is clean and does not look dried or fungus-ridden, I do not bother peeling it. Do not freeze the root because it gets extremely waterlogged when thawed, ruining its flavor.

Jaggery (vellum/gur): Sugarcane juice is cooked and dried in clumps to yield unrefined sugar called jaggery. This is cloyingly sweet and provides an earthy, molasses-like flavor to many Indian dishes. You can use firmly packed dark brown sugar as an alternative.

Karhi leaves (kauvapillai/karhi patta): A distant member of the citrus family, this small to midsized leaf is highly aromatic. It is a crucial ingredient in many a south Indian dish. Buy karhi fresh or don't buy it at all. Some Indian grocery stores stock it dried, but the flavor doesn't compare. The fresh leaves will keep in refrigerator for 2 weeks in a zip-lock bag. You can freeze them for a month and use them in recipes without thawing.

Sesame seed (til): This is used extensively in everything from snacks to desserts. These seeds are tiny, tear-shaped, and vanilla ice cream white in appearance when the black skin is discarded. The skin-on variety is crucial to many of south India's religious functions. The white sesame seed's light-colored oil (*nalla yennai*), called unrefined sesame seed oil in natural food stores in the United States, is a must in Tamilian-speaking homes and quite dissimilar to the dark-colored sesame seed oil extracted from toasted seed (used in classic Chinese cooking).

Split and hulled black lentils (udhtham paruppu/urad dal): These lentils are the basis of much south Indian cooking, used in batters of steamed cakes, dumplings, pancakes, and crepes. They are tiny, oval-shaped grains with an off-white color. These lentils are also used as a spice to flavor oils, and when roasted, they are blended with other "traditional" spices to provide an essential nutty flavor.

Split and hulled pigeon peas (torram paruppu/toovar dal): A bastion of south Indian cooking, these brownish-yellow grains are flatter than the yellow split peas. They are sold in Indian grocery stores in two forms: oiled and unoiled. The grains are coated with vegetable oil to mask the sweetness that attracts bugs. The oil is always thoroughly rinsed before use. If you do not expect to use these grains very often, I recommend buying them in this form. I prefer the unoily variety because it doesn't require the extra step of thoroughly rinsing and drying for spice blends that use them after they have been roasted. Refrigerate the oily peas to prevent them from turning rancid.

Tamarind (puli/imli): This fruit of the tamarind tree (with tart, fernlike leaves that are edible) is encased in an olive green pod when fresh. Once they are dried, the shell turns milk chocolate brown and brittle. Throw away the shell and soak the fruit in warm water for about 20 minutes. Loosen the pulp and remove the seeds, which are extremely hard. Squeeze as much of the pulp into the soaked liquid as possible and discard the rest; strain the liquid into a bowl. The strained tamarind liquid provides a sharp, acidic balance to many of south India's curries and chutneys. Dried tamarind pulp is sold as compressed bricks (seedless or with seed) in Indian and other Asian grocery stores. The extracted pulp is also sold in plastic jars as tamarind concentrate. A teaspoon of concentrate usually sours four servings of a dish. The dried brick and the concentrate need not be refrigerated. They will keep for many months.

Turmeric (manjal/haldi): Fresh turmeric root is a rhizome (bulbous root) and an important cousin to gingerroot. It is a staple in Indian homes, especially in the south where it is used in social and religious events. The dried root, when ground, yields a sharp yellow powder that makes its way into many commercial curry powders (a mixture that doesn't exist in classic Indian cuisine; curry, a sauce-based dish, comes from the Tamil word *karhi*, meaning "sauce"). A little amount goes a long way, and the sharp and slightly pungent aroma and flavor from dried root are very different from its sweet-smelling, fresh counterpart.

Yellow split peas (kadalai paruppu/chana dal): These sun-yellow disk-shaped lentils are a cinch to cook in less than 30 minutes. They continue to maintain a nutty-firm texture even when cooked.

OTHER HERBS, SPICES, AND LEGUMES
USED IN MY KITCHEN

Bay leaves (tez patta): Both dried and fresh leaves are available in supermarkets. The dried ones are commonly used in north Indian spice blends, whole as well as dry-roasted and ground. When cooking with whole leaves, remove them from the dish before serving.

Bishop's-weed (ajwain): A wild-growing member of the cumin family in India's western region, this spice has a chemical in it (thyminol) that is also found in thyme. You can use thyme instead, but you will miss bishop's-weed's underlying peppery flavor.

Black salt (kala namak): This pinkish-gray, smoky-tasting, sulfur-smelling compound is mined from stone quarries. The complex-tasting salt is extremely tart and is used to flavor many of India's snacks as well as legume-based preparations from the north because of its flatulence-reducing powers.

Brown lentils/French lentils (sabud masoor dal): These muddy brown, lens-shaped lentils, widely used in French cuisine, are ubiquitous in supermarkets in the United States. This is considered truly humble peasant food in northern India. These are quick-cooking lentils and do not require prior soaking.

Cinnamon stick (dal chini): Sri Lanka and China provide cinnamon to the world. The sticks come from the tree's bark and differ in flavors (the Sri Lankan variety is not as strong as its Chinese cousin). The sticks are used to delicately flavor many of north India's dishes and, when broken into smaller pieces, they make their way into roasted blends, the most common being Garam Masaala (page 206). Whole spices like these are often left in the dish because they continue to infuse it with aromas and tastes. The sticks are not meant to be eaten whole.

Cloves (lavang): These black-colored, nail-shaped dried flower buds pack a strong flavor when ground. Their anesthetic qualities are still used by many a dentist in India (I took solace from clove oil when I was subjected to painful braces during my teenage years).

Fennel seed (saunf): This light green spice has a shape similar to caraway and cumin. The seed is a member of the anise family, with a strong licorice flavor. The bulb is widely used in Italian cooking, but the seed's haunting flavor and inherent sweetness are most prized in dishes from eastern India. I love candy-coated fennel seed—it is a powerful digestive and breath freshener.

Garbanzo beans (kabuli chana): These are by far one of the most popular legumes all across India (they are also called chickpeas in the United States). The flour (besan/gram flour) is made from dried beans and is omnipresent in foods all across India, from appetizers to desserts. These nutty-flavored beans are hard to cook and require soaking overnight. Indian kitchens are equipped with pressure cookers that expedite cooking time. Canned beans are just fine, but rinse and drain off the brine.

Kidney beans (rajmah): Red kidney beans are widely used in north Indian cooking. Punjabi-speaking households in the north take great pride in making one of their tomato-based dishes simply called Rajmah.

Mango powder (amchur): A variety of unripe green mango provides the tart flavor of this spice. Its pulp is cut and sun-dried and then ground into a powder (*aam* meaning "mango," *chur* is "powder"). This sour-tasting spice provides an essential tartness to many of north India's dishes.

Saffron (kesar): Saffron is the orange-yellow stigma of the crocus flower. The stigma is handpicked, and it takes about 4,000 crocus flowers to produce one ounce of saffron. No wonder it is the world's most expensive spice. Whenever friends returned from a trip to any of the Middle Eastern countries, they would always present us with a box of saffron, which was stored in my sister's jewelry box under lock and key. A little goes a long way, so you need only a few threads to aromatically permeate an entire dish. The rich yellow hues are visually appealing. I never buy powdered saffron, as it might be adulterated. We often steep the threads in a warm liquid to unleash the fully perfumed potential.

Split and hulled green lentils (mung dal): These whole green lentils (similar in shape and size to the whole black lentils), when split and hulled, reveal yellow-colored grains that have very short cooking times. In southern India, during the thirteen-day mourning period after a loved one's death, mung dal is used to flavor many dishes, since daily-used lentils like urad dal (split and hulled black lentils) are not allowed in meal preparations.

White poppy seed (khus khus): This variety of poppy seed and its black brother are derived from the opium plant, but don't plan on getting high with this very legal seed, as it is stripped of all the hallucinogenic elements of its parent. The white seed is delicately nutty and lacks the bitterness found in the black seed. It is commonly available in Indian grocery stores.

Whole black lentils (sabud urad): It is well worth your time to make a special trip to the Indian grocery store for these black, oval-shaped, pebble-like lentils. They are popular in northern India, but when they are split and hulled, they are much sought after in southern India too.

Whole green lentils (sabud mung): These tiny dark green lentils, similarly shaped to whole black lentils, are also available in natural food stores and Asian grocery stores. Their cooking time is comparable to that of whole black lentils, about 45 minutes to an hour. When these lentils are soaked and kept in a dark place, they produce tender sprouts, offering yet another deliciously nutritious resource to India's vegetarians.

Baahar Ka Khaana
Street Foods of Mumbai

Meetha Chutney
Sweet and Sour Condiment

Mirchi Chutney
Green Chilies Condiment

Paani Pooris
Crispy Hollowed Breads with Two
Chutneys

Dahi Batata Pooris
Crispy Hollowed Breads with Mung Beans

Sev Batata Pooris
Crispy Flat Breads with Potato, Mango,
and Noodles

Gilla Bhel
Puffed Rice with Two Chutneys

Sukha Bhel
Puffed Rice with Green Mango

Ragada Patties
Breaded Potato Shells with Yellow Peas

Kaanda Pakodi
Onion Fritters

Seekh Kebabs
Grilled Lamb on Skewers

Subzi Kebabs
Assorted Vegetable Cutlets

Dahi Vadaas
Lentil Croquettes in Yogurt Sauce

Vadaa Paav
Garlic Potato Sandwiches

Chaat
Spicy Sprouted Beans with Yogurt

Paav Bhaaji
Vegetable Pâté with Griddle Bread

Mumbai Samosas
Seasoned Vegetables in Crispy Wrapper

Chana Bhatura
Garbanzo Bean Stew with Puffy Bread

Falooda Kulfi
Cellophane Noodles with Rose Syrup and
Ice Cream

Adrak Chai
Ginger-Spiked Milk Tea

Pista-Baadam Paal
Steamed Milk with Pistachio Nuts and
Almonds

The Queen's Necklace: Mumbai

Though many Westerners still call it Bombay, Mumbai reclaimed her Indian name on the fiftieth year of independence, August 15, 1997. It is a city for the senses. Locals and tourists alike make their way up to the Hanging Gardens at night to see Mumbai's coastline against the moonlit sky. The jeweled buildings studding the shores of the Arabian Sea bear a strong resemblance to Queen Victoria's diamond necklace. In this bustling metropolis, legacies of the British Raj linger in the majestic Gateway of India and the sprawling Victoria Terminus, while the aromas of ragada patties (golden fried potatoes with hot and sweet sauce) and spicy chai (tea) are pure India.

Just saying the name Mumbai, I think of the forbidden dishes on the street corners, of the smell of frying onions and cumin seeds, of ginger, garlic, and chilies. I can hear my sister, the doctor, admonishing me, "Don't eat the foods on the streets. You have no idea under what hygienic conditions they were all prepared." Still, I'd sneak out to see the budhiya mai (old woman), dressed in her cotton saree, jade green with a red border, draped over her head to protect her from the searing rays of the sun. She resembled my grandmother, stacking her guavas just so. I'd reach into my pocket for a char anna (a quarter of a rupee, barely a penny), and she would pluck that light green ripe guava and, with her shiny pen knife, slice off the end and cut the fruit three-fourths of the way in four quarters, then smother it with salt and potent cayenne pepper to elevate the fruit's intensity.

In the sweltering heat of the early afternoon sun, vendors, men wearing white half-sleeved vests with dhotis, white sheets wrapped around their waists, set up their folding tables and kerosene stoves, lighting them underneath in a heavy kadhai (wok). By late afternoon, the heavy scent of frying and spices thickens the dusky air, tempting hungry office workers heading to their homes, ready to shore themselves up after a long day and keep their appetites at bay until their late suppers at 9 P.M.

No one uses silverware on the streets. It's impractical and unnecessary. Far better to hold this food in your hands or eat it from the bowls fashioned from leaves held together by toothpicks. Once emptied, these "bowls" are fed to the wild dogs, cows, and monkeys that roam Mumbai's streets.

Mumbai draws people from all corners of India and its street food reflects a mosaic of cultures. One vendor from Old Delhi sells chana bhatura, garbanzos simmered in a tart mango sauce with puffy fried breads; the next, a hawker from Madras, is selling vadaa sambhar, split black lentil fritters bathed in a sweet yellow lentil stew sweetened with coconut and spiked with red chilies. Here you'll find vadaa paav, garlic potatoes spiked with green chilies and cilantro, served in a soft bun with garlic and red pepper chutney, or chili-stuffed vadaas. With your mouth on fire, find the toothless sixty-year-old man in a garb similar to that worn by Gandhi ready to offer a cup of freshly brewed chai, Darjeeling tea brewed in whole milk and many spices, to provide soothing relief.

When it is 6 o'clock in the evening in Mumbai and 4:30 in the morning in the United States and you get a craving for a taste of that great food you savored on the street corner near Chowpatty Beach, whip up one of the favorites in this chapter.

Meetha Chutney
Sweet and Sour Condiment

This chutney, along with Mirchi Chutney (page 17), is a staple in many a Mumbai vendor's cart. Since quite a few recipes in this chapter call for this date-tamarind delicacy, you can make a double batch and freeze half of it for future use.

1½ cups water
1 tablespoon tamarind concentrate
1½ cups chopped seedless dates

Pinch of ground red pepper
  (cayenne)
Pinch of salt

1. In a 1-quart saucepan, whisk together the water and tamarind until the tamarind dissolves. Add the remaining ingredients and bring to a boil over medium-high heat. Lower the heat to medium and simmer, uncovered, 4 to 6 minutes or until the mixture is slightly thickened. Remove from the stove and cool 5 to 10 minutes.
2. Transfer the mixture to a blender and puree until smooth. Refrigerate in a glass, plastic, or stainless steel container (the highly acidic tamarind will react with certain metals) for up to a week or freeze for up to a month.

Makes about 1¼ cups

Tamarind concentrate is available in plastic jars in Indian, Latin, Asian, and Middle Eastern grocery stores. The ethnic section of certain supermarkets and natural food stores also stocks this tart ingredient. It is not necessary to store the concentrate in the refrigerator, but refrigeration won't harm it.

Fresh dates are delicious in this recipe. Most of the gourmet varieties from the Middle East contain the pits. The pits are long and narrow and are easy to remove. Pry the date apart with your hands and pull out the pit. I prefer the variety known as Medjool for its cloying sweetness. About 15 medium dates will yield the amount you need for the recipe.

Mirchi Chutney
Green Chilies Condiment

½ cup coarsely chopped fresh
cilantro

¼ cup water

8 to 10 fresh Thai, cayenne, or
serrano chilies

1 teaspoon coarsely chopped
gingerroot

½ teaspoon salt

Puree all the ingredients in a blender until smooth.

Makes about ⅓ cup

❀ Adventurous
"endorphin-rush
seekers" may want to
throw in a few extras
chilies in the blender.

❀ This will keep in the
refrigerator for 4 days
or in the freezer for a
month.

PAANI POORIS
Crispy Hollowed Breads with Two Chutneys

❧ Small hollow pooris (about 1 to 2 inches in diameter), also known as paani pooris or gol gappas, are available in Indian grocery stores and by mail order. This specialty from the northwestern state of Gujarat is a craze in Mumbai. The pooris are extremely crispy and tender, so be extra careful when poking a small hole in the center of the top. The hole should be big enough to push through one or two cooked garbanzo beans.

❧ Paani poori masaala is sold at Indian grocery stores. It is a blend of spices that includes mango powder, black salt, cumin, coriander, and black pepper, among others. The sulfur-like smell in the blend is from black salt, a product mined from stone quarries and considered a powerful digestive.

Of course our big sister and family doctor Lali forbade us to eat paani pooris during the monsoons in Mumbai. Her medical sensibilities were painfully aware of the tainted waters, especially during the rainy season, and hence she cautioned us with enormous fervor. The clay pot–cooled water, spiked with pungent black salt and chili-fortified chutney, in which we dunked the pooris, was enough to bring me to the brink of defiance of her wishful command.

It was too much discipline for a weak-minded little Mumbaiite like me, and with guilt-ridden pleasure, I hid under the vendor's ample umbrella, salivating with glee as I watched him gently poke a hole in a crispy, hollow poori with his right thumb. He stuffed it with tender-cooked garbanzo beans and dunked the poori in his earthen pot of spiced water that would unleash its fiery tirade against my stomach's cast-iron lining. He placed my filled poori on my handheld pipal leaf plate as my mouth anticipated its eggshell-thin crispness crumbling with a gush of cool, hot, pungent, tart, and sweet water attacking every taste bud with forceful furor. And I was not disappointed as poori after poori appeared on my leaf with tantalizing speed. I caved in to its flavor-packed brilliance, short-lived and satiating, only to pay for it later on as Lali had predicted. But it was well worth the discomfort!

2 cups cold water
5 tablespoons Meetha Chutney (page 16)
2 teaspoons Mirchi Chutney (page 17)

2 tablespoons finely chopped fresh cilantro
2 teaspoons paani poori masaala
30 round, hollow pooris (see note)
1 cup cooked garbanzo beans

1. In a medium bowl, combine all the ingredients except the pooris and beans.
2. Place a poori in the palm of one hand. With the forefinger of your other hand, gently poke a hole through each poori's top, taking care not to puncture the bottom. Fill each poori with one or two garbanzo beans.
3. Dunk the stuffed poori into the spiced water (stir before each dunking to ensure that spices do not sink to the bottom), filling it completely. Eat immediately in a single bite.

Serves 6

Vendor selling Paani Pooris in Mumbai

- If you are using canned garbanzo beans, drain and rinse off the brine.

- Double the recipe and serve it as a light dinner on hot summer evenings.

- Garbanzo bean flour noodles (sev) of various sizes and flours are widely available in Indian grocery stores. For this recipe, choose the ones that are very thin, pale-yellow in color, and spicy-mild.

- When I serve these, I always encourage my guests to leave their shyness and dainty "northward pointing pinky finger" at my doorstep and insist that they devour each poori with all its filling in one single bite. Food should sing in your mouth, and in my opinion, this dish choreographs the song with Shiva's Ananda Tandam (Lord Shiva's dance of bliss)—full of vigor, smoothness, and vitality.

Dahi Batata Pooris
Crispy Hollowed Breads with Mung Beans

※ Chaat masaala (*chaat* is Hindi for "lick") is a spice blend consisting of black salt, mango powder made from dried pulp of unripe green mangoes, dried pomegranate seeds, and other seasonings. Snack foods in India (especially in the north and northwest) usually include this tart, finger-licking, addictive spice blend. Sprinkle it on fresh fruit for a unique flavor combination, or on potatoes, onions, and legumes as in Chaat (page 35). You can make your own or purchase it at your favorite Indian store.

※ Because the pooris get soggy quickly after they are assembled, make only as many as you can eat at any given time. If the pooris become soft as a result of exposure to humidity, rewarm them uncovered on an ungreased cookie sheet at 300° for about 5 minutes. Cool before filling.

All vendors who sell Paani Pooris (page 18) also offer these hot and sweet delicacies topped with a dollop of plain yogurt. When I entertain friends at home, I always serve these as an appetizer, giving each guest a dahi batata poori kit (pooris, mung bean mixture, the two chutneys, yogurt, and cilantro) to assemble and devour, as is often the practice in Mumbai's dining establishments. The street vendor, on the other hand, assembles them for you, offering that extra level of personal service. When someone else is making them as you wolf them down, you don't know when to quit eating!

¼ cup sabud mung (whole green lentils), sorted and rinsed
2 cups water
1 medium potato, peeled, boiled, cooled, and finely chopped
1 teaspoon salt
¼ teaspoon ground turmeric
30 round hollow pooris (see note page 18)

¼ cup Mirchi Chutney (page 17)
½ cup Meetha Chutney (page 16)
½ cup plain yogurt, whisked
¼ cup finely chopped fresh cilantro
Chaat masaala for dusting (optional) (see note)

1. In a 1-quart saucepan bring the sabud mung and water to a boil over medium-high heat. Skim off any foam that forms on its surface. Lower the heat to medium and simmer, partially covered, stirring occasionally, for 15 minutes, or until the beans are partially cooked. Lower the heat and simmer, covered, stirring occasionally, for 12 to 15 minutes, or until the beans are cooked. Drain off excess water.

2. In a small bowl, combine the cooked beans, potato, salt, and turmeric.

3. Place one poori at a time in the palm of one hand. With the forefinger of your other hand, gently poke a hole through each poori's top surface, being careful not to puncture the bottom. Arrange them in a single layer on a serving platter.

4. Stuff each poori with 1 teaspoon mung bean mixture followed by ¼ teaspoon mirchi chutney, ½ teaspoon meetha chutney, and ½ teaspoon plain yogurt. Sprinkle with cilantro and dust with chaat masaala (optional). Eat each poori in one single bite to experience its full flavors and textures.

Serves 6

Sev Batata Pooris
Crispy Flat Breads with Potato, Mango, and Noodles

Kailash Parbat, the phallic-shaped mountain towering over 22,000 feet in the mighty Himalayas, is considered to be the home of Shiva and his consort Parvati. Shiva, whose lingam (phallus) is a widely worshiped symbol of fertility, is a member of Hinduism's trinity of gods: Brahma the creator, Vishnu the preserver of life, and Shiva the destroyer of evil. Pilgrimages to Mount Kailash are cherished, but only a handful of brave souls are willing to challenge the snow and bone-chilling cold. Nimble Tibetans, who know how to master the unforgiving elements of this majestic, holy splendor, usually guide this arduous trek.

Luckily, Mumbaiites have to travel a very short distance in not-so-harsh conditions to the restaurant Kailash Parbat, an icon that provides blissful comfort for Mumbai's teeming millions. In my opinion, this restaurant, nestled in the southern part of downtown Mumbai, makes the best sev pooris in the world. Like the other customers, I have waited patiently for my turn to gulp mouthfuls of these crispy, hot, tart, sweet delicacies. After all, a pilgrimage to appease the stomach is just as important as one that soothes the soul. If only Shiva savored these sev pooris, he might reconsider his chilling abode.

> ℞ These small, flat, crispy golden-brown pooris roughly 2 inches in diameter and cracker thin, are made of all-purpose, whole-wheat, and semolina flours in a fairly time-consuming process. A better option is to purchase them from a mail-order source that specializes in Indian groceries. These pooris will keep at room temperature for six weeks in an airtight container or zip-lock plastic bag. I have made similar-tasting pooris by using large flour tortillas. Cut out 2-inch circles of tortillas with a cookie cutter and deep-fry in 350° oil for 30 seconds to 1 minute until they are golden brown. Remove with a slotted spoon and drain on paper towels.

¼ cup finely chopped peeled, unripe green mango
¼ cup finely chopped red onion
¼ cup finely chopped peeled, boiled potato
½ teaspoon salt
24 flat mini-pooris

2 tablespoons Mirchi Chutney (page 17)
½ cup Meetha Chutney (page 16)
½ cup thin garbanzo bean flour noodles (sev)
1 tablespoon finely chopped fresh cilantro

1. In a bowl, combine the mango, onion, potato, and salt.
2. Arrange pooris in single layer on a serving platter. Top each poori with a heaping teaspoon of the mango mixture, followed by ¼ teaspoon mirchi chutney and 1 teaspoon meetha chutney. Sprinkle on the noodles and cilantro and serve immediately. Eat each poori in one single bite to experience its full flavor and textures.

Serves 6

GILLA BHEL
Puffed Rice with Two Chutneys

❧ Leftovers will not keep since they will lose their wonderful textural contrast of crisp against wet. I of course cannot imagine reaching that predicament!

❧ A potato peeler is the perfect tool for peeling an unripe mango.

Bhel is to Mumbai as hot dogs are to Coney Island. Bhel is a hodgepodge of puffed rice, crispy garbanzo bean flour noodles, and crunchy vegetables tossed with two antithetical chutneys: one sweat-inducing chili-spiked hot, the other mellow and smooth with a fine balance of sweet and tart flavors. The resulting combination will bring a smile to your face and make you fall in love with Mumbai again and again!

1 large unripe green mango, peeled and cut into ¼-inch cubes
2 medium potatoes, peeled, boiled, cooled, and cut into ¼-inch cubes
1 medium red onion, finely chopped
1 medium tomato, finely chopped
⅓ cup Meetha Chutney (page 16), or more as desired

3 tablespoons Mirchi Chutney (page 17), or more as desired
1 teaspoon salt
1 package (1 pound) bhel mix (see note page 23)
¼ cup finely chopped fresh cilantro

1. In a large mixing bowl, thoroughly combine all ingredients except bhel mix and cilantro.
2. Stir in the bhel mix and sprinkle with cilantro. Serve immediately.

Serves 10

SUKHA BHEL
Puffed Rice with Green Mango

The word sukha *is really a misnomer, since it means "dry," and this dish is wet thanks to the tart lime juice. I prefer this combination to the one with Gilla Bhel (page 22) because I love the freshness and clean taste of freshly squeezed lime juice that barely coats the vegetables without overpowering them.*

1 cup finely chopped peeled, unripe green mango
1 cup finely chopped red onion
1 medium potato, boiled, peeled, cooled, and finely chopped
¼ cup finely chopped fresh cilantro
1 teaspoon salt
2 to 3 fresh Thai, cayenne, or serrano chilies, finely chopped
Juice of 1 large lime
1 package (1 pound) bhel mix (see note)

1. In a large bowl, combine all ingredients except the bhel mix.
2. Just before serving, add the bhel mix and toss well. Serve immediately.

Serves 8

≈ Bhel mix is available in Indian grocery stores. It is a mixture of turmeric-stained puffed rice (murmura/moori), very fine fried garbanzo bean flour noodles (sev), and pieces of flat crispy bread (poori). It has a relatively long shelf life (like potato chips) and can also be eaten as a snack.

≈ The texture of this dish is very important—since you want to experience the bhel mix's crunchiness with the vegetables' relative softness. For this reason, combine the wet and dry ingredients just before serving.

≈ The vegetable mixture can be prepared up to two days ahead and stored, covered, in the refrigerator.

RAGADA PATTIES
Breaded Potato Shells with Yellow Peas

❧ Dried yellow peas are available in Indian grocery stores, natural food stores, and through mail-order sources. Resembling whole green peas, these bright yellow, slightly shriveled peas need to be soaked before cooking, as do most dried beans. They have a sweet, nutty flavor, reminiscent of garbanzo beans. Whole yellow peas are split and hulled to yield chana dal (yellow split peas). As an alternative, use canned (2 cans, 15 ounces each) and drained or freshly cooked garbanzo beans.

❧ To cook 1 cup of dried yellow peas, rinse well under running water. In a 3-quart saucepan, bring the peas and 4 cups of water to a boil over medium-high heat. Remove from heat and let the peas soak 8 to 24 hours. Drain and bring to a boil with 4 cups fresh water over medium-high heat. Cook, covered, on low heat for 1½ hours, or until tender. Discard any skin that separates from the peas. This will yield about 3 cups cooked.

Ragada patties are synonymous with Mumbai's beaches. Along the crowded shore-line of Chowpatty Beach, vendors secure their carts into the hot sand. As the fierce sun retreats into the western sky, the peddlers light their kerosene lamps, studding the seashore like Queen Victoria's diamond necklace in the dusky light. The aromas of fresh cilantro and pungent Thai chilies mingle with the salty air of the Arabian Sea, and children build sand castles mimicking the killas (forts) of Shivaji, the Maratha warrior. A young couple hides behind the rocks, protected from the crazed waves. She is happy to sneak in a few kisses while her lover places a small garland of jasmine flowers in her black tresses that smell of sandalwood, hearts beating fast for fear of being caught. Eventually, the scent of fried potato shells beckons them into the lantern light—ragada patties, voluptuously brown, smothered with hearty yellow peas, perked up with fiery, curvaceous chilies, and kissed with sweet-sour tamarind-date chutney.

PATTIES
(POTATO SHELLS)

4 large white potatoes (about 2 pounds), peeled, boiled, and mashed
1½ teaspoons salt
8 to 10 slices white bread, or as needed
2 tablespoons vegetable oil
Additional vegetable oil for pan-frying

RAGADA
(YELLOW PEAS)

3 cups cooked yellow peas (see note)
2 cups water
1 cup finely chopped red onion
1 teaspoon salt
1 teaspoon ground red pepper (cayenne)
½ teaspoon ground turmeric

GARNISH

3 tablespoons Mirchi Chutney (page 17)
¾ cup Meetha Chutney (page 16)

¾ cup plain yogurt, whisked
½ cup finely chopped fresh cilantro

TO MAKE PATTIES

1. Preheat the oven to 200°.

2. In a large bowl, mix the potatoes and salt. Moisten 4 to 5 slices of bread at a time under running water. Squeeze the slices to remove the excess water. Add the bread to the potatoes and knead the mixture well. Repeat with the remaining bread slices, as needed, to form soft, smooth dough similar to bread dough. Add 2 tablespoons vegetable oil and knead for 1 to 2 minutes.

3. Divide the dough into 12 equal portions and shape each portion into a round. Cover with a clean, slightly damp cloth or plastic wrap.

4. Grease the palms of your hands with a little oil. One at a time, press a potato round between your hands to form a patty roughly ½ inch thick and 3 inches in diameter.

5. In a 10-inch nonstick skillet, heat 1 tablespoon of oil over medium heat. Fry 4 patties at a time for 5 to 7 minutes, or until the bottom is crispy and golden brown. Turn the patties and fry for 5 to 7 minutes, or until crispy and golden brown. Drain the patties on paper towels and keep warm, uncovered, in the oven.

TO MAKE RAGADA

Place all the ingredients in a 3-quart saucepan and bring to a boil over medium-high heat. Lower the heat to medium and simmer, uncovered, for 8 to 10 minutes to blend the flavors. Remove from the heat and coarsely mash the mixture.

TO SERVE

Arrange the patties in a single layer on a large platter. Spoon the pea mixture over the patties. Top with ½ teaspoon (or more, as desired) mirchi chutney, followed by 1 tablespoon of meetha chutney, and 1 tablespoon yogurt. Sprinkle with cilantro.

Serves 6

As a child, I first observed a vendor squeezing moist bread slices to create instant dough by kneading the bread with mashed potatoes. I was instantly intrigued, drawn by the oddity of taking perfectly good white, pasty bread and drenching it under tap water to yield a sticky blob of wetness that binds structurally challenged mashed potatoes to form firm shells housing yellow peas. Don't use flavored breads, which provide unwanted flavors and textures.

These patties are extremely filling. I have often gorged myself at teatime to tide me over until dinner, but mealtime comes and goes while the flavors and fullness pleasantly linger on. The patties freeze well (cooked or otherwise) and will keep for a month. Thaw overnight in the refrigerator, then follow the recipe for uncooked patties. Reheat cooked patties in a lightly greased pan or uncovered at 300° in the oven for 12 to 15 minutes, or until warm.

KAANDA PAKODI
Onion Fritters

A candy thermometer inserted in the oil should register 350°. If you do not have a thermometer, a drop of water placed in the oil should immediately rise to the top without making a splattering sound. A fryer, though not essential, is ideal.

Marathi is the official language in Mumbai, but signs are written in Hindi and English as well. Everyone understands kaanda, Marathi for "onions," and eats kaanda pakodi (onion fritters). In inner-city Mumbai, the densely populated area of Girgaum has a large Maharashtrian (Marathi-speaking) community and vendors who have stalls sandwiched between chawls (single-room apartment buildings).

One hot and sultry summer day, while visiting family friends, we awoke from afternoon siestas, struggling in the oppressive heat. Mrs. Nabar, our hostess, insisted that we drink adrak chai (milk tea perfumed with coarsely crushed fresh gingerroot) and sent her seventy-year-old husband off to the kaanda pakodi vendor, insisting that they were the best in Mumbai. I did not have the heart to tell her that in this heat, hot tea and fried onions were unthinkable.

We waited, struggling to breathe. Mr. Nabar appeared almost forty minutes later with a huge bundle of pakodis wrapped in grease-stained Marathi newspapers. He explained that the vendor was just getting the oil ready when he arrived, and he could not cook the onions until it was plenty hot.

The hot, spicy tea actually cooled us, and the light, airily crisp onions were so delicious that they commanded our complete attention and broke our obsession with the heat and its overwhelming demands. We soon were refreshed and lightened.

1½ cups thinly sliced onions	1 teaspoon salt
1 cup garbanzo bean flour, sifted	½ teaspoon cumin seed, ground
1 teaspoon coriander seed, ground	¼ teaspoon ground turmeric
1 teaspoon ground red pepper (cayenne)	½ cup water
	Vegetable oil for deep-frying

1. In a large bowl, thoroughly combine all ingredients except the water and oil. Stir in the water, mixing well.
2. In a wok or 3-quart saucepan, heat the vegetable oil (about 2 to 3 inches deep) over medium heat until a thermometer registers 350°.
3. With your hand, gently place half of the batter-smothered onion slices in the hot oil. Fry for 3 to 5 minutes, turning occasionally, until golden brown. Remove with a slotted spoon and drain on paper towels. Repeat with the remaining onions. Serve as is, or with a chutney of your choice.

Serves 6

Seekh Kebabs
Grilled Lamb on Skewers

Near the train depot in Andheri, a suburb of Mumbai, vendors sell everything from used books to imported soaps and perfumes from the West on makeshift tables or permanent stalls like the newsstands of Manhattan. A distinguished older Muslim man looms above the rest with a traditional white turban wrapped carefully around his head of shocking white hair. He sells seekh kebabs along with a salad of fresh mint, raw red onions, cilantro, and wedges of plump lime. He squats on the sidewalk over a grill he's fashioned out of a broken grate set on four large stones. His twelve-year-old son fans the coals to keep them burning, learning his father's trade. The father purses his lips, barely visible through his majestic beard and mustache, yellowed with age hastened by fatigue, and draws on his long hookah, making a childish bubbling sound while inhaling the intoxicating tumbaako (raw tobacco). Long seekhs (metal skewers) of compressed ground mutton (mature goat) lie across the grates spitting grease, and the wafting aroma makes even a Brahmin vegetarian like me hungry.

❧ I like to serve these kebabs with a simple salad of raw red onions, slivers of green chilies, sprigs of cilantro, fresh mint, and wedges of lime.

❧ In place of lamb, you can use ground turkey, chicken, or even beef. Adjust your cooking time since they vary for each of these meats. Turkey and chicken will cook in about 10 minutes while beef will require the same amount of time as lamb.

12 bamboo skewers, 6 to 8 inches long
1 pound ground lamb
½ cup finely chopped red onion
2 tablespoons finely chopped fresh cilantro
1 tablespoon finely chopped garlic
1 tablespoon Garam Masaala (page 206)
1 teaspoon salt

1. Soak the skewers in water for ½ hour so they won't burn.
2. In a medium bowl, combine the remaining ingredients. Divide the mixture into 12 equal parts. Wrap each part around a skewer, pressing it with your hand to cover about half the length of skewer.
3. Preheat the broiler or grill. Place the skewers on the broiler pan or grate. Broil or grill, turning occasionally, for 5 to 6 minutes, or until the lamb is barely pink in the center. Serve immediately.

Serves 6

Subzi Kebabs
Assorted Vegetable Cutlets

Potatoes are essential to the cutlets to hold them together, but you can use any vegetable combination with them for variation.

I often treat myself to these cutlets at breakfast, topped with a dollop of tomato cat-sup and sandwiched between two slices of white bread, just as Indians do in boxcars during long railroad journeys, served by dark-skinned waiters in spotless-white elbow-length gloves.

3 medium potatoes (1 pound), peeled, boiled, and mashed
1 cup frozen green peas, thawed and drained
1 cup firmly packed mint leaves, finely chopped
2 tablespoons finely chopped fresh cilantro
2 teaspoons salt
1 teaspoon Garam Masaala (page 206)

6 to 8 fresh Thai, cayenne, or serrano chilies, finely chopped
1 tablespoon vegetable oil
1 teaspoon cumin seed
2 medium carrots (1 cup), peeled and finely chopped
1 large egg, lightly beaten
1 cup plain, dry breadcrumbs
Additional vegetable oil for pan-frying

1. In a medium bowl, combine the potatoes, peas, mint, cilantro, salt, garam masaala, and chilies.
2. In a 10-inch nonstick skillet, heat 1 tablespoon oil over medium-high heat; sizzle the cumin seed for 15 to 20 seconds. Add the carrots and stir-fry for 2 to 3 minutes, or until partially cooked. Add the carrot-cumin mixture to the potato mixture and combine throughly.
3. Divide the potato mixture into 16 equal parts. Shape each part into a patty roughly 3 inches in diameter and ¼ inch thick. Dip each patty in the beaten egg and then coat with breadcrumbs.
4. Coat the same skillet with about 2 tablespoons oil and heat over medium heat. Arrange 5 to 6 cutlets at a time in the skillet without overcrowding. Cook each side for 4 to 6 minutes, or until golden brown. Drain on paper towels.

Makes 16 cutlets (serves 8)

DAHI VADAAS
Lentil Croquettes in Yogurt Sauce

"Arré, we must go to Elco to eat their dahi vadaas," insisted Geeta, my newly arrived sister-in-law, her charcoal-black eyes widening with emphatic glee. She was taking us all out for the evening, bribing her way into our hearts with her favorite street vendor's offerings. "It is in Bandra West and very close to the railway station. Chalo chalo, if we hurry we can catch the fast train and be there under a half hour," she chattered as she herded us out the door. I was exhausted and in no mood to catch a bus, hop on a train, and battle Mumbai's millions. I had been wrongfully accused of talking in class (and undeservedly slapped, I might add) by Miss DeSouza, my otherwise favorite French teacher. Her five-fingered impression on my soft dimpled cheek still smarted from the afternoon, my tears threatened to brim with hatred—but that would disappear within the hour.

There's nothing like Mumbai street life to diminish the shock of a slap. The piercing horn of the three-wheeled rickshaw, noisy as a pressure cooker's whistling, and the angry ringing of the bicyclist's bell jarred me back from my self-pity to the life-risking task at hand—crossing the street to catch the red double-decker bus to Andheri station. The fifteen-foot-wide road was home to everyone and everything that breathed; black and yellow taxis with their Fiat emblems glistening in the hot afternoon sun sped toward their destination on both sides of the two-way street. The vegetable vendor pulled his wooden pushcart stacked with orderly vegetables in an otherwise uncontrollable world. The irritating rickshaws dashed like frenzied black mice in and out of traffic with sperm-like, crazed recklessness, threatening to make unwanted contact with hapless pedestrians and the pack of stray dogs that claimed every open space in this stretch of concrete that was mistakenly called a road. Although this would appear as utter chaos in the outsider's eyes, to us Mumbaiites it is a well-conducted orchestra, overseen by everyone's desire to survive, thrive, and respect each other's space, whatever little of it is available.

Once all of us made it to the safety of the other side of the street, we waited patiently for bus number 254. We filed onto the bus and scurried to its top deck. I grabbed a window seat and looked down on the unstoppable drama of street life. The evening traffic was as unbearable as the heat as the bus pushed its way amid the sea of people toward the station. An otherwise ten-minute trip took forty minutes, but we made it to the railway station and caught the next fast train to Bandra. By now all of us were hungry and irritable, and Geeta was slipping to the lower rungs of my popularity ladder. Soon we reached Elco Shopping Center's street-side restaurant, the object of our pilgrimage, and plopped our tired behinds on hard

The recipe can be made up to 4 days in advance and stored in the refrigerator.

wooden seats. Geeta ordered for us since this was her deal, and we waited with grow-
ing impatience. Soon came the first plates of cilantro-dusted yogurt hiding mounds of
fried lentil croquettes. After the first mouthfuls, I understood Geeta's zealous fervor
for these dahi vadaas. Suddenly I was a disciple too, having been blessed by their
divine presence that nudged me to open up my heart's doors to my brother's wife.

VADAAS (CROQUETTES)

1 cup urad dal (split and hulled
   black lentils), sorted
½ cup water
1 teaspoon salt
½ teaspoon hing (asafetida)
4 to 6 fresh Thai, cayenne, or
   serrano chilies
Vegetable oil for deep-frying

DAHI (YOGURT SAUCE)

1 cup plain yogurt
¼ cup water
1 tablespoon sugar
2 tablespoons finely chopped fresh
   cilantro
1 teaspoon ground red pepper
   (cayenne)

TO MAKE VADAAS

1. In a medium bowl, place the dal and water. With your fingers, gently
   wash the dal for 30 seconds until the water becomes cloudy (not unlike
   my original mood), then drain. Repeat 5 or 6 times, until the water looks
   clear. Cover the lentils with warm water and soak at room temperature for
   at least 2 to 3 hours, or overnight. Drain.
2. In a blender, combine the dal and the remaining ingredients except oil
   and grind until smooth. Transfer the batter to mixing bowl and beat it with
   a wooden spoon or spatula for 3 to 5 minutes to incorporate air.
3. In a wok or 3-quart saucepan, heat the vegetable oil (about 2 to 3 inches
   deep) over medium heat until a thermometer registers 350°.
4. Add tablespoonfuls of batter to the hot oil, without overcrowding (unlike a
   Mumbai intersection) and fry for 6 to 8 minutes, turning 2 to 3 times, until
   golden brown. Remove with a slotted spoon and drain on paper towels.

TO MAKE DAHI

In a medium bowl, whisk together the yogurt and water until smooth. Stir in
the sugar.

TO SERVE

1. Soak the vadaas in warm water for about 1 to 2 minutes. Flatten the vadaas between the palms of your hands to completely squeeze out the water. Stir the vadaas into the yogurt sauce and marinate for 1 to 2 minutes. Place them in a single layer on a serving platter.
2. Pour the yogurt sauce over the vadaas, then sprinkle with cilantro and ground red pepper. Serve at room temperature or chilled (whenever a hectic day or foul mood needs soothing).

Makes about 20 vadaas. Serves 10

VADAA PAAV
Garlic Potato Sandwiches

Although she might never admit it, my mother was secretly grateful to the vendor across the street who made vadaa paav. Every evening as we rushed in after school, noisy and starved, she was in the thick of her dinner preparations. So she ushered us out the door and across the street. We never ate before 9 P.M., and Amma's dinners were simple yet laborious, so our 5 P.M. snack was essential.

We, on the other hand, were openly grateful to escape our chores in exchange for the sizzling potato sandwiches Ramlal hustled up for us with a wink and good-humored magic. We enjoyed his burlesque, his rugged good looks, and his half-sleeved white tunic folded around his tanned biceps that revealed a black-stringed amulet with a picture of Hanuman, the god of bachelors, the prince of virility.

He'd take a bowl of mashed potatoes spiked with green chilies and cilantro and scoop up golf ball–sized pieces, flattening them between his calloused palms into half-inch-thick disks, then drop them into a thick yellow batter of garbanzo bean flour. With his fingers dripping batter, he'd slide the patties into the sizzling oil, and we'd watch as they floated up, golden and crisp. With a chaalni (slotted spoon), he'd lift them out and set them on slices of soft white bread, rubbed with fiery dry red chili chutney. "Do you want the chutney with garlic or the one without?" he would ask. My brother Ravi, sister Mathangi, and I replied in unison, "Without," because at that age we never ate garlic. It was foreign to our rigid southern Indian palates and banished from our kitchens in accordance with our priestly community's teachings. Ramlal handed us the buns, and we stood by the stall devouring our sandwiches—a perfect snack to help me tackle the fifteen chemistry equations that needed to be balanced that evening.

LASOON CHUTNEY
(GARLIC AND RED CHILIES CONDIMENT)

¼ cup blanched Spanish peanuts, or
   dry-roasted unsalted
1 tablespoon coriander seed
1 teaspoon cumin seed
5 to 6 dried red Thai, cayenne, or
   serrano chilies

1 tablespoon sesame seed
6 medium cloves garlic, thinly sliced
1 teaspoon salt

VADAAS (FRITTERS)

1 cup garbanzo bean flour, sifted
1½ teaspoons salt
¼ teaspoon ground turmeric
¼ teaspoon baking soda
½ cup water, or as needed
4 medium potatoes, boiled, peeled, and mashed
½ cup coarsely chopped fresh cilantro

1 tablespoon coarsely chopped gingerroot
5 medium cloves garlic
3 to 4 fresh Thai, cayenne, or serrano chilies
Vegetable oil for deep-frying
6 hamburger buns (sliced)

TO MAKE CHUTNEY

1. Heat a 6-inch skillet over medium-high heat. Add the peanuts and roast, stirring constantly, for 2 to 3 minutes, or until patchy golden brown spots appear (see note). Transfer the nuts to small bowl. If you are using dry-roasted peanuts, roast for 30 seconds to 1 minute to warm them.
2. In the same skillet, add the coriander, cumin, and chilies. Roast, stirring constantly, for 20 to 30 seconds, or until the seed crackles and the chilies slightly blacken. Mix with the peanuts.
3. Add the sesame seed to the skillet and toast, stirring constantly, for 10 to 15 seconds, or until the seed crackles and turns golden brown; add to the peanut mixture.
4. Add the garlic slices to the skillet and stir-fry for 2 to 3 minutes, or until golden brown; add to the peanut mixture. Let the mixture cool.
5. In a blender or spice grinder, grind the peanut mixture until it is the texture of coarse breadcrumbs. Add the salt and mix well.

TO MAKE VADAAS

1. In a medium bowl, combine the flour, ½ teaspoon salt, turmeric, and baking soda. Whisk in water, a few tablespoons at a time, to make a thick, pancake-like batter.
2. In a separate bowl, combine the potatoes with 1 teaspoon salt.
3. In food processor, finely mince the cilantro, gingerroot, garlic, and chilies. Add to potatoes and mix well.
4. Divide the potato mixture into 12 equal portions. Shape each portion into a ball, then press the ball between your palms into a ½-inch-thick patty.

⋇ The chutney recipe yields about ¾ cup. You can refrigerate any remaining chutney for 10 days and use it as a topping for salads, or sprinkle it on slices of hot buttered toast for a perky breakfast.

⋇ Enjoy these sandwiches with a hearty glass of dark beer, a cup of steaming Adrak Chai (page 43), or a Bombay Gin martini, extra dry.

5. In a wok or 3-quart saucepan, heat the vegetable oil (about 2 to 3 inches deep) over medium heat until a thermometer registers 350°.

6. Completely coat 6 potato patties with batter and slide them gently into the hot oil. Fry for 3 to 5 minutes, turning occasionally, until golden brown. Remove with a slotted spoon and drain on paper towels. Repeat with the remaining patties.

TO ASSEMBLE

Spread 1 tablespoon chutney (or more) on the insides of each hamburger bun. Place two vadaas between each bun. Serve immediately.

Serves 6

CHAAT
Spicy Sprouted Beans with Yogurt

Anything and everything mixed together, no restrictions, no constraints, tolerance for all—this could easily be a description of the large metropolis of Mumbai. But it really is what chaat is all about. Chaat, which literally means "licking," aptly defines the lip-smacking flavors that make this combination so popular on street corners and beaches. A combination of vegetables, legumes, and even fresh fruits with herbs and spices, served cold or at room temperature, usually constitutes the basis of chaat. I particularly like the textural contrasts between this recipe's vegetables and legumes.

3 medium potatoes, boiled, peeled, and cut into ½-inch cubes
1 medium tomato, finely chopped
1 small red onion, finely chopped
1 cup mixed bean sprouts
1 cup plain yogurt, whisked

¼ cup finely chopped fresh cilantro
4 to 6 fresh Thai, cayenne, or serrano chilies, finely chopped
2 teaspoons Chaat Masaala (see note page 20)
Juice of 1 large lime

Combine all the ingredients in a bowl and mix well. Serve at room temperature or chilled.

Serves 6

Paav Bhaaji
Vegetable Pâté with Griddle Bread

❧ Paav bhaaji masaala is available at any store that sells Indian groceries. This commercially prepared masaala (blend) usually combines 15 to 20 different spices to create flavors associated with this Mumbai favorite. You can substitute a good-quality commercially prepared curry powder for a different—but delicious—flavor.

❧ Often, a salad of red onions marinated in freshly squeezed lime juice, ground red pepper (cayenne), and cilantro accompanies the paav bhaaji. Sprinkle it on top of the bhaaji for a nirvana-like experience.

Many favorite Mumbai dishes originated in the pans of street vendors. This paav bhaaji (paav is "bread" in Marathi, and bhaaji is "vegetable") is from a vendor who still cooks outside the downtown Regal Cinema. He sautés the chopped vegetables down into a chunky pâté atop his kadhai (wok), then pushes them aside to keep them warm. To serve a customer, he melts some butter in the center of the wok, adds a healthy portion of the bhaaji, and stir-fries the warm pâté. Then he spreads it on a soft paav bun, crisping it facedown on the wok, and serves it, along with some extra bhaaji, in a bowl made from leaves.

2 cups finely chopped onions
1½ cups finely chopped tomatoes
2 tablespoons finely chopped fresh cilantro
2 to 3 fresh Thai, cayenne, or serrano chilies
1 teaspoon cumin seed
½ cup butter
1 tablespoon finely chopped gingerroot
1 teaspoon salt
1 teaspoon paav bhaaji masaala (see note)

2 medium potatoes, boiled, peeled, and finely chopped
1 cup finely chopped cauliflower florets
1 medium green bell pepper, cored, seeded, and finely chopped
½ cup frozen green peas
16 half-inch-thick slices French bread
Additional butter for brushing

1. In a blender, puree 1 cup onion, 1 cup tomato, cilantro, chilies, and cumin until smooth.
2. In a wok or deep 12-inch skillet, melt ¼ cup butter over medium-high heat. Add the remaining onions and gingerroot and stir-fry for 4 to 6 minutes, or until golden brown.
3. Sir in the pureed mixture, salt, and paav bhaaji masaala. Lower the heat to medium and cook uncovered, stirring occasionally, for 10 to 12 minutes, or until the sauce slightly thickens and a thin coating of oil starts to separate from the sauce.

4. Add the remaining tomatoes, potatoes, cauliflower, green pepper, and green peas. Cook, stirring occasionally, for 10 to 12 minutes, or until the vegetables are thoroughly cooked. Add the remaining ¼ cup butter and stir-fry the mixture for 2 to 3 minutes to blend the flavors.

5. Spread 1 tablespoon of the vegetable mixture on one side of each French bread slice.

6. In a 10-inch nonstick skillet, heat 1 tablespoon butter over medium heat. Place 4 to 6 slices of French bread in single layer without crowding, vegetable side down. Heat for 2 to 3 minutes, or until the underside is crusty brown. Repeat with the remaining slices. Serve immediately with the rest of the additional vegetable mixture on the side.

Serves 8

Customers enjoying Paav Bhaaji on Mumbai street corner

Mumbai Samosas
Seasoned Vegetables in Crispy Wrapper

⁂ These samosas can be assembled up to a day ahead and stored loosely wrapped in the refrigerator. You can also freeze them uncooked for a month. To cook, slide unthawed samosas in 350° oil and fry for 2 to 4 minutes, or until golden brown. Leftover fried samosas can be rewarmed uncovered on a cookie sheet in a 200° oven for about 5 minutes.

Samosas wrapped in a pastry crust, most popular in north Indian restaurants, are known as Punjabi samosas, after their place of origin. The wrappers in Mumbai's streets are much thinner, similar in texture to wonton and egg roll skins. The filling varies, depending on what is in season. Potatoes and carrots, being yearlong inexpensive staples, always make their appearance in these delectable crunchy shells.

2 tablespoons vegetable oil

1 teaspoon cumin seed

½ cup finely chopped carrot

½ cup frozen green peas

3 medium potatoes (1 pound), boiled, peeled, cooled, and finely chopped

2 tablespoons finely chopped fresh cilantro

2 teaspoons Garam Masaala (page 206)

1½ teaspoons salt

4 to 6 fresh Thai, cayenne, or serrano chilies, finely chopped

¼ cup water

1 teaspoon cornstarch

20 wonton wrappers

Vegetable oil for deep-frying

1. In a 10-inch skillet, heat the oil over medium-high heat. Add the cumin seed and sizzle for 10 to 15 seconds.
2. Add the carrots and stir-fry for 2 to 3 minutes until they are slightly cooked. Fold in the green peas and continue cooking for 1 to 2 minutes until the peas are just warm.
3. Stir in the potatoes, cilantro, garam masaala, salt, and chilies. Transfer the vegetable mixture to a bowl to cool.
4. In a small bowl, combine the water and cornstarch to make a thin paste.
5. Working with one wonton wrapper at a time (keeping the remaining ones covered in plastic wrap or a slightly damp paper towel), place a heaping tablespoon of vegetable mixture diagonally along the lower two-thirds of the wrapper. Smear the edges with cornstarch slurry and seal the edges firmly together to form a triangle.
6. In a wok or 3-quart saucepan, heat the vegetable oil (about 2 to 3 inches deep) over medium heat until a thermometer registers 350°.
7. Fry 5 samosas at a time, turning once, for 2 to 3 minutes, until golden brown. Remove with a slotted spoon and drain on paper towels.

Makes about 20 samosas

CHANA BHATURA
Garbanzo Bean Stew with Puffy Bread

There are few things that come to mind when I am coerced into being thankful to Father Netto, the Jesuit principal of my boyhood elementary school, St. Xavier's Boys' Academy. He was a native Indian of medium stature with thin, grayish-black hair, the color of smoked tamarind pulp, adorning his olive-drab pate. His substantial ears, along with more woolly hair clumps, offered ample resting spots for his thick black-rimmed glasses, which often dangled around his short neck from the end of a long rope garland. He always wore a body-length, long-sleeved, white robe with that familiar priestly banded collar. A pair of well-creased, ivory-colored, slightly frayed, all-cotton pant legs jutted out from under the robe, accentuating his pointed black shoes. His intimidating personality matched his perennially folded brow, and he instilled fear in all his gray-white uniformed charges.

But I must confess that I was secretly grateful to him for detaining me after school for catching me, on rare occasions, eating in class, talking to a friend during math test, or being late for the morning assembly. Normal school hours ended at 1:30 P.M., but the detention earned me two extra, excruciating hours. Each time I ascertained my afternoon predicament, I set aside two rupees of my pocket money (out of twenty rupees a month) for my street pal and cook, Kulbushan Singh. In his turmeric-yellow dyed turban, the strapping sardarji—a Sikh from India's wheat-growing capital in northern India's Punjab—stood with his cart of soul-satisfying food across from the school's courtyard. His spicily tart kabuli chana (garbanzo beans), fortified with potent chilies, acidic amchur (mango powder), and a heaping dose of attention and a beatific smile were the reward at the end of my midafternoon confinement. "Come, oh king of mine, let me make you strong with my garbanzo bean stew and puffy fried bread," he bellowed through his barely visible lips immersed within a neatly braided beard and mustache.

With a twirl of his bushy mustache, he heaped a serving of chana in a bowl fashioned with leaves held together by a toothpick. His just-slapped piece of dough puffed gently in his hot oil-filled wok. Within seconds I was perched on his tall cane stool, legs dangling in midair, my canvas book bag by the concrete wayside, shoving into my eager mouth mounds of chana wrapped in morsels of fluffy bhatura. Between bites he listened to my day's mishaps, clucking his tongue in sympathy for the fear and injustice that was Father Netto's wrath. A full belly brought on by the gift of an extra bhatura eased my afternoon's self-pity and the cumbersome one-hour train ride back to my suburban home in Andheri.

Kulbushan often served this dish with a side of raw beets and red onions marinated in lime juice, cilantro, finely chopped chilies, and salt. Since I was not a "beet person" at that age, I skipped it. Do try that accompaniment if you wish.

The chana can be made up to a day ahead, and so can the dough for bhaturas. For an optimum flavor experience, fry the bhatura just before serving. You will be glad you did!

CHANA
(GARBANZO BEAN STEW)

½ cup coarsely chopped onion
1 tablespoon coarsely chopped
  gingerroot
3 large cloves garlic
1 to 2 fresh Thai, cayenne, or
  serrano chilies
1 tablespoon vegetable oil
1 tablespoon amchur (mango
  powder) or 2 tablespoons freshly
  squeezed lime juice
1 teaspoon salt
1 teaspoon coriander seed, ground
¼ teaspoon ground turmeric
1 cup water
1 can (15 ounces) garbanzo beans,
  rinsed and drained
1 medium potato, peeled and cut
  into 1-inch cubes

1 medium tomato, cut into
  1-inch cubes
3 tablespoons finely chopped fresh
  cilantro
1 teaspoon cumin seed, roasted and
  ground

FOR BHATURAS
(PUFFY BREAD)

2 cups all-purpose flour
1 teaspoon salt
½ teaspoon baking soda
½ cup yogurt
Warm water as needed
Vegetable oil for deep-frying
1 medium lime, cut into wedges

TO MAKE CHANA

1. In a food processor finely mince the onion, gingerroot, garlic, and chilies.
2. In a 2-quart saucepan, heat the oil over medium-high heat. Add the onion mixture and stir-fry for 3 to 4 minutes until golden brown. Stir in the amchur, salt, coriander, and turmeric. Cook for 30 seconds.
3. Add the water, garbanzo beans, potato, tomato, and 1 tablespoon cilantro. Bring the mixture to a boil, then reduce the heat to low and simmer, covered, stirring occasionally, for 10 to 12 minutes, or until the potatoes are fork-tender. Simmer uncovered, stirring occasionally, for 8 to 10 minutes, or until the sauce slightly thickens.
4. Stir in the cumin and sprinkle the remaining cilantro on top.

TO MAKE BHATURAS

1. In a medium bowl, combine the flour, salt, and baking soda. Spoon in 2 tablespoons of yogurt at a time, mixing with your hand or a spoon, until it comes together into a ball to form soft dough. Add enough yogurt to make

smooth, pliable dough that is neither sticky nor dry. You can add additional warm water to bring the dough together into a ball. Brush with oil and knead 1 more minute.

2. Cut the dough into 4 equal portions. Shape each portion into a smooth round and brush with oil. Let the dough rounds rest under plastic wrap for at least 30 minutes. (You can refrigerate the dough at this point, covered, up to 24 hours. Bring it back to room temperature before proceeding.)

3. In a wok or 3-quart saucepan, heat the vegetable oil (about 2 to 3 inches deep) over medium heat until a thermometer registers 375°.

4. Flatten each dough round into a patty (keep the remaining patties covered). Evenly roll out the patty with rolling pin, without tearing, to form a circle roughly 6 inches in diameter and about ¼ inch thick. One at a time slip the rolled dough in the hot oil. With the bottom of a slotted spoon, gently and repeatedly submerge the dough until it puffs up. Flip it once and cook for 10 seconds until golden brown. Remove from oil and drain on paper towels.

5. Serve the piping-hot bhaturas with chana and wedges of lime.

Serves 4

FALOODA KULFI
Cellophane Noodles with Rose Syrup and Ice Cream

Mumbaiites are never afraid of combining disparate objects or even cultures to create uniqueness in a metropolis that defies uniformity of any kind. So why not noodles with ice cream and crushed ice? This delicacy is a must when you visit Mumbai, especially when the sun bears down on you relentlessly. The ice cream, often served with these noodles, comes from Parsee Dairy Farm, a one-of-a-kind dessert specialty store that makes living in Mumbai all the more exciting!

❧ Yellow-colored cellophane noodles, made from cornstarch, are available in Indian grocery stores. You can substitute similar cellophane noodles, widely available in other Asian markets.

❧ Sweetened rose syrup, in tall bottles, is also found in Indian and Middle Eastern grocery stores.

8 cups whole milk
½ cup fat-free, cholesterol-free egg product (like Egg Beaters)
½ cup sugar
½ cup teaspoon vanilla extract

1 package (1¾ ounces) cellophane noodles
2 cups hot water
¼ cup sweetened rose syrup
1 cup crushed ice cubes

1. In a large, wide-rimmed saucepan or Dutch oven, bring the milk to a boil over medium-high heat, stirring constantly to prevent scorching. Continue cooking the milk down, for 50 minutes to 1 hour, stirring occasionally and scraping the sides of the pan to release collected milk solids, until the milk is reduced to 2 cups.
2. Cool the reduced milk and refrigerate it for at least 2 hours until well chilled.
3. In a large bowl, with an electric mixer on medium speed, beat together the egg substitute and sugar, scraping the bowl constantly, until the mixture is smooth and creamy yellow.
4. Add the reduced milk and vanilla extract and continue beating for 2 to 3 minutes until well blended.
5. Transfer the ice cream batter to an ice cream maker and freeze per manufacturer's instructions.
6. Place the noodles in a medium bowl. Pour 2 cups hot water over the noodles and soak for 2 to 3 minutes, until soft; drain. Dunk the noodles in ice-cold water for 3 to 5 minutes; drain. Toss the noodles with the rose syrup.
7. Divide the noodles into 6 individual serving bowls. Top each bowl with 2 scoops of ice cream. Serve immediately, sprinkled with crushed ice.

Serves 6

ADRAK CHAI
Ginger-Spiked Milk Tea

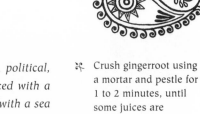

Chai, that milky sweet and spicy brew, is the lifeblood of India's social, political, and business gatherings. In a store selling silk sarees, when you are faced with a choice between the flame-red silk laced with gold or the midnight purple with a sea green border and green leaves, the owner will offer you a cup of hot chai in a stainless steel tumbler to enlighten your decision. Visit your best friend or close a hostile business deal, but first sip chai. Stroll down the dry streets of summer Mumbai or wade through a foot of standing water in the harsh monsoons, but do take a moment to sip chai, available on every street corner, hawked by vendors everywhere. Chai: Darjeeling tea steeped with milk, ginger, cloves, cinnamon, cardamom, and a kick of black pepper. This adrak chai is quintessential Mumbai: bold, spicy, and sensuous.

The double-decker bus waded through the murky waters on a typical gray June morning—ah, monsoons in Mumbai, you've got to love them! Pervasive dampness clinging to moist skin and polyester clothing, climbing up a woman's petticoat under her six-yard saree, seeping through leather clogs by Bata Shoes, failing to keep the virulent waters from invading the core of your being. Raincoats, umbrellas, and gumboots are ineffectual in their battle with the pregnant clouds. I gingerly stepped from the bus into knee-deep water and waded to the entrance of the college canteen, joining my friends huddled together, deep in discussion of the upcoming practical on frog, earthworm, and cockroach dissection. The gory details never bothered even the daintiest stomach as gulps of steaming hot chai provided comfort against the angry downpour.

2 cups water
4 teaspoons loose Darjeeling black
   tea leaves (or 5 tea bags)
2 cups whole milk
2 tablespoons coarsely chopped
   gingerroot, crushed

1 teaspoon cardamom seed (removed
   from pods), crushed
4 tablespoons sweetened condensed
   milk or 4 teaspoons sugar

1. Bring the water to a rapid boil in a 2-quart saucepan over medium-high heat. Add the tea leaves and brew for 1 to 2 minutes.
2. Add the remaining ingredients and bring to a boil, taking care not to let the milk boil over.
3. Strain the tea into cups. Serve immediately.

Serves 4

- Crush gingerroot using a mortar and pestle for 1 to 2 minutes, until some juices are released. Use the crushed gingerroot along with any residual liquid to flavor the chai.

- Crush cardamom seed with a mortar and pestle until they are coarsely cracked. You can also place the seed between layers of plastic wrap and crush with a rolling pin.

- You can use reduced-fat milk, but whole milk results in a richer tasting and creamier brew.

Pista-Baadam Paal
Steamed Milk with Pistachio Nuts and Almonds

We were a monetarily poor but richly loved bunch. Appa was the only earning member of the extended family, consisting of his wife, mother, brother, sister-in-law, and the kids, fourteen in all. We lived in a 300-square-foot chawl, a single-room unit in a crowded apartment building within the heart of Matunga, Mumbai's Tamilian district. The kitchen was squished in a corner of the room, the few pots and pans and two kerosene-burner stoves stacked neatly against the wall. A lonesome tap with erratic water supply jutted from the same corner's wall. We shared a communal bathroom across the hall with three other units, making bathtimes something of a logistical nightmare. Clothes were washed under the kitchen's tap and hung on three roped rows outside on the balcony, a cacophony of fabrics swaying in the wind.

Kindhearted and generous Appa was never frugal in showering his children with love and affection, especially his firstborn, my sister Lali. Once a week on his day off from working for the Indian Navy, after almost everyone was asleep, his ritual journey began. He quietly stepped over the sea of sleeping bodies, clutching a few coins in his right hand, a tall stainless steel tumbler in his left, his white dhoti tightly wrapped around his nimble waist, his nine-stringed poonal thread draped over his tired left shoulder, a light Brahmin reminder of his heavy responsibility to wife, mother, children, brother, and family. He stepped bare-chested, a cotton angostram draped over his left shoulder, with no shoes or slippers on his calloused feet, down the chipped stairs onto the quiet street and around the corner to the dairy vendor's stall. A gargantuan wok filled halfway with simmering milk rested on a massive kerosene stove. No words were spoken as coins exchanged hands. The vendor grabbed two urnlike brass containers and ladled hot milk into one of them. He pitched in some sugar, finely chopped unsalted pistachio nuts, and almonds. With one deft motion, he poured the mixture into the other jug. Soon the motion was repeated between the two vases, back and forth, without a drop of milk spilling on the ground, fashioning an image of milk suspended in air like a thick strand of rice noodle, creating a frothy, steamed beverage. He poured it into Appa's waiting tumbler to the brim, a halolike fizz crowning its rim.

Appa shuffled back to the room, holding the hot drink with his angostram, careful not to lose even a single drop. Lali was the only one awake, huddled in a corner on the balcony, poring through her medical books under the light of the moon aided by an oil lamp that threw a dancing glow across the pages. Appa gingerly stepped over the sleeping bodies once again and handed the glass to his oldest pride and joy. Lali sipped the beverage, the foam forming a white mustache above her lip, the sweetened milk warming her throat. Appa crawled into a little space next to Amma and smiled in the dark, proud of his daughter who fought the odds and was well on her way to becoming a physician. He caressed Amma's bare wrists, white rings visible in the moonlight against her tanned skin where her gold wedding bangles used to be. Now they rested in the jeweler's window display, pawned to pay for medical school, the family sacrifices offset by encouraging warm, nutty milk that would remain embedded in Lali's memory forever.

8 cups whole milk	¼ cup blanched almonds
¼ cup raw pistachio nuts	4 teaspoons sugar

1. In a large, wide-rimmed saucepan or Dutch oven, bring the milk to a boil over medium-high heat, stirring constantly to prevent scorching. Continue cooking the milk down, for 30 to 40 minutes, stirring occasionally and scraping the sides of the pan to release the collected milk solids, until it is reduced to 4 cups.
2. In a food processor, pulse the pistachio nuts and almonds until they are the texture of coarsely ground black peppercorns.
3. Stir the nuts and sugar into the reduced milk.

Serves 4

Naashta

Snacks

Bette Davis's Subzi Pakoras
Vegetable Fritters

Mirchi Pakoras
Batter-Dipped Chilies

Thuviyal Bhujiyas
Batter-Dipped Chutneyed Bread Slices

Malabar Pakoras
Garbanzo Bean Flour Ribbons

Urulikazhangu Vadaas
Potato Croquettes with Lime Juice

Muri
Puffed Rice with Fennel and Cucumber

Medu Vadaas
Black Lentil Fritters with Potatoes

Aloo Kebabs
Minted Onions Stuffed in Potato Shells

Fafda
Garbanzo Bean Flour Strips with Black Salt

BETTE DAVIS'S SUBZI PAKORAS
Vegetable Fritters

- Do not be confined by the recommended vegetable combination. I have made these pakoras with many other blends. If you are using frozen chopped spinach, thaw it first and completely squeeze out the water.

- The baking soda aerates the batter and makes for an airily crisp fritter. A family friend who operates a Maharashtrian restaurant in Mumbai once advised me to add the same amount of hot oil to the batter instead of water. I was amazed at the result: a crispier exterior housing tender, delectable vegetables with every bite.

- Pakoras are ideal when served hot and crispy immediately after frying. The batter will keep in the refrigerator for 2 days.

I was mesmerized as I peeked out the window of my stodgy, "garden-level" one-bedroom apartment. I had never seen this before: Pillows of velvety whiteness tumbled down the darkened sky, stacking up in layers on the frozen ground. Snow! I was used to seeing inches of collected murky water during Mumbai's monsoons, but never this bone-chilling, fluffy purity of softly frozen water. This was my first winter in the tundra of Marshall, Minnesota, my debut into the lonesome student world in a foreign land.

As the heaps increased and covered my view, the room darkened, matching my sunsetting demeanor. A mounting yearning for the warm, comforting familial love of my mother and siblings washed over me like the angry waves of the Arabian Sea. I shuddered with iced desire and my sorrow-filled mind drifted to comforting food. I longed for some crispy batter-soaked vegetables spiced with Amma's touch and Lali's love.

I dragged myself to the pitiful excuse for a kitchen and coarsely chopped onions and potatoes on the acrylic cutting board with my dull serrated knife. I had the oil heating in my only saucepan, worn with overuse, yellowed with age and turmeric. Soon the garbanzo bean floured clumps of spiced vegetables lay on paper towels, draining off excess grease.

I grabbed the full plate of pakoras and plopped myself on the weather-beaten couch in front of the 14-inch black-and-white television set. The only clear channel announced the Saturday Afternoon Movie, and soon All About Eve flashed on my Lilliputian screen. When she glided across the screen, I couldn't even bear to bite my pakoras for fear of drowning out her haunting voice with my ruminating greed. Bette Davis ascended the winding stairs in her gorgeous long, black, off-shoulder dress, holding a pencil-thin cigarette in her left hand. With her right gloved hand, she lifted her dress up to her ankles to reveal her stilettos, and as she stepped onto the next marbled step, threw back her tresses and hissed, "Fasten your seat belts. It's going to be a bumpy night." Suddenly I was drawn into her voluptuously devious world, unaware of the outside winter storm, my own blues diminishing with each savory fritter flavored with Bette Davis's allure.

1 cup garbanzo bean flour, sifted
½ cup finely chopped cabbage
½ cup finely chopped peeled carrot
½ cup finely chopped peeled, unripe
  green mango
½ cup finely chopped onion
½ cup finely chopped peeled potato
½ cup frozen green peas
2 tablespoons finely chopped fresh
  cilantro

1 teaspoon cumin seed
1 teaspoon Garam Masaala
  (page 206)
1 teaspoon salt
¼ teaspoon ground turmeric
¼ teaspoon baking soda
3 to 4 fresh Thai, cayenne, or
  serrano chilies, finely chopped
½ cup water
Vegetable oil for deep-frying

1. In a medium mixing bowl, combine all ingredients except water and oil
   and mix well. Add the water a few tablespoons at a time until the batter
   clumps up.
2. In a wok or 3-quart saucepan, heat the vegetable oil (about 2 to 3 inches
   deep) over medium heat until a thermometer registers 350°.
3. Gently drop tablespoonfuls of batter into the oil, without overcrowding, and
   fry for 3 to 5 minutes, turning once or twice, until golden brown. Remove
   with a slotted spoon and drain on paper towels. Serve immediately.

Serves 6

MIRCHI PAKORAS
Batter-Dipped Chilies

The longest beach in India is Marina Beach in Chennai (Madras)—sand the color of speckled vanilla ice cream, the blue-green Indian Ocean with its surface calm masking a turbulent underbelly within its icy depth. The gentle warm breeze blowing from its horizon offers little relief from the oppressive heat. But when the sun hides his fiery head in sultry shame behind the sea's unending jade green sareelike horizon, the wind exhales a deep-rooted cool breath, exuberant from its scorching release. The shore draws tourists, families, lovers, and vendors peddling freshly extracted sugarcane juice, plump corn on the cob roasted over hot coals and smothered with lime juice, ground red pepper, and coarsely crushed sea salt, and curvaceous banana peppers blanketed with garbanzo bean flour batter and fried golden brown.

❧ Light green banana peppers are quite spicy, so when you are seeding them, either wear rubber gloves or be sure to thoroughly wash your hands with warm water and soap afterward. The chemical capsaicin that lurks in the pepper's vein and seeds will leave a smarting impression on your hands and lips. Use 1-inch-thick strips of green bell peppers, cut lengthwise, if banana peppers are not available.

❧ I find Boondi Raita (page 211) particularly comforting with these addictive pakoras.

1 pound banana peppers
1 cup garbanzo bean flour
2 tablespoons rice flour
1 teaspoon salt
½ teaspoon ground red pepper (cayenne)

¼ teaspoon ground turmeric
½ cup water
Vegetable oil for deep-frying

1. Cut off the stem end of the peppers. With a paring knife, slit each pepper lengthwise three-quarters of the way without cutting through the pepper. Slip your forefinger and thumb in the slit and remove the seeds (see note for handling instructions).
2. In a medium bowl, combine the two flours, salt, red pepper, and turmeric. Whisk in water, a few tablespoons at a time, to make a thick pancakelike batter.
3. In a wok or 3-quart saucepan, heat the vegetable oil (about 2 to 3 inches deep) over medium heat until thermometer registers 350°.
4. Dip the peppers into the batter to completely coat them. Slip them into the hot oil, a few at a time, without overcrowding, and fry for 3 to 5 minutes, turning occasionally, until golden brown. Remove with a slotted spoon and drain on paper towels.

Serves 4

Street vendor on Marine Beach selling Mirchi Pakoras

Thuviyal Bhujiyas
Batter-Dipped Chutneyed Bread Slices

How could you possibly go wrong with fried bread, especially if it is slathered with chili-spiked cilantro chutney? It is even better dipped in a garbanzo bean flour batter spiced with ground red pepper and fried golden brown. Serve these with Tamatar Chutney (page 225) and Adrak Chai (page 43) for a scrumptious teatime snack.

The rice flour in the batter adds an extra crunch to the fried sandwiches. You can substitute ½ teaspoon baking soda.

I always dip and fry thick slices (about ½ inch) of potato, onion, and green pepper if I have any leftover batter.

Thuviyal (Chutney)

½ cup coarsely chopped fresh cilantro
¼ cup water
½ teaspoon tamarind concentrate
½ teaspoon salt
3 to 4 fresh Thai, cayenne, or serrano chilies
½ small onion, coarsely chopped

Batter

1 cup garbanzo bean flour
2 tablespoons rice flour
1 teaspoon salt
½ teaspoon ground red pepper (cayenne)
¼ teaspoon ground turmeric
½ cup water
8 slices white bread, crusts trimmed
Vegetable oil for deep-frying

TO MAKE THUVIYAL
Puree all the ingredients in a blender until smooth.

TO MAKE BATTER AND ASSEMBLE SANDWICHES
1. In a medium bowl, combine the two flours, salt, red pepper, and turmeric. Whisk in the water, a few tablespoons at a time, to make a thick pancake-like batter.
2. In a wok or 3-quart saucepan, heat the vegetable oil (about 2 to 3 inches deep) over medium heat until a thermometer registers 350°.
3. Liberally spread the thuviyal on one side of each bread slice. Sandwich two bread slices together, thuviyal side in. Cut the sandwiches diagonally (or any shape you prefer). Dip the sandwiches into batter to completely coat them. Slip them into the hot oil, 4 at a time, and fry for 3 to 5 minutes, turning occasionally, until golden brown. Remove with a slotted spoon and drain on paper towels.

Serves 4

MALABAR PAKORAS
Garbanzo Bean Flour Ribbons

These addictive fried noodles are a specialty from India's southern coast of Malabar, home to the world's best black peppercorns. They are often made during Diwali, a festival of great importance to the Hindus of India that is a tribute to Lakshmi, the goddess of wealth and prosperity.

1 cup garbanzo bean flour
1 cup rice flour
1 teaspoon ground red pepper
  (cayenne)
1 teaspoon salt

½ teaspoon hing (asafetida)
2 tablespoons unsalted butter
½ cup warm water
Vegetable oil for deep-frying

1. In a medium bowl, combine the flours, cayenne, salt, and hing. Cut in the butter with a pastry cutter; using the palms of your hands, rub the flour mixture and butter until mixture looks like coarse breadcrumbs.
2. Make a small well in the center of the flour and pour in half of the water. With your fingers, combine the ingredients to form dough. Add additional water, 2 tablespoons at a time, until the dough forms a ball. Knead for 2 to 3 minutes, until the dough is soft and smooth. Cover with plastic wrap and set aside for 10 to 15 minutes. (You can refrigerate dough at this point, covered, up to 24 hours; bring it back to room temperature before proceeding.) Divide the dough into 2 equal portions.
3. In a wok or 3-quart saucepan, heat the vegetable oil (about 2 to 3 inches deep) over medium heat until a thermometer registers 350°.
4. Push the dough through a noodle press (use the noodle mold with the flat, slit-like holes) directly into the hot oil. Fry for 2 to 3 minutes, turning once or twice, until the noodles are golden brown. Drain on paper towels.
5. Cool the noodles, then store them in an airtight container or zip-lock plastic bag at room temperature in a cool spot for up to 2 months.

Makes about 12 ounces

URULIKAZHANGU VADAAS
Potato Croquettes with Lime Juice

Various versions of these addictive croquettes appear at every south Indian wedding; they are traditionally served for breakfast on the day of the ceremony. Piping-hot stainless steel tumblers of coffee with sweetened steamed milk offer an ideal match for these savory-spicy treats.

❧ I love the flavors of these vadaas with Vengayam Thuviyal (page 221).

❧ You might want to double the quantity; one of me can eat 20 of these during the course of an evening!

❧ You can substitute chana dal (yellow split peas) for the urad dal. If karhi leaves are unavailable, eliminate them from the recipe.

❧ Before squeezing fresh limes, roll them on a countertop to soften the skin to get more juice. (You will be amazed at how much more juice you get out of a lime that appears hard and dry.) Cut the lime in half crosswise and use a juicer, reamer, or fork to squeeze the juice out.

3 medium potatoes (1 pound) peeled, boiled, and mashed
1 cup garbanzo bean flour
¼ cup freshly squeezed lime juice
2 tablespoons coarsely chopped fresh karhi leaves
2 tablespoons finely chopped fresh cilantro
1 teaspoon salt
¼ teaspoon ground turmeric

4 to 5 fresh Thai, cayenne, or serrano chilies, finely chopped
1 tablespoon vegetable oil
1 teaspoon black mustard seed
1 tablespoon urad dal (split and hulled black lentils), sorted
1 tablespoon raw cashews, coarsely chopped
Vegetable oil for deep-frying

1. In a medium mixing bowl, combine all the ingredients except the oil, mustard seed, urad dal, and cashews.
2. In a small skillet, heat 1 tablespoon oil over medium-high heat; add the mustard seed. When it begins to pop, cover the skillet. As soon as the seed finishes popping, add the urad dal and cashews. Stir-fry for 30 seconds, or until the dal and cashews turn golden brown. Pour the oil mixture over the potato mixture and mix well.
3. Divide the potato mixture into 20 equal portions. Shape each portion into a ½-inch-thick patty. If the potatoes are a little sticky, grease your palms before shaping them.
4. In a wok or 3-quart saucepan, heat the vegetable oil (about 2 to 3 inches deep) over medium heat until a thermometer registers 350°.
5. Gently drop 5 to 6 patties at a time into the oil and fry for 3 to 5 minutes, turning once or twice until golden brown. Remove with a slotted spoon and drain on paper towels.

Makes 20 Vadaas. Serves 10

MURI
Puffed Rice with Fennel and Cucumber

In this classic street food from Calcutta, India's capital city during the British regime, the cool crispness of cucumbers offsets the pungent mustard oil and the very robust dried red chilies. I love the potatoes in this dish, especially when they are stir-fried long enough to get that crouton-like crunch.

2 tablespoons mustard or vegetable oil

1 teaspoon fennel seed

1 teaspoon cumin seed

½ teaspoon fenugreek seed

3 to 4 dried red Thai, cayenne, or serrano chilies

1 medium potato, peeled and cut into ¼-inch cubes

4 cups puffed rice, lightly toasted (see note)

1 teaspoon salt

½ teaspoon ground red pepper (cayenne)

1 large cucumber, peeled, seeded, and cut into ¼-inch cubes

2 tablespoon finely chopped fresh cilantro

1. In a wok or 12-inch skillet, heat the oil over medium-high heat. Sizzle the fennel, cumin, fenugreek, and chilies for 10 to 15 seconds.
2. Immediately add the potatoes and stir-fry for 8 to 10 minutes, or until dark brown and crispy. Remove the pan from the burner.
3. Meanwhile, combine the puffed rice, salt, and red pepper in a large serving bowl. Add the potato mixture, cucumber, and cilantro, and toss well. Serve immediately.

Serves 6

❧ To toast puffed rice, spread it on an ungreased cookie sheet and bake for about 5 minutes in a 300° oven until crispy. Do not overbake or the rice will turn brown and shrivel up.

❧ Mustard oil is a highly pungent delicacy in eastern Indian cooking. Since this flavorful oil is very potent, it is sold in a slightly diluted form blended with soybean oil. It is widely available in Indian grocery stores and natural food stores.

❧ Leftover muri will turn soggy, so make sure you eat every last morsel.

MEDU VADAAS
Black Lentil Fritters with Potatoes

❧ The flavors from urad dal are essential for these vadaas. You can use chana dal (yellow split peas) instead for a much different texture and taste.

❧ If the karhi leaves are unavailable, you can eliminate them, but they do add a special taste.

❧ The batter will keep in the refrigerator for 3 days or in the freezer for a month. When the batter thaws, the moisture level increases and the batter becomes stickier. A few tablespoons of rice flour will bring it together to a manageable consistency.

❧ If you have trouble shaping the vadaas, just drop teaspoonfuls of hot batter in the hot oil and fry until golden brown. They are delicious any shape.

When Rama's wife Sita was kidnapped by the evil demon Ravana and taken to Lanka (what is now Sri Lanka), it was Hanuman who gathered his troop of monkeys and flew Rama in the palm of his hands over the Indian Ocean to Lanka. Once there, in the heat of the battle, he wrapped a long piece of cloth along the length of his gargantuan tail and dipped it in kerosene. He set fire to his tail and flew around burning Lanka to create a diversion to enable Rama to save his beloved Sita. Dassera's ten-day festival includes a tribute to his tail.

At the crack of dawn on a chilly morning in October, my mother's premier task was to bathe and wrap a clean nine-yard saree around her diminutive body before entering her very small and cluttered kitchen. Amma grabbed the small kerosene stove that sat in a corner, shaking it ever so gently to make sure there was enough fuel, lit it, then sat a dilapidated vanaali (wok) gingerly on its burner. She added enough vegetable oil to fry the vadaas. The previous night, she and Akka, my grandmother, had ground the batter, flavoring it with fresh gingerroot, hot Thai chili peppers, and sweet-smelling karuvapillai (karhi leaves). Amma rested her left thigh on her armamanai, a plank of wood with a sharp blade at one end, to pry open the large pile of fresh banana leaves that my brother had purchased the previous evening for serving food on this special day to our family priests. She deftly cut in half a large leaf and sprinkled it with cold water. She removed the plate that covered the batter in the stainless steel stockpot, releasing the unmistakable citrus smell of the fresh karhi leaves, awakening all my senses.

Amma placed a heaping tablespoon of batter on the lush banana leaf and spread it evenly to 3 inches in diameter. She made a hole similar to a doughnut's in the center of the vadaa. She dripped a drop of water in the hot oil to make sure that it bounced off gently from the surface. When I asked her if it was ready, she nodded her head.

She slipped the vadaa into the hot oil, and the scent of gingerroot and black peppercorns filled the tiny kitchen. "We need at least thirty vadaas," Amma sighed, "for the maala [garland]." It seemed an impossible task, but within moments she had reached that goal. The vadaas had to be in increments of 30. When I asked why, Akka, who was within earshot, mumbled, "That's just the way it is." The vadaas looked so tempting—all evenly round and golden brown. I knew I had to wait to eat them until the priest had blessed the offering.

The armamanai took on the role of a pair of scissors for the long piece of string that would hold the vadaas together. I was in charge of stringing the perfect vadaas and tying the loose ends to make the garland. "What a horrible way to torture a poor hungry boy," I mused out loud, holding the garland high as I walked barefoot away from the kitchen toward the priest who sat in front of Hanuman's framed portrait. His incessant chanting in Sanskrit was haunting and kept me mesmerized for the duration of the tribute. The word samarpayamee *signified the end of the ritual and was permission for me to run to the kitchen to grab a vadaa fresh from the wok. "Heaven on earth," I thought, as I sought to appease the Ravana in my belly.*

1 cup urad dal (split and hulled black lentils), sorted

½ cup uncooked long-grain rice

2 to 3 dried red Thai, cayenne, or serrano chilies

1 tablespoon coarsely chopped gingerroot

3 to 4 fresh Thai, cayenne, or serrano chilies

2 medium potatoes, peeled and shredded (1 cup)

2 tablespoons coarsely chopped fresh karhi leaves

2 tablespoons finely chopped fresh cilantro

1 teaspoon salt

½ teaspoon hing (asafetida)

Vegetable oil for deep-frying

I go the traditional way and inhale these vadaas with Sambhar (page 110) and Thénga Chutney (page 226). They are equally delicious as is.

1. In a medium bowl, cover the dal and rice with water and gently use your fingers to wash the grains for 10 to 20 seconds; drain. Repeat 5 or 6 times until the water in the bowl is clear. Add the dried chilies. Cover with warm water and soak at room temperature for at least 1 to 2 hours, or overnight (about 8 hours); drain.

2. In a food processor, grind the dal-rice mixture with the gingerroot and fresh chilies until smooth. The batter will be fairly thick and feel slightly gritty. Transfer the batter to a bowl and fold in the remaining ingredients. With a wooden spoon or spatula, beat the batter for 2 to 3 minutes to incorporate air.

3. In a wok or 3-quart saucepan, heat the vegetable oil (about 2 to 3 inches deep) over medium heat until a thermometer registers 350°.

4. Generously grease the palms of your hands with oil. Place 2 tablespoons of batter in one palm and with the fingers of your other hand shape into ½-inch-thick patties about 3 inches in diameter. The mixture will be very sticky, so use as much oil as necessary to shape the vadaa. With a forefinger, bore a hole similar to a doughnut's in the center of each vadaa. Gently "peel" the vadaa from your palm and drop it in the hot oil. Fry for 5 to 7 minutes, turning once or twice, until richly golden brown. Remove with slotted spoon and drain on paper towels. Repeat with the remaining batter.

Makes about 10 vadaas

ALOO KEBABS
Minted Onions Stuffed in Potato Shells

My friend Jiten stopped over for lunch when I happened to test this recipe. His first bite and resulting expression said it all. His winsome smile followed by a widening of his dark brown eyes told me that the spicy minted onions in the kebab's center achieved the intended purpose. The appetizer became the entrée, since neither of us could stop at one. Three apiece did not leave much room for anything else, but it really did not matter. We both had fallen madly in love with the same temptress!

❧ In India, kebabs are variously shaped bite-sized pieces of meat, fish, or vegetables that are grilled, deep-fried, or cooked in a griddle. In the Western world they are always considered chunks of meat or vegetables that are skewered and grilled.

❧ This is a great "do-ahead" dish that can be reheated in the oven at 300°. The crispy potato shells regain their crunchy exterior when rewarmed. Due to this fact alone, they also can be frozen for a month. Place the frozen shells on a cookie sheet and reheat at 300° for 20 minutes or until warm in the center.

SHELL

3 medium potatoes (1 pound), peeled, boiled, and mashed
1 teaspoon salt
¼ teaspoon ground turmeric
5 to 6 slices white bread
1 tablespoon vegetable oil

FILLING

½ cup finely chopped onion
3 tablespoons finely chopped fresh cilantro
3 tablespoons finely chopped fresh mint leaves
1 teaspoon salt
6 to 7 fresh Thai, cayenne, or serrano chilies, finely chopped
Vegetable oil for deep-frying

TO MAKE SHELLS

1. In a large bowl, combine the potatoes, salt, and turmeric. Briefly moisten the bread slices under running water, then squeeze them to remove excess water. Add the bread to the potatoes. Knead the mixture well to form soft, smooth dough not unlike bread dough. Add the vegetable oil and knead for 1 to 2 minutes.
2. Divide the dough into 12 equal portions. Shape each portion into a round. Cover with a clean, slightly damp cloth or plastic wrap.

TO MAKE FILLING

In a small bowl mix all the ingredients. Divide into 12 equal portions.

TO ASSEMBLE AND FRY KEBABS

1. Grease your palms with a little oil. One at a time, press a potato round between your palms to form a patty roughly ¼ inch thick and 3 inches in diameter. Place 1 portion of the filling in the center. Gather up the corners of the potato shell and bring them toward the center to cover the filling. Pinch together the gathered edges to seal shut. Gently shape into a patty ½ inch thick and roughly 2 inches in diameter.

2. In a wok or 3-quart saucepan, heat the vegetable oil (about 2 to 3 inches deep) over medium heat until a thermometer inserted in oil registers 350°.

3. Gently slide 6 patties at a time into hot oil and fry 4 to 6 minutes, turning once or twice, until golden brown and crispy. Remove with a slotted spoon and drain on paper towels.

Makes 12 kebabs

If you are averse to deep-frying, these kebabs can be pan-fried in a skillet. Heat 2 tablespoons oil in a nonstick skillet over medium heat. Arrange as many kebabs as possible in a single layer without over-crowding. Cook for 5 to 7 minutes until golden brown and crispy. Flip the kebabs and cook the other side for 5 to 7 minutes until golden brown and crispy. Drain on paper towels. Repeat with remaining kebabs.

FAFDA
Garbanzo Bean Flour Strips with Black Salt

Gujarati-speaking households in India's northwestern region always stock this snack. An early morning cup of tea or a mid-afternoon glass of fresh lemonade laced with black salt usually accompanies a plateful of crispy, addictive fafda. A double batch of this in my house usually does not make it past two days!

1 cup garbanzo bean flour

½ cup urad flour (see note)

1 teaspoon salt

½ teaspoon baking soda

⅓ cup warm water

Vegetable oil for deep-frying

1 teaspoon black salt (see note)

1 teaspoon ground red pepper
 (cayenne)

❧ Urad flour is made by grinding urad dal (split and hulled black lentils) into an ever-so-slightly grainy white flour. This flour is also used for making those delectable lentil wafers called papads (papadums in the south). It is widely available in Indian grocery stores.

❧ Black salt, called kala namak, is a pinkish-gray, smoky-tasting, sulfur-smelling compound mined from stone quarries. The complex-tasting salt is extremely tart and is used to flavor many of India's snacks and legume-based preparations from the north because of its flatulence-reducing powers. There is no substitute for this salt, but if this is the only ingredient not stocked in your pantry that prevents you from preparing this recipe, by all means use regular salt instead.

1. In a medium bowl, combine the two flours, salt, and baking soda. Add water a few tablespoons at a time to bring dough together to form a ball. Knead for 2 to 3 minutes until the dough is fairly stiff. Wrap the dough in plastic wrap.
2. With a meat pounder, gently pound on the plastic-wrapped dough for about 5 minutes until it softens. With lightly greased hands, roll the dough into a log about 15 inches long and 1 inch thick. Cut the log into 10 equal pieces. Shape each piece into a ball. Roll each ball into a circle about ⅛ inch thick and 5 to 6 inches in diameter. Cut the circle into ½-inch-thick strips with kitchen shears. Spread the strips on cookie sheets or paper towels for 5 to 6 hours or overnight until dry.
3. In a wok or 3-quart saucepan, heat the vegetable oil (about 2 to 3 inches deep) over medium heat until a thermometer registers 350°.
4. Fry the strips in hot oil in small batches without overcrowding, for about 5 minutes or until golden brown. Drain on paper towels.
5. Toss with black salt and ground red pepper.

Makes about 8 ounces

Subzi
Vegetables

Mirch Ka Salan
Bell Peppers in Coconut–Poppy Seed Sauce

Bésan Mirch Subzi
Assorted Bell Peppers with Roasted
Garbanzo Bean Flour

Makkai Curry
Corn with Roasted Chilies and Coconut Milk

Bharit
Grilled Pureed Eggplant with Peanuts

Bésan Vanghee
Garbanzo Bean Flour–Crusted Eggplant

Kotorangai Poriyal
Green Beans with Coconut

Vendakkai Bhaaji
Stuffed Fresh Okra

Kaanda Goshtu
Red Onions with Tamarind

Vazhaipazham Curry
Plantain Curry with Sesame Seed

Dum Aloo
Potatoes in Red Chilies–Sesame Sauce

Urulikazhangu Varuval
Spicy Potato Fry

Aloo Baingan
Potatoes with Eggplant

Mrs. Kalia's Aloo Mutter
Chunky Potatoes with Peas

Urulikazhangu Kotorangai Bhaaji
Potatoes and Green Beans with Coconut

Malai Kofta Curry
Potato Croquettes in an Almond-Cream
Sauce

Keerai Masiyal
Stewed Spinach with Coconut Milk

Sarson da Saag
Mustard Greens with Garlic

Sindhi Saai Bhaaji
Mixed Greens with Yellow Split Peas

Palak Paneer
Homemade Cheese with Spinach

Shorakai Curry
Summer Squash with Coconut

Undhiyu
Stuffed Mixed Vegetables with Coconut

MIRCH KA SALAN
Bell Peppers in Coconut–Poppy Seed Sauce

⅔ In Hyderabad, this
recipe is often
anointed with a spicier
pepper, similar to
banana peppers. Use
banana peppers if
available. I have also
used fresh poblano
peppers for an even
hotter version.

⅔ White poppy seeds
provide a nutty but
mellow flavor in this
recipe. If unavailable,
use black poppy seeds
instead for a slightly
bitter but nonetheless
very appealing dish.

I have sampled quite a few renditions of this classic dish from Hyderabad, a city in south central India with a strong Islamic population living in peaceful harmony with the predominantly Hindu majority in the surrounding states. Having tried everything from fiery presentations to mellow combinations, I fell in love with this version, a harmonious balance that truly represents this charming city.

½ cup freshly shredded coconut
  (page 6)
½ cup coarsely chopped onion
2 tablespoons raw cashews
2 tablespoons white poppy seed
4 large cloves garlic
2 to 3 fresh Thai, cayenne, or
  serrano chilies

2 tablespoons Ghee (page 204) or
  vegetable oil
1 pound assorted bell peppers,
  seeded and cut in ½-inch cubes
1 cup water
1 teaspoon salt
2 tablespoons finely chopped fresh
  cilantro

1. In a food processor, finely mince the coconut, onion, cashews, poppy seed, garlic, and chilies.
2. In a 2-quart saucepan, heat the ghee over medium-high heat. Add the coconut mixture and stir-fry for 1 to 2 minutes, or until the mixture turns golden brown.
3. Stir in the remaining ingredients except cilantro and bring to a boil. Reduce the heat to medium and cook, covered, stirring occasionally, for 12 to 15 minutes, or until the peppers are fork-tender. Sprinkle with cilantro.

Serves 4

BÉSAN MIRCH SUBZI
Assorted Bell Peppers with
Roasted Garbanzo Bean Flour

This curry is a specialty of the northeastern region of India. Its roasted garbanzo bean flour base forms delectable clumps around the wok-seared peppers. The flour's nutty flavor is intrinsic to the recipe's success.

½ cup garbanzo bean flour
2 tablespoons vegetable oil
1 teaspoon cumin seed
1 pound assorted bell peppers,
    seeded and cut into 1-inch cubes
2 tablespoons finely chopped fresh
    cilantro

1 teaspoon salt
½ teaspoon ground red pepper
  (cayenne)
½ cup water

1. Preheat a wok or 12-inch skillet over medium-low heat. Add the flour and cook, stirring constantly, for 5 to 7 minutes until golden brown and with a nutty aroma. Transfer the flour to a small bowl or plate to cool. Wipe out the wok with a paper towel or a cloth.

2. In the same wok, heat the oil over medium-high heat. Add the cumin seed and sizzle for 10 to 15 seconds. Add the peppers and stir-fry for 5 to 7 minutes until they are well seared and their skin is slightly blackened and blistered.

3. Stir in the cilantro, salt, red pepper, and roasted flour. Remove the pan from the heat and fold in the water.

Serves 4

✿ Resist the temptation to crank up the heat under the wok to expedite the flour's roasting. Higher temperatures will burn the flour.

✿ A well-seasoned wok or heavy-bottom pan will sear the peppers very well to add complexity to the dish. As the peppers roast, they sweat, and the juices collect in the pan's bottom. When the peppers are not crowded into a too small pan, the liquid will evaporate; otherwise they stew in their own juices. So use at least the recommended pan size.

MAKKAI CURRY
Corn with Roasted Chilies and Coconut Milk

The sweetness of corn is enhanced by coconut milk delicately spiked with roasted red chilies in this delectable side dish from the southwestern state of Kerala. I always serve this with a bowl of steamed rice and a basket of flame-roasted papads (lentil wafers).

🌿 You can substitute frozen corn for fresh when it is not available or at its seasonal best. Be sure to thaw and drain the corn to avoid watering down the delicate curry.

🌿 Dry-roast chilies in a small 6-inch skillet over medium-high heat. Shake the skillet occasionally for 1 to 2 minutes until the chilies slightly blacken. Cool them and pound coarsely with a mortar and pestle until some of the endorphin enhancers are released—also known as its seeds.

2 tablespoons vegetable oil
1 teaspoon black mustard seed
1 cup coconut milk
1 tablespoon finely chopped fresh cilantro
1 teaspoon salt

12 to 15 fresh karhi leaves
2 dried red Thai, cayenne, or serrano chilies, dry-roasted and coarsely pounded (see note)
4 cups fresh corn kernels

1. In a 12-inch skillet, heat the oil over medium-high heat. Add the mustard seed. When it starts to pop, cover the skillet. As soon as the seed finishes popping, stir in the remaining ingredients.
2. Bring the mixture to a boil, then lower the heat and simmer uncovered, stirring occasionally, for 4 to 6 minutes or until the corn is warm and still slightly crunchy.

Serves 6

BHARIT
Grilled Pureed Eggplant with Peanuts

This specialty from India's western state of Maharashtra brings together smoky-flavored eggplant and freshly shredded coconut. I find this recipe especially welcome during the summer months when I take home more than my share of eggplant from the farmers' market.

1 medium eggplant (about
  1½ pounds), stem removed
½ cup freshly shredded coconut
  (page 6)
¼ cup dry-roasted peanuts, finely
  chopped
2 tablespoons finely chopped fresh
  cilantro
1 teaspoon salt

½ teaspoon ground turmeric
20 to 25 fresh karhi leaves, coarsely
  chopped
4 to 6 fresh Thai, cayenne, or
  serrano chilies, finely chopped
1 tablespoon Ghee (page 204) or
  vegetable oil
½ cup finely chopped onion

✎ I serve this pâté with Makkai Ki Roti (page 193) for a simple weekend meal. For a special entertaining menu, you can whip this up as an impressive accompaniment to the main course.

1. Preheat the broiler or outdoor grill for direct heat.
2. Pierce the eggplant with a knife or fork in 4 to 6 places to vent steam when broiling or grilling. Place the eggplant in the broiler pan or on the grill rack and roast it, turning occasionally, for 8 to 10 minutes, or until the skin is completely blistered and almost charcoal-black. Set the eggplant aside covered for 5 to 10 minutes to "steam" the skin for easy peeling. When the eggplant is cool to the touch, peel and discard skin. Mash the eggplant with potato masher.
3. Combine the remaining ingredients, except ghee and onion, with the eggplant.
4. In a wok or 10-inch skillet, heat the ghee over medium-high heat. Add the onions and stir-fry for 3 to 4 minutes until golden brown. Add the eggplant mixture and stir-fry for 8 to 10 minutes to blend the flavors.

Serves 4

Bésan Vanghee
Garbanzo Bean Flour–Crusted Eggplant

This makes a great snack during lazy Sunday afternoons in chilly weather, especially when served with a cup of Adrak Chai (page 43).

1 large eggplant (about 2 pounds),
  stemmed and cut crosswise into
  ½-inch-thick slices
Juice of 1 medium lime (¼ cup)
1 cup garbanzo bean flour

1 teaspoon cumin seed, ground
1 teaspoon ground red pepper
  (cayenne)
1 teaspoon salt
Vegetable oil for pan-frying

1. Moisten the eggplant slices with the lime juice.
2. In a medium bowl, combine the flour, cumin, red pepper, and salt.
3. In a 10-inch nonstick skillet, heat 1 tablespoon oil over medium heat. Evenly coat each eggplant slice with the flour mixture. Place the slices in a single layer in the pan and cook for 3 to 5 minutes, or until golden brown and slightly crispy. Flip the slices and cook for 3 to 5 minutes or until golden brown and crispy. Drain on paper towels.

Serves 4

Kotorangai Poriyal
Green Beans with Coconut

Poriyals are dry coconut-based vegetable dishes usually served at south Indian weddings and other auspicious festivities. I especially love the flavor of fresh green beans when they are at their tender peak during the summer months.

1 tablespoon chana dal (yellow split peas), sorted

12 to 15 fresh karhi leaves

2 dried red Thai, cayenne, or serrano chilies

2 tablespoons Ghee (page 204) or vegetable oil

1 teaspoon black mustard seed

1 tablespoon urad dal (split and hulled black lentils), sorted

1 pound fresh green beans, trimmed and cut into 1-inch pieces

1 cup freshly shredded coconut (page 6)

½ cup water

1 teaspoon salt

2 tablespoons finely chopped fresh cilantro

1. Preheat a 10-inch skillet over medium-high heat. Add the chana dal, karhi leaves, and chilies. Roast the ingredients, shaking the pan occasionally, for 2 to 3 minutes, or until the dal turns golden brown and the chilies slightly blacken. Let cool. In a spice grinder or blender, grind the mixture until it has the texture of finely ground black pepper.
2. In the same skillet, heat the ghee over medium-high heat; add the mustard seed. When the seed begins to pop, cover the skillet. As soon as the seed finishes popping, add the urad dal and stir-fry for 30 seconds, or until the dal is golden brown.
3. Stir in the spice blend and the remaining ingredients except cilantro. Bring to a boil, then lower the heat and steam, covered, stirring occasionally, for 12 to 15 minutes, or until the beans are fork-tender. Sprinkle with cilantro.

Serves 4

VENDAKKAI BHAAJI
Stuffed Fresh Okra

* I love the flavor and texture of fresh okra— not at all like the mouth feel affiliated with Louisiana's gumbo. Friends and students of mine who do not care for okra's "slimy" texture are truly amazed when I reveal the secret to preventing its slippery tendencies: Wash fresh okra under running water and drain on paper towels; allow the okra to dry *completely* before cutting its stem.

* Do not substitute frozen whole okra for fresh.

Imagine my surprise when Mathangi grudgingly picked up a shattuvam (spatula) to flip the dosai (crepe) under Akka's watchful eye.

My sister was always a tomboy who would rather pick up a hockey stick than a karandi (cooking spoon). She insisted on playing ground hockey for her all-woman Sophia College, diligently keeping up with her daily practice, but found every excuse in her convent-educated mind to not learn the tricks of popping black mustard seed the south Indian way. Finally Akka had it and said, "Arré, who will marry you if you don't know how to cook? At least make an attempt to learn to make the bare minimum of sambhar, rasam, shaadum. What face can we show your prospective in-laws who will wonder what happened in your 'education'?" So Mathangi, with tears threatening to flow like the Ganges from her big black eyes, stirred the pigeon peas, strained the rice, and stir-fried the potatoes spiked with Amma's Sambhar Masaala (page 208). My chiding only made matters worse and "the look" from my other sister Lali was enough to send me scampering for safety.

Now Mathangi is married to a wonderful man with "understanding" in-laws. She has two lovely sons and makes all her family's meals to her resident mother-in-law's grudging satisfaction. She weaves in the right spices with the appropriate lentils, vegetables, and rice. She has a penchant for creating her own flavors and takes great pride in combining spices from the north (amchur) and south (mustard seed), a silent rebellious tribute to Akka's rigid Tamilian cooking. This okra recipe is her favorite and over the years has become mine too. I can imagine Akka's almost tooth- less smile, her beaming pride for her "boy-like" granddaughter who learned to be such a fine wife, loving mother, and "educated" cook.

1 pound fresh okra	1 teaspoon cumin seed, ground
½ cup dry-roasted peanuts, ground	1 teaspoon ground red pepper (cayenne)
2 tablespoons finely chopped fresh cilantro	1 teaspoon salt
1 tablespoon coriander seed, ground	¼ cup vegetable oil
1 tablespoon amchur (mango powder)	1 teaspoon black mustard seed
	25 to 30 fresh karhi leaves (see note)

1. Wash the okra and pat it completely dry with paper towels; trim off the stem end. With a paring knife, make a slit about ¼ inch deep from the stem end three-quarters of the way down each okra.
2. In a small bowl, combine all the ingredients except the oil, mustard seed, and karhi leaves.
3. With your fingers, gently pry open an okra to reveal the cavity. Snugly stuff as much peanut-spice blend as possible into the cavity. Repeat with the remaining okra. You can save any remaining peanut-spice blend refrigerated for a week and add it to other vegetable dishes.
4. In a 10-inch skillet or wok, heat the oil over medium-high heat; add the mustard seed. When it begins to pop, cover the skillet. As soon as the seed finishes popping, reduce the heat to low.
5. Add the stuffed okra and karhi leaves to the skillet. Cook, covered, stirring occasionally and gently, for 40 to 45 minutes, or until the okra is fork-tender.

Serves 4

❉ You can substitute an equal amount of grated lemon or lime peel for the amchur.

❉ Fresh karhi leaves provide a highly aromatic but subtle flavor to the okra, but if they are unavailable, don't worry.

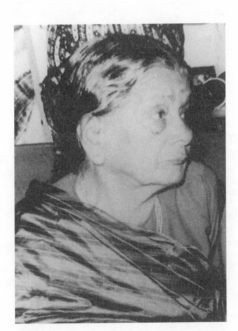

Akka

KAANDA GOSHTU
Red Onions with Tamarind

Each time Amma made goshtu, a stew of coarsely mashed vegetables, she had to make it three different ways: one with eggplant, the second with eggplant and onions, and the third with only onions. You see, eggplant was a bone of contention in our house. My sister Mathangi hated it—"Chi, just like fish," she crinkled her nose, raised her right eyebrow, and nodded her head in that oh-so-Indian way. She loved cooked onions (raw was even better). I, on the other hand, craved eggplant. Its grainy, velvety softness made my temple's bells resonate and I could not imagine diluting its flavors and textures with onions. I did not mind the purity of sweetly caramelized red onions all by their lonesome. And then there were the moderates who wanted it all! So goshtu made its presence known at the dinner table in all its three glorious incarnations, appeasing one and all.

This is a simple side dish I like to serve with fluffy hot Rotlis (page 182) and Keerai Molaghutal (page 94) along with a platter of steamed basmati rice. Leftover steamed rice, when mixed with goshtu and topped with Ghee (page 204), makes for a well-spiked lunch the next day, especially when served with a bowl of cool plain yogurt.

Avoid using a metal wok or a cast-iron pan, since the tamarind's acidity will react with the metal to produce unwanted flavors and colors.

2 tablespoons vegetable oil
1 tablespoon coriander seed
2 dried red Thai, cayenne, or serrano chilies
1 teaspoon black mustard seed

1 large red onion, cut into ½-inch cubes
1 teaspoon tamarind concentrate
1 cup water
½ teaspoon salt

1. In a 1-quart saucepan, heat the oil over medium-high heat. Stir-fry the coriander and chilies for 30 seconds to 1 minute, or until the seed turns reddish-brown and the chilies slightly blacken. Turn off the burner, and with slotted spoon transfer the seed-chilies mixture to a plate to cool. Then grind the mixture in spice grinder until it has the texture of finely ground black pepper.

2. Reheat the oil over medium-high heat; add the mustard seed. When it starts to pop, cover the pan and continue cooking until all the seed has popped. Immediately add the onion and stir-fry on low to medium heat for about 10 minutes, or until caramel brown.

3. Dissolve the tamarind in the water and add it to the onions along with the ground spices and salt. Cook, uncovered, over medium heat, stirring occasionally, for about 15 minutes, or until the liquid evaporates.

Serves 4

VAZHAIPAZHAM CURRY
Plantain Curry with Sesame Seed

This simple curry is offered to the past three generations of male ancestors during the yearly tribute to Appa's demise. The priest folds leaves from the pious pipal tree and fills them with grains of steamed rice. He washes the grains into the fire with clarified butter, invoking the souls of my father's grandfather and his previous male ancestors. Following the purification of the pipal leaves, the priest fills them up yet again with thick slices of plantains bathed in roasted ground sesame seed, black peppercorns, and fresh karhi leaves.

2 large plantains, peeled and cut crosswise into ¼-inch-thick slices

2 cups water

1 tablespoon uncooked long-grain rice

1 tablespoon sesame seed

1 teaspoon black peppercorns

2 tablespoons Ghee (page 204) or vegetable oil

1 teaspoon black mustard seed

1½ teaspoons salt

15 to 20 fresh karhi leaves

> Plantains, widely available in large supermarkets, are a variety of large bananas that have a slightly waxy flavor when cooked. Choose plantains that are olive green and very firm to the touch. Even slightly soft plantains signify ripeness that will impart an unwanted sweetness to the dish.

1. In a 2-quart saucepan, bring the plantains and water to a boil over medium-high heat. Lower the heat to medium and cook, uncovered, stirring occasionally, for 5 to 7 minutes, or until the plantains are fork-tender. Drain the plantains in a colander placed in a bowl. Reserve ½ cup liquid and discard the rest.

2. In a 6-inch skillet, toast the rice, sesame seed, and peppercorns over medium heat, shaking the pan occasionally, for 1 to 2 minutes, or until the rice and sesame seed turn golden brown. Let cool. Transfer the blend to a spice grinder and grind until the mixture is the texture of finely ground black pepper.

3. In a wok or 10-inch skillet, heat the ghee over medium-high heat; add the mustard seed. When it starts to pop, cover the skillet until all seed has popped. Immediately add the plantains, roasted ground spices, salt, karhi leaves, and reserved liquid.

4. Simmer the curry for 1 to 2 minutes, or until the sauce thickens.

Serves 4

Dum Aloo
Potatoes in Red Chilies–Sesame Sauce

I was never allowed to travel outside Mumbai on my own, even when I was eighteen and invincible. So when the opportunity knocked on my door, I was beside myself with anticipated adulthood. I had just spent two weeks in Vadodara, north of Mumbai, under the watchful eyes of my cousin and his wife. His accent intrigued me, that distinct American twang he had cultivated during his tenure in Minneapolis–St. Paul while teaching at the University of Minnesota. I wanted to imitate the way he enunciated "can't" in that slow nasal drawl. I unfortunately mouthed it just as the Jesuits had taught me to, in that proper English way.

The modest bungalow with its sprawling mango groves in the front yard and the four karhi leaf trees in the back made the stay more memorable. It was bittersweet to leave the sweetly romantic wake-up call of two peacocks fanning their glory in a show of male bravado for the constant cacophony of car and bicycle horns in the concrete jungle called Mumbai.

Off I was whisked to the railway station at Vadodra and tucked away securely into the cool comforts of the first-class sleeper compartment of the Rajdhani Express that had made its way from New Delhi. My heart was aflutter and I felt a curious vulnerability mixed in with a false sense of independence. I was, in reality, more interested in finding out what my dinner tray would contain when the train pulled into Surat, a city that balanced contrasting flavors of garlic, chilies, and jaggery (a raw form of cane sugar). Along with airily puffy whole wheat breads, freshly pureed Alphonso mangoes, and split lima beans bathed in a spicy green chili sauce was this mound of chunky potatoes surrounded by a sesame paste darkened with exotica that to me was Surat. I had ordered the "no-garlic" dinner, but over the years I have grown to like this pervasively flavorful bulb and the true gusto that lifts this humble tuber to an elevation touched only by Rama himself.

6 medium cloves garlic

3 dried red Thai, cayenne, or serrano
  chilies

1 teaspoon cumin seed

1 teaspoon salt

¼ teaspoon ground turmeric

2 tablespoons vegetable oil

2 tablespoons sesame seed, ground

3 medium potatoes (1 pound),
  peeled, boiled, and cut into
  1-inch cubes

½ cup water

1 tablespoon finely chopped fresh
  cilantro

1. In a food processor finely mince the garlic, chilies, cumin, salt, and turmeric.
2. In a 10-inch skillet, heat the oil over medium-high heat. Add the garlic mixture and stir-fry for 1 minute, or until the garlic turns golden brown and the mixture acquires a pungent aroma.
3. Add the sesame seed and stir-fry for 30 seconds or until golden brown.
4. Stir in the potatoes and water. Lower the heat and simmer, uncovered, stirring occasionally, for 3 to 5 minutes, or until the water is almost absorbed. Sprinkle with cilantro.

Serves 4

URULIKAZHANGU VARUVAL
Spicy Potato Fry

If there had been a group called Potatoes Anonymous while I was growing up in Mumbai, my family would have insisted that I become a card-carrying member. I, on the other hand, never considered my condition an issue. I coveted my favorite tuber daily, and there came a point in my existence when my own Amma quit asking my opinion on what vegetable she should make for the evening's meal. Urulikazhangu, aloo, batata, pomme de terre, potato, batéta—in all six languages that I spoke, they boiled down to that ubiquitous tuber. Soon I was known as "Aloo Baba" (Potato Child), destined to become Mumbai's leading starch head.

While growing up in Appa's naval quarters overlooking the Arabian Sea, my habit was generously fed. Amma succumbed to my constant demands for homemade shoe-string fries. The thick alkaline breeze wafted through the open balcony of our sixth-floor apartment, mingling with the aroma of potatoes sizzling in hot fat. I yelled above the momentary splutter of salted water being sprinkled in sizzling oil to ask if they were ready. "Patience, patience," she cried, and soon the crispy potatoes smothered with ground red pepper, fresh karhi leaves, and cilantro lay in my small thali (plate), my fingertips losing all sensation against their heat, my mouth afire with an unabashed passion for their gusto.

- Use any kind of potato you like. I prefer baking potatoes for their higher starch content. Amma always peeled her potatoes, but skin-on tubers can be extra tasty (and nutritious).

- Skip the karhi leaves if they are unavailable.

Vegetable oil for deep-frying
2 large white potatoes, peeled and cut lengthwise into ¼-inch-thick strips
1 tablespoon finely chopped fresh cilantro
1 tablespoon coarsely chopped fresh karhi leaves
½ teaspoon salt
½ teaspoon ground red pepper (cayenne)

1. In a wok or 3-quart saucepan, heat the vegetable oil (about 2 to 3 inches deep) over medium heat until a thermometer registers 350°.
2. Fry half the potatoes in the hot oil without overcrowding, turning occasionally, for 6 to 8 minutes, or until crispy and golden brown. Remove with a slotted spoon and drain on paper towels. Repeat with the remaining potatoes.
3. In a medium bowl, combine the fried potatoes with the remaining ingredients. Toss well to coat.

Serves 4

Aloo Baingan
Potatoes with Eggplant

Home cooks in Calcutta create miracles by combining spices we would rarely think of putting together. They are masters at creating special vegetable combinations with eggplant. This one with potatoes makes me sing all day long.

2 tablespoons Ghee (page 204) or
  vegetable oil
1 teaspoon fennel seed
1 teaspoon cumin seed
2 to 3 dried red Thai, cayenne, or
  serrano chilies
3 medium potatoes (1 pound),
  peeled and cut into 1-inch cubes
1 tablespoon coriander seed, ground
1 teaspoon salt

½ teaspoon ground red pepper
  (cayenne)
¼ teaspoon ground turmeric
1 medium eggplant (about 1 pound),
  cut into 1-inch cubes
½ cup water
1 medium tomato, cut into
  1-inch cubes
2 tablespoons finely chopped fresh
  cilantro

1. In a wok or 12-inch skillet, heat the ghee over medium-high heat. Add the fennel, cumin, and chilies and sizzle for 10 to 15 seconds until the seeds turn reddish brown and fragrant and the chilies slightly blacken.
2. Reduce the heat to low and add the potatoes, coriander, salt, red pepper, and turmeric. Cook, covered, stirring occasionally, for 15 minutes, or until the potatoes are partially cooked.
3. Stir in the eggplant and water. Simmer, covered, stirring occasionally, for 15 to 20 minutes or until the potatoes and eggplant are cooked.
4. Add the remaining ingredients and cook, covered, for 5 minutes until the tomato is warm.

Serves 6

Mrs. Kalia's Aloo Mutter
Chunky Potatoes with Peas

I was still exhausted from the twenty-four-hour flight as the car driven by a family friend made its way through the cornfields of southwestern Minnesota. It was the fall of 1982 and my second day in the United States. Lost in numbed thought, I was beginning to fully understand that I was alone and for the first time away from my familiar life in Mumbai. Panic washed over me as the white station wagon approached the small town of Marshall, and the four-story buildings of the university campus towered above the flat fields. What was my one-hundred-pound, brown-skinned body doing here? But more important, what was I going to do for meals? My dormitory arrangements did not include food. It was getting obvious to me that the local restaurants would not serve the food I was used to, especially since I was, like many Indians, a vegetarian. Lali's nagging words reverberated within my shivering being: "You better learn to cook or you will be sorry."

An hour later, standing amid the clutter of my large suitcases in the small dorm room, I pried open a window to watch my friend drive away. I had known that leaving home would be the start of a journey, but the whiff of the chilled autumn breeze, carrying with it the fresh-mown grass smell of harvested corn, mixed with the acrid odor of pig farms, gave me no clue to the culinary odyssey ahead of me.

Like a parched man drawn to the oasis in the desert of Rajasthan, I found myself looking for an Indian surrogate mother to make familiar foods that would coat my tongue with succulent, spicy treats. And so I was drawn to the Kalias. Dr. Kalia, who taught mathematics on campus, and his kind and very pregnant wife, with a gentle face and big-framed glasses that kept slipping off her dainty nose, were my apsaras—angels of mercy, warmhearted in a land frozen shut by the harsh, merciless winter. It did not matter that they predominantly ate north Indian foods, a far cry from my noodles, crepes, and dumpling heritage; I was eternally grateful for the familial companionship that nurtured my soul with warm rotis wrapped around cardamom-scented kidney beans and spicy potatoes and peas curry.

1 cup coarsely chopped onion

2 tablespoons coarsely chopped
   gingerroot

2 large cloves garlic

2 tablespoons vegetable oil

1 teaspoon cumin seed

3 medium potatoes (1 pound),
   peeled, boiled, and cut into
   1-inch cubes

2 cups frozen green peas

2 medium tomatoes cut into
   1-inch cubes

1 cup water

1 teaspoon Garam Masaala
   (page 206)

1 teaspoon ground red pepper
   (cayenne)

1 teaspoon salt

¼ teaspoon ground turmeric

2 tablespoons finely chopped fresh
   cilantro

1. In a food processor finely mince the onion, gingerroot, and garlic.
2. In a wok or 12-inch skillet, heat the oil over medium-high heat. Add the
   cumin seed and sizzle for 15 to 20 seconds. Add the onion mixture and
   stir-fry for 3 to 5 minutes until golden brown.
3. Stir in the remaining ingredients except cilantro. Lower the heat and cook,
   covered, stirring occasionally, for 12 to 15 minutes until the potatoes are
   warm, the peas are cooked, and the sauce slightly thickens. Sprinkle with
   cilantro.

Serves 6

Urulikazhangu Kotorangai Bhaaji
Potatoes and Green Beans with Coconut

If you are using frozen green beans, purchase the precut ones and do not thaw them before adding to the potatoes. The moisture from the frozen beans will help steam the vegetables along with the liquid from the freshly shredded coconut.

When green beans were at the peak of their season, Amma made this side dish that highlighted their inherent sweetness. The potatoes were incorporated to appease me and to ensure that I ate four Rotlis (page 182) the nights this combination graced our dinner table.

2 tablespoons vegetable oil

1 teaspoon black mustard seed

3 medium potatoes (1 pound), peeled and cut into ½-inch cubes

½ pound fresh green beans, cut into ½-inch pieces

1 cup freshly shredded coconut (page 6)

1 teaspoon salt

½ teaspoon ground red pepper (cayenne)

¼ teaspoon ground turmeric

12 to 15 fresh karhi leaves

1. In a wok or 12-inch skillet, heat the oil over medium-high heat; add the mustard seed. When it begins to pop, cover the skillet. As soon as the seed finishes popping, add the potatoes and stir-fry for about 3 to 4 minutes, or until partially brown.
2. Stir in the remaining ingredients and simmer, covered, stirring occasionally, for about 15 minutes until the potatoes and beans are fork-tender.

Serves 6

Coconut and flower vendor outside a temple in Mumbai

MALAI KOFTA CURRY
Potato Croquettes in an Almond-Cream Sauce

❧ Shape the koftas into
balls immediately after
you have mixed the
ingredients. The salt in
the mixture along with
the liquid from the
potatoes continues to
add moisture, which
makes the mixture
difficult to handle if
you wait.

❧ Do not be afraid of
adding half-and-half to
the hot-tempered
almond-tomato
mixture, since the
extra fat in the dairy
will prevent the sauce
from breaking or
curdling.

This sinfully rich curry should be relished in small bites to prolong your sensual dining experience. The first time I met this creamy almond sauce draped over golden brown rounds of fried potato croquettes was at my friend Anand's sister's wedding. His northern Indian heritage was evident in his light skin, thick dark eyebrows, and full lips—his ethnic appearance diluted over the centuries from Aryan ancestry. His sister Sheetal was a close replica, her dark hair covered with strands of gold jewelry, and her body masked in deep red bridal wear.

Sheetal sat demurely next to her husband while Anand and I sat across from them, ready to stick our tongues out should she glance in our direction. When the waiter served these koftas, Sheetal blushed, which made Anand and me giggle, our nervous laughter laced with the knowledge of her looming departure to her stranger husband's abode. This was an arranged marriage and her only third "viewing" of her husband. Anand eagerly dove his fingers into the smooth, creamy, delectable rounds and moaned with joyful gluttony. I had never tasted these before and so followed his actions with blind faith—and the soft, succulent, spicy koftas did not disappoint.

If weddings were the only time one could savor this treat, I of course wanted to get married for that reason alone. Later I found out the real reason for Sheetal's beet-red face—these koftas were considered a sign of fertility, a symbol of promise and hope that she would yield many sons in the years to come.

KOFTAS

Vegetable oil for deep-frying
3 medium potatoes (about 1 pound),
   peeled and shredded
1 cup finely chopped red onion
1 cup garbanzo bean flour

2 tablespoons finely chopped fresh
   cilantro
1 teaspoon salt
4 to 6 fresh Thai, cayenne, or
   serrano chilies, finely chopped

MALAI CURRY

2 tablespoons Ghee (page 204) or
  vegetable oil
1 teaspoon cumin seed
1 cup finely chopped red onion
1 tablespoon finely chopped
  gingerroot
4 medium cloves garlic, finely
  chopped

1 cup finely chopped tomato
¼ cup blanched almonds, ground
1 teaspoon salt
½ teaspoon ground red pepper
  (cayenne)
2 cups half-and-half
2 tablespoons finely chopped fresh
  cilantro

TO MAKE KOFTAS

1. In a wok or 3-quart saucepan, heat the vegetable oil (about 2 to 3 inches deep) over medium heat until a thermometer registers 350°.
2. In a medium bowl, combine all ingredients and mix well. Divide the mixture into 18 equal portions. Shape each portion into a round ball. The mixture will feel wet, but rest assured that the balls will not fall apart while cooking.
3. Gently drop half the balls in hot oil (without overcrowding). Fry for about 3 to 5 minutes, turning them occasionally, until golden brown. Remove with a slotted spoon and drain on paper towels. Repeat with the remaining balls.

TO MAKE MALAI CURRY

1. In a 3-quart saucepan, heat the ghee over medium-high heat. Sizzle the cumin seed for 10 to 15 seconds.
2. Add the onion, gingerroot, and garlic and stir-fry for 3 to 4 minutes, or until golden brown.
3. Stir in the tomato, almonds, salt, and cayenne. Cook, stirring occasionally, for 2 to 3 minutes, or until the tomato softens.
4. Fold in the fried koftas and half-and-half. Bring to a boil, then lower heat to medium and simmer, uncovered, stirring gently and occasionally, for 4 to 6 minutes, or until the sauce slightly thickens. Sprinkle with cilantro.

Serves 6

Keerai Masiyal
Stewed Spinach with Coconut Milk

You can use frozen chopped spinach. Thaw it, then squeeze out the water.

You line up one thousand nine-yard-saree-wearing, single-studded-nose-ringed Tamilian ammas, hand them a bunch of fresh spinach, and ask them to make keerai masiyal, and I guarantee you will taste as many renditions. Here's one of my favorites.

2 tablespoons vegetable oil
1 teaspoon black mustard seed
1 tablespoon urad dal (split and hulled black lentils), sorted
1 package (10 ounces) fresh spinach leaves, finely chopped

1 teaspoon Sambhar Masaala (page 208)
½ teaspoon salt
½ cup unsweetened coconut milk
½ cup water

1. In a 2-quart saucepan, heat the oil over medium-high heat; add the mustard seed. When it begins to pop, cover the skillet. As soon as the seed finishes popping, add the urad dal and stir-fry for 30 seconds, or until golden brown.
2. Stir in the spinach, a handful at a time (if using fresh), and cook until just wilted, 1 to 2 minutes.
3. Add the remaining ingredients and continue cooking, uncovered, stirring occasionally, for 3 to 4 minutes to blend the flavors.

Serves 4

SARSON DA SAAG
Mustard Greens with Garlic

Saag means greens; sarson da saag specifies mustard greens, and palak da saag is spinach. This flavorful side dish often accompanies hearty whole-wheat griddle breads in Punjab, the wheat-growing capital of India. I love this recipe with Makkai Ki Roti (page 193) for a simple lunch.

½ cup coarsely chopped onion
1 tablespoon coarsely chopped gingerroot
4 large cloves garlic
2 tablespoons Ghee (page 204) or vegetable oil
¼ teaspoon hing (asafetida)
1½ pounds fresh mustard greens, finely chopped

½ teaspoon ground turmeric
1 large tomato, blanched, skinned, and finely chopped (see note)
1 teaspoon Garam Masaala (page 206)
1 teaspoon salt
Juice of 1 medium lime

1. In a food processor finely mince the onion, gingerroot, and garlic.
2. In a wok or 3-quart saucepan, heat the ghee over medium-high heat; sizzle the hing for 5 to 10 seconds. Add the onion mixture and stir-fry for 3 to 5 minutes until golden brown.
3. Stir in the mustard greens and turmeric. Cook, stirring occasionally, for 8 to 10 minutes, or until the greens wilt and almost all the liquid leaching from the greens evaporates.
4. Add the remaining ingredients and cook, stirring occasionally, 5 minutes to blend the flavors.

Serves 4

❧ The slight bitterness of mustard greens provides a complex balance to this earthy dish. Trim off and discard the tough stems before use.

❧ You can substitute spinach leaves for a smoother, less bitter flavor, or use a combination of the two greens.

❧ To blanch a tomato, bring a small saucepan of water to a boil over medium-high heat. Simmer the tomato for 2 to 3 minutes until the skin starts to tear. Remove with a slotted spoon and cool until easy to handle. Core the tomato and slip its skin off easily with a paring knife or your bare hands.

SINDHI SAAI BHAAJI
Mixed Greens with Yellow Split Peas

Sindhis are a community of Indians with roots from the northwestern region. They are extremely hospitable and are known for their sharp business acumen. Many of our close family friends are Sindhis, including the Chandwanis, our neighbors across the hall. I always enjoyed Mrs. Chandwani's company, her "everything is all right" attitude providing perennial joy. She always wore white sarees, even when her husband was alive, with her shocking gray-white hair tightly knotted in a bun. Her beautifully tanned smooth skin was taut even at sixty-five years of age, a tightness that mirrored her relationship with her large family. I loved visiting her home on Sunday evenings to watch the Hindi movie of the week on her black-and-white television set, the only one in our apartment building during the early seventies. The familiar clacking of knitting needles as she sat in her oversized wicker chair offered background noise to Lata Mangeshkar's nightingale voice emanating from Waheeda Rehman's hauntingly full lips. The occasional crunch of Mrs. Chandwani's home-made, airily crisp papads peppered my palate and soul.

Mrs. Chandwani's hospitality always warmed my heart, especially when Appa succumbed to his malignant brain tumor. The Sunday he died, soon after an uninvited visit by Yaman, the god of death, all cooking came to a standstill in our home. We wore our grief on our sleeves as the hours ticked by and his body lay prostrate on the hard terrazzo floor of the master bedroom covered by a clean white sheet of hand-woven cotton. None of us felt like it, but we had to eat in order to be strong for battling the soulful sadness coming over us. We took turns crossing our Yaman-kissed threshold to Mrs. Chandwani's dining table, which was filled with heaps of sympathetic love, plates of steamed rice, delicately spiced potatoes, mounds of fluffy rotis, and bowls filled with dark green saai bhaaji drizzled with cumin-scented homemade ghee. My growling stomach prodded my guilt-ridden mind to help myself to a large helping of the pureed vegetables, my eyes brimming with salty, heavy-hearted tears.

¼ cup chana dal (yellow split peas), sorted and rinsed

3 cups water

½ pound fresh mustard greens, coarsely chopped

½ pound fresh spinach leaves, coarsely chopped

1 cup diced eggplant

1 small potato, peeled and diced

1 small onion, coarsely chopped

1 large tomato, coarsely chopped

2 to 4 fresh Thai, cayenne, or
  serrano chilies

2 tablespoons Ghee (page 204) or
  vegetable oil

1 teaspoon cumin seed

6 medium cloves garlic, finely
  chopped

1 teaspoon salt

1. In a 3-quart saucepan, bring the dal and water to a boil over medium-high heat. Skim off any foam that forms on its surface. Lower the heat to medium and simmer, partially covered, stirring occasionally, for 10 minutes, or until the dal is partially cooked.
2. Stir in the remaining ingredients except ghee, cumin, garlic, and salt. Continue simmering, covered, stirring occasionally, for 15 to 20 minutes, or until the vegetables are fork-tender. Let the mixture cool for about 30 minutes.
3. In a blender or food processor, puree the mixture until smooth. Return the mixture to the saucepan and rewarm over low heat.
4. Meanwhile, heat the ghee in a small skillet over medium heat. Add cumin seed and sizzle for 15 to 20 seconds. Stir in the garlic and stir-fry for 1 to 2 minutes until golden brown. Stir in the salt. Add the ghee mixture to the pureed vegetable blend and continue simmering 5 minutes to blend the flavors.

Serves 6

Palak Paneer
Homemade Cheese with Spinach

❧ This version of palak paneer differs from the norm as it adds a unique south Indian twist of sambhar masaala and includes no garlic.

❧ For a delicious, slightly bitter twist, combine mustard greens with the spinach.

❧ Enjoy this dish with any of the breads in this book.

I was eight and had just spent the morning sitting by Appa's hospital cot on a cold, round, stainless steel three-legged stool. It was the day after his brain surgery and he was sleeping in numbed comfort. It was lunchtime and Lali, tired from hospital duty and antiseptic smells, took me to my first north Indian restaurant across the street from King Edward Memorial Hospital's Victorian, weather-beaten splendor. The smells permeating the dining room were unfamiliar to me, and the waiters carrying trays of red-colored meats to an adjacent table made my dark brown eyes widen with horror. "That's tandoori murghi," Lali chided. "Do you want some?" "Chi, no," I clucked, forcing the wave of nausea back down my throat. She ordered palak paneer, aloo gobhi, subzi pulao, and naan—standards that I encountered during my later years in every north Indian restaurant in America. I enjoyed the aloo gobhi, pulao, and naan—but the palak paneer was another story.

The firm white cubes of paneer (homemade cheese, I was told) with their surface blistered golden brown by hot oil lay nestled in a mass of spinach greens. My fingers prodded a cube gently to see whether it would move, but it lay perfectly still in its Gandhian non-violent response. The first bite delicately crunched its thin brown skin and sank into a firm-textured, slightly chewy interior. My palate didn't quite know what to think of this texture since it was more familiar with pillow-soft dumplings and lacy-crisp crepes. I shelved the experience in my vegetarian brain in the folder marked "meat," promising never to retrieve it from the archives of the unappetizing.

Fortunately, during my teenage years I became more comfortable with textures of all kinds and unlocked the file from my memory database, discovering the true beauty of nutritious and tasty paneer folded in a robust blend of caramelized onions, ginger, pureed spinach, and spices. Now I always keep chunks of fried paneer in my freezer to give a boost of protein to vegetable dishes at a moment's notice and to fondly reminisce about that first encounter with "meat."

2 tablespoons Ghee (page 204) or vegetable oil

1 teaspoon cumin seed

1 medium onion, thinly sliced

1 tablespoon finely chopped gingerroot

1 pound fresh spinach leaves, washed and coarsely chopped

½ cup finely chopped fresh tomato

1 teaspoon Sambhar Masaala (page 208)

1 teaspoon Garam Masaala (page 206)

1 teaspoon salt
½ teaspoon ground red pepper
  (cayenne)

¼ cup heavy (whipping) cream
1 cup ½-inch cubes fried Paneer
  (page 210)

1. In a 2-quart saucepan, heat the ghee over medium-high heat. Add the cumin seed and sizzle for 10 to 15 seconds.
2. Add the onion and gingerroot and stir-fry for about 5 minutes until dark brown. Stir in the spinach, a handful at a time, and cook until wilted. Mix in the remaining ingredients except the cream and paneer. Transfer the mixture to a blender or food processor and puree until smooth.
3. Return the pureed spinach to the saucepan and add the cream. Cook over low heat, uncovered, stirring occasionally, for about 5 minutes to blend the flavors.
4. Fold in the paneer and cook for about 5 minutes until the paneer warms through.

Serves 4

SHORAKAI CURRY
Summer Squash with Coconut

Akka refused this harmless-looking, bowling pin–like summer squash entry into her kitchen. My grandmother had strong opinions about everything: why girls should never have short hair; how gaudy her daughter-in-law's sarees were; which vegetable could or could not be eaten in a Brahmin household. When asked the reasoning for any of her opinions, she simply would say, "What gall. I am your grandmother, I know many things you don't, so please don't ask weird questions." I of course rarely argued with her, except to pester her at times by pushing those forbidden buttons.

Shorakai, also known as opa squash in supermarkets in the United States, was never eaten in my grandmother's kitchen. She said it would make you scratch your skin uncontrollably and break into hives, and that a true Brahmin would never eat this lowly vegetable, reserved only for the shudras (lower castes). So of course I had to try it at a (non-Brahmin) friend's house whose mother had no qualms about making this squash. I nervously remembered Akkas's warnings when I took my first bite, waiting for my body to break out in sheer punishment for disobeying her. It of course never happened, and the delicious flavors of the tender squash bathed in the nutty, hot-sweet coconut sauce soon engulfed me in its low-caste devilish comfort. I fondly remember Akka's unsubstantiated tales and I momentarily hesitate each time I devour this humble squash even today!

- Shorakai or opa squash is a pale-green-skinned summer squash shaped like a bowling pin, widely available in supermarkets and Asian grocery stores. I have seen it in various shapes and sizes, oftentimes even 1 foot long at local farmers' markets. Choose squash that is firm and smooth with an unblemished skin.

- You can substitute yellow squash, unpeeled and unseeded, or try any of your favorite squashes as variations.

- A potato peeler is great for peeling this squash. Cut off the stem end and peel the squash to reveal a white flesh. Cut the squash lengthwise and, with a spoon, scoop out and discard the seeds with any surrounding fibrous pulp.

- Omit karhi leaves from recipe if they are unavailable.

2 medium opa squashes (about 1 pound each), peeled, seeded, and cut into 1-inch cubes
1 cup water
1 cup freshly shredded coconut (page 6)
3 to 4 fresh Thai, cayenne, or serrano chilies

2 tablespoons Ghee (page 204) or vegetable oil
1 teaspoon cumin seed
2 tablespoons finely chopped fresh cilantro
1 teaspoon salt
15 to 20 fresh karhi leaves

1. In a 2-quart saucepan bring the squash and water to a boil over medium-high heat. Lower the heat to medium and cook, uncovered, stirring occasionally, for 10 to 12 minutes, or until the squash is fork-tender.
2. In a blender, puree the coconut and chilies until smooth. Use any resid-

ual liquid from the squash, if needed, for grinding coconut mixture. Add to the squash, stir well, and simmer, uncovered, for 3 to 5 minutes.

3. Meanwhile, in a 6-inch skillet, heat the ghee over medium-high heat. Add the cumin seed and sizzle for 30 seconds. Remove the skillet from the heat and stir in the remaining ingredients. Pour the ghee mixture into the saucepan, stir, and continue simmering, uncovered, for 3 to 5 minutes to blend the flavors.

Serves 6

I usually enjoy this curry with a bowl of steamed rice, pickle, and Rotlis (page 180) for a simple evening meal.

UNDHIYU
Stuffed Mixed Vegetables with Coconut

This is one of those classic Gujarati dishes that appear at every wedding and other very special family gatherings. The mixture of vegetables varies among households, some incorporating seasonal purple yams (very rarely available in the United States) as an unusual ingredient. Fresh fenugreek-flavored croquettes also sneak their way into the mix, making the dish more time-consuming but well worth it.

- Undhiyu is a great combination with Rava Pooris (page 194). Throw in some homemade pickle from this book, and you have a winning meal. Savor every bite as if it were your last.

- Fafda are flat, light green pea pods often found in Indian grocery stores. They are seasonal (usually available in the United States in the late spring and summer), so grab them as quickly as you can. Off-season, you can use frozen fafda. If you are in a bind, use the more commonly available Chinese pea pods.

- Baby eggplant is found in the produce section of Indian grocery stores. These are dark purple in color and are usually no larger than plum tomatoes. If unavailable, use regular eggplant. Choose the thinnest and smallest one you can find. Remove the stem end and slice it crosswise into 2-inch-thick slices.

½-pound baby eggplant, stem end removed

3 medium potatoes, peeled

1 large sweet potato, peeled

1 large plantain, peeled

1 cup freshly shredded coconut (page 6)

¼ cup finely chopped fresh cilantro

2 tablespoons coriander seed, ground

2 tablespoons cumin seed, ground

2 tablespoons sugar

2 teaspoons salt

2 teaspoons ajwain (bishop's-weed)

2 teaspoons ground red pepper (cayenne)

½ cup vegetable oil

1 cup fafda (flat pea pods), stem end removed

1. Cut open the eggplant by making X-shaped cuts from the stem end, three-quarters of the way down, without cutting all the way through.
2. Cut up the potatoes, sweet potato, and plantain into 2-inch slices. Slit each slice similar to the eggplant.
3. In a medium bowl, combine the coconut, cilantro, coriander, cumin, sugar, salt, ajwain, and cayenne.
4. Stuff each of the slit vegetables with as much of the coconut-spice mixture as it will hold.
5. In an 8-quart saucepan or Dutch oven, heat the oil over low heat. Add the stuffed vegetables and fafda. Cook, covered, stirring very gently and occasionally, for about 2 hours, or until the vegetables are fork-tender. Some of the stuffed vegetables will fall apart, along with their filling. That's okay.

Serves 6

Dals
Lentil-Based Stews

Murghi Dhansaak
Multilentil Stew with Chicken and Vegetables

Keerai Molaghutal
Spinach Stew with Pigeon Peas

Mung Nu Dal
Split Green Lentils with Peanuts

Sabud Masoor Dal
Brown Lentils with Garlic

Dahi Pakodi
Spinach Croquettes in Spicy Yogurt Sauce

Dal Maharani
Black Lentils with Kidney Beans

Kashmiri Chana
Garbanzo Beans with Mushrooms

Shundal
Black-Eyed Peas with Coconut and Jaggery

Cauliflower Kootu
Cauliflower Stew with Yellow Split Peas

Molaghu Rasam
Pepper Soup with Tamarind

Sambhar
Pigeon Pea Stew with Vegetables

Mendia Kozhumbu
Onions in Tamarind-Fenugreek Sauce

Yezhai Kariha Kootu
Seven-Vegetable Curry with Jaggery

Chana Dal Usli
Steamed Yellow Split Peas with Green Beans

MURGHI DHANSAAK
Multilentil Stew with Chicken and Vegetables

⚜ All the lentils used in this recipe are widely available in stores and mail-order resources that sell Indian groceries. Fresh fenugreek leaves are hard to come by, but you should be able to find dried leaves (called kasoori méthi) in Indian stores nationwide.

⚜ This classic combination of vegetables and lentils is finger-licking good, but use any other permutation of ingredients for variations. I have even made a vegetarian version, sans chicken, on many an occasion.

⚜ Eliminate karhi leaves if they are not available.

Here's a question to ponder: What do Zubin Mehta (formerly conductor of New York's Philharmonic Orchestra), Freddie Mercury, born Farrokh Balsara (the late lead singer of the musical group Queen), and the well-known, affluent industrialist Birla and Tata families from Mumbai have in common? Their roots trace back to a group of Persians who fled Iran when the Islamic powers took over, needing to protect their religion based on the teachings of Zoroaster, worshiper of the sacred fire. Zoroastrians, later known as Parsees, eventually settled in Bombay, bringing with them Persian cooking techniques and adapting to locally available spices and legumes. This lentil-chicken powerhouse of a dish is a must in every Parsee home.

¼ cup masoor dal (red lentils), sorted

¼ cup vaal nu dal (split lima beans), sorted

¼ cup mung dal (split and hulled green lentils), sorted

¼ cup toovar dal (split and hulled pigeon peas), sorted

4 cups water

2 pounds bone-in chicken pieces, skin removed

1 small butternut squash, peeled, seeded, and coarsely chopped

1 small Asian eggplant, coarsely chopped

1 medium potato, peeled and coarsely chopped

2 tablespoons Ghee (page 204) or vegetable oil

1 teaspoon cumin seed

1 medium red onion, halved and thinly sliced

4 medium cloves garlic, finely chopped

1 cup finely chopped fresh fenugreek leaves, or ½ cup dried, crumbled

2 tablespoons finely chopped fresh cilantro

2 teaspoons salt

1 teaspoon ground red pepper (cayenne)

¼ teaspoon ground turmeric

15 to 20 fresh karhi leaves

1. In a Dutch oven or large saucepan, cover the four dals with water. With your fingers, gently wash the dals for 30 seconds until the water becomes cloudy; drain. Repeat 5 or 6 times until the water is clear.
2. Add the water, chicken, squash, eggplant, and potato. Bring to a boil over medium-high heat; lower the heat and simmer, uncovered, stirring occa-

sionally, for about 45 minutes, or until the lentils are almost cooked, the chicken pieces are no longer pink when cut, and the vegetables are tender.

3. Transfer the chicken to a plate. Cool the dal-vegetable mixture for about 15 minutes, then puree in a blender or food processor. Transfer the pureed blend back into the saucepan and add the chicken pieces. Keep the pan warm over low heat.

4. In a 10-inch skillet, heat the ghee over medium-high heat. Add the cumin seed and sizzle for 10 to 15 seconds. Add the onion and stir-fry for about 3 to 5 minutes, or until golden brown. Stir in the remaining ingredients and cook 1 minute.

5. Add the skillet's contents to the chicken mixture. Continue cooking, covered, stirring occasionally, for 10 minutes to blend the flavors.

Serves 6

KEERAI MOLAGHUTAL
Spinach Stew with Pigeon Peas

* I usually serve this with a bowl of steamed rice or some fluffy, piping-hot Rotlis (page 182). During the chilly months, I sometimes serve it as is, for a delectable soup course along with a basket of airily crisp pappadums (lentil wafers).

* Use chana dal (yellow split peas) as an alternative to toovar dal (split and hulled pigeon peas) for a slightly different flavor. If urad dal (split and hulled black lentils) are unavailable, you can substitute chana dal for that too.

* When using fresh spinach, trim the stems and thoroughly wash the leaves to remove all the dirt. If time is of the essence, buy prewashed spinach leaves.

Poor Appa never lived long enough to see any of his children get married. So when my brother Shankar married Geeta, the first wedding in our family since Appa's demise, it turned out to be a bittersweet event. Akka, Appa's mother, was still with us and periodically wiped her saddened, tear-filled eyes with her dark green, gold-bordered nine-yard silk saree pullow, soaking it all in so she could share this with her son. She hoped to be joining his spiritual side soon, wishing to discard her smothering blanket of life, the same sheath that offered comfort when he was alive.

The nadaswaram pierced her near-deaf ears, bolstered by the heart-thumping beat of the mridangam (drum). She wiped yet another tear as the vaadyar (priest) sprinkled holy Ganges water on the bride and groom. Shankar reached over and tied the 22-karat-gold mangalsutram (wedding necklace), dangling from the end of a turmeric-stained blessed string, around his bride's neck, competing with the other necklaces for prominence against her dark skin glistening with pearls of sweat. Agni, the god of fire, burned with heightened passion as the vaadyar poured ghee from a silver spoon onto heaps of sweet-smelling, sun-cooked cow dung. Akka reached for the uncooked rice kernels, mottled with more turmeric and blessed by the vaadyar, and showered them over the couple, wishing them wealth, prosperity, and the prospect of procreating eight sons, an age-old blessing that seemed more like a curse in these modern times.

Geeta came into our house with her trousseau of sarees, gold, diamonds, stainless steel thalis (platters), katoris (small bowls), and tumblers, and her brand of cooking the Keralite way. Her southwestern roots reflected different flavors from those found in our southeastern Tamilian kitchen—a pervasive use of coconut oil, freshly shredded coconut, and an abundance of dried red chilies. She tried winning over her in-laws with her hard work and charm, all under the scrutiny of the household matriarch, Akka. Her Tamil words were laced with Malayalam verbiage, a phenomenon we found highly amusing. For a Sunday meal she decided to impress us with her molaghutal (chili-spiked stew), which really was a Keralite's way of saying molagha (chilies) kootu (stew)—a similar-flavored stew in Akka's kitchen. One bite of her molaghutal convinced me of her cooking prowess while her husband watched me eat with a proud grin on his face, wanting to take credit for his "find."

¼ cup toovar dal (split and hulled pigeon peas), sorted, rinsed, and drained

3½ cups water

1¼ pounds fresh spinach leaves, finely chopped, or 2 packages (10 ounces each) frozen chopped spinach

1 teaspoon salt

¼ teaspoon ground turmeric

2 tablespoons Ghee (page 204) or vegetable oil

½ cup freshly shredded coconut (page 6)

2 tablespoons urad dal (split and hulled black lentils), sorted

1 teaspoon cumin seed

2 dried red Thai, cayenne, or serrano chilies

1 teaspoon black mustard seed

1. In a 1-quart saucepan, bring the toovar dal and 2 cups water to a boil over medium-high heat. Lower the heat and simmer, partially covered, stirring occasionally, for 20 minutes, or until the dal is tender.

2. Meanwhile, in a 2-quart saucepan, bring 1 cup water, spinach, salt, and turmeric to a boil over medium-high heat. Lower the heat to medium and simmer, uncovered, stirring occasionally, for 10 minutes, or until the spinach is cooked. If using frozen spinach, cook until thawed.

3. Meanwhile, in a small skillet, heat 1 tablespoon ghee over medium-high heat. Add the coconut, urad dal, cumin seed, and chilies. Stir-fry for 2 to 4 minutes, or until the mixture turns golden brown; add ½ cup water and stir well. Add the contents of the skillet to the cooked toovar dal.

4. In a blender or food processor, puree the toovar dal mixture until smooth; add to the spinach.

5. In a small skillet, heat 1 tablespoon ghee over medium-high heat; add the mustard seed. When it starts to pop, cover the skillet until all the seed has popped. Immediately pour the seed-ghee mixture into the spinach mixture and stir well.

Serves 4

MUNG NU DAL
Split Green Lentils with Peanuts

This dal, which my friend Pinank's mother makes, is fairly thin and spicy sweet. It is delicious when eaten with Rotlis (page 182) or steamed rice for a simple meal. I have often served it as a soup course to my dinner guests.

1 cup mung dal (split and hulled green lentils), sorted and rinsed

5 cups water

2 tablespoons Ghee (page 204) or vegetable oil

1 teaspoon cumin seed

¼ cup dry-roasted peanuts, coarsely chopped

1 tablespoon finely chopped fresh cilantro

1 tablespoon sugar

1 teaspoon salt

¼ teaspoon ground turmeric

12 to 15 fresh karhi leaves

4 to 6 fresh Thai, cayenne, or serrano chilies, finely chopped

1. In a 2-quart saucepan, bring the mung dal and 3 cups water to a boil over medium-high heat. Lower the heat to medium and cook, uncovered, for 15 to 20 minutes, stirring occasionally and skimming off any foam that forms on top, until the dal is tender.
2. Meanwhile, in a 6-inch skillet, heat the ghee over medium-high heat. Add the cumin seed and sizzle for 10 to 15 seconds. Stir in the remaining ingredients and cook for 30 seconds.
3. Scrape the skillet's contents and remaining 2 cups water into the saucepan containing the dal. Continue simmering, uncovered, for about 5 minutes to blend the flavors.

Serves 6

SABUD MASOOR DAL
Brown Lentils with Garlic

I was exposed to masoor dal at the home of my friend Anil, whose roots are from Lucknow, a city in the north-central state of Uttar Pradesh. I remember hearing a reference to this lentil in an old black-and-white Hindi movie, in which the drop-dead gorgeous Madhubala turned to her tireless suitor, pouted her lower lip, and crooned, "This face of yours, ugly as it is, reminds me of the dirty, muddy shabbiness of brown lentils." Needless to say, when I tasted Anil's mother's creation, brought to the table for a quick lunch, I couldn't help wondering why this was compared to hideous faces. I was drawn into its haunting muddy looks, its darkness-enveloping nutty-sweet aroma of cumin seed sizzled in ghee. One bite convinced me that Madhubala was wrong—she never would have said such horrible things if she was in that room savoring each morsel with me. How could she have judged a lentil by its looks?

1 cup sabud masoor dal (whole brown lentils/French lentils), sorted and rinsed

4 cups water

2 tablespoons Ghee (page 204) or unsalted butter

1 teaspoon cumin seed

4 large cloves garlic, finely chopped

1 cup finely chopped tomato

1 tablespoon finely chopped fresh cilantro

1 teaspoon salt

¼ teaspoon ground turmeric

3 to 4 fresh Thai, cayenne, or serrano chilies, slit open lengthwise

1. In a 2-quart saucepan, bring the dal and water to a boil over medium-high heat. Skim off any foam that forms on its surface. Lower the heat to medium and simmer, uncovered, stirring occasionally, for 20 minutes until the dal is partially cooked.

2. Meanwhile, in a 10-inch skillet, heat the ghee over medium-high heat. Add the cumin seed and sizzle for 10 to 15 seconds.

3. Immediately add the garlic and stir-fry for 30 seconds, or until golden brown. Stir in the remaining ingredients and cook for 2 to 3 minutes until the tomato softens. Combine the tomato sauce with the dal.

4. Lower the heat and continue simmering the dal, covered, stirring occasionally, for 8 to 10 minutes until cooked.

Serves 4

❧ You can give me dal seven days a week and I will survive just fine, thank you very much! This is a very simple dish that I often enjoy served over a plateful of steamed basmati rice. By adding Maangai Urughai (page 220) and a bowl of plain yogurt to the combination, I join the ranks of millions in India who follow this humble diet almost daily.

❧ Try other types of lentils, beans, and peas with the same tomato-based seasoning "packet" for variety and guilt-free pleasure.

❧ When slit open, the chilies reveal the vein and seeds that house the potent capsaicin. When you disturb the sleeping giant by chopping the chilies, its anger and fieriness escape to bring you closer to a superior power often known as an endorphin rush. So when you just barely slit them open, you can still continue to enjoy its hushed presence with a very faint wisp of hotness.

Dahi Pakodi
Spinach Croquettes in Spicy Yogurt Sauce

❧ I always serve saucy dishes like this with steamed basmati rice. The simplicity of the rice provides a mellow background to the robust flavors in this curry. The entire dish can be made a day ahead and reheated before serving. This also freezes well, but some of the croquettes will fall apart when thawed.

❧ We are blessed with a wonderful array of greens. Use mustard, kale, or collard greens instead of spinach for a nice variation.

For the first twenty-one years of my life, I could count on the fingers of one hand how many times I ate commercially prepared yogurt. This cultured beauty was always homemade, given the hot, humid weather almost nine months of the year in Mumbai.

The routine never changed in Amma's kitchen. Vishu, my oldest brother, would be the annoying morning bird, too buoyant, chatty, and obnoxiously loud for my taste. Before he got married and went his separate way, he was the official "doodhwallah" (milkman) of our house. He gathered the empty, liter-size glass milk bottles that were washed the previous night and placed in their wire mesh compartments. The rattling of glass against metal melodiously followed him, like bells around a cow's neck, as he stepped down the two flights of stairs and tumbled onto the chipped concrete sidewalk. The government-run Aarré milk booth sat just outside our building, half a block from the bus stop. The tiny blue-striped wooden shed had space for two chairs and two employees to squeeze into their seats. Crates of filled milk bottles lay stacked outside the shed, sweating in chilled harmony against the morning dew and rising humidity. The queue was already twelve individuals long at the ungodly hour of 5 A.M. The barely awake bodies scurried toward the open window with their rupees in one hand and their empty milk bottles in the other.

When Vishu's turn came, he handed the money to Radhika, a doe-eyed girl with hair tumbling down to her waist in that familiar braid, her tamarind-colored tresses glistening with morning sweat mixed with coconut oil, fresh jasmine flowers inter-twined with her locks. She took his money and stamped his passport-sized ration card with the amount of liters purchased—the allowed quota of 1 liter per household member. We could get 10 liters, but we never needed that much, except when festivals and company pushed us over the rationed edge. On cue, Bacchubhai took the empty bottles and gave Vishu the holy cow's nectar, filled to the brim and capped with thin blue-striped aluminum foil.

Once the milk arrived upstairs, Lali or Amma emptied it into a large stainless steel vessel. The milk was brought to a boil atop a burner connected to the bright red portable propane gas tank and then allowed to cool at room temperature. Amma always saved a little yogurt from the previous batch to culture 2 liters of the warm milk every morning. A separate stainless steel vessel with the warm, now cultured milk sat at the corner of the dining table, and within four hours the lid was removed to unveil jelly-firm sweet yogurt that was still warm to the touch under the hot, humid sunshine that filtered through the window.

Even today I yearn for her warm, sweet yogurt but have succumbed to the comforts of commercially purchased yogurt instead. If I ever simplify my lifestyle and no longer worry about doing 500 chores during the course of 24 hours, the first order of business on my then-clean slate will be to make yogurt just as Amma did and Lali still does day after humid day.

PAKODIS (CROQUETTES)

1 bag (10 ounces) fresh spinach, washed and finely chopped, or 1 package (10 ounces) frozen chopped spinach, thawed and squeezed to drain
1 cup garbanzo bean flour
1 cup finely chopped onion
1 teaspoon Garam Masaala (page 206)
1 teaspoon salt
2 tablespoons water, if needed
Vegetable oil for deep-frying

DAHI (YOGURT SAUCE)

1 cup coarsely chopped onion
1 tablespoon coarsely chopped gingerroot
4 to 6 fresh Thai, cayenne, or serrano chilies
2 large cloves garlic
2 cups plain yogurt
½ cup water
2 tablespoons garbanzo bean flour
½ teaspoon ground turmeric
½ teaspoon salt
2 tablespoons Ghee (page 204) or melted butter
1 teaspoon cumin seed
1 tablespoon finely chopped fresh cilantro

TO MAKE PAKODIS

1. In a medium bowl, combine all the ingredients except water and oil. If the mixture is dry, add 2 tablespoons water. The consistency should be that of smooth dough. Divide the dough into walnut-size pieces and shape each piece into a ball.
2. In a wok or 3-quart saucepan, heat the vegetable oil (about 2 to 3 inches deep) over medium heat until a thermometer registers 350°F.
3. Gently drop 5 to 6 croquettes at a time into the oil and fry for 3 to 5 minutes, turning once or twice until golden brown. Remove with a slotted spoon and drain on paper towels.

TO MAKE DAHI

1. In a food processor, finely mince the onions, gingerroot, chilies, and garlic.
2. In a medium bowl, whisk together the yogurt, water, garbanzo bean flour, turmeric, and salt until smooth.
3. In a 2-quart saucepan, heat the ghee over medium-high heat. Add the cumin seed and sizzle for 10 to 20 seconds. Add the onion mixture and stir-fry for 3 to 5 minutes until golden brown.
4. Stir in the yogurt mixture and simmer, uncovered, for 5 minutes to blend the flavors. Add the fried croquettes and continue simmering, uncovered, stirring very gently and taking care not to break up croquettes, for 15 to 20 minutes, or until the sauce slightly thickens. Sprinkle with cilantro.

Serves 6

Dal Maharani
Black Lentils with Kidney Beans

Dal is integral to every Indian meal. It can range from simple to complex as the occasion commands. Always served with flat breads and/or rice, it forms a complete protein when combined with starch. This lentil-based stew is truly the queen (maharani) of them all as it combines two of north India's prized grains: sabud urad (whole black lentils) and rajmah (red kidney beans). Plain yogurt, when whisked in before serving, provides a creamy texture without the fat, but by all means use heavy (whipping) cream if you want to live like a queen (or king).

1 cup sabud urad (whole black lentils), sorted and rinsed

7 cups water

1 medium onion, coarsely chopped

2 tablespoons coarsely chopped gingerroot

10 medium cloves garlic

3 to 5 fresh Thai, cayenne, or serrano chilies

¼ cup Ghee (page 204) or melted butter

1 teaspoon cumin seed

1 can (15 ounces) red kidney beans, rinsed, drained, and coarsely mashed

3 tablespoons finely chopped fresh cilantro

1 teaspoon salt

1 cup plain yogurt, whisked

1. In a 3-quart saucepan, bring the sabud urad and 4 cups water to boil over medium-high heat. Lower the heat to medium and simmer, partially covered, stirring occasionally, for 30 minutes, or until almost all the water evaporates. Stir in an 2 cups water and continue simmering, covered, stirring occasionally, for 15 to 20 minutes, or until the sabud urad is cooked.

2. Meanwhile, in a food processor, finely mince the onion, gingerroot, garlic, and chilies.

3. In a 10-inch skillet, heat the ghee over medium-high heat. Add the cumin seed and sizzle for 10 to 15 seconds. Add the onion mixture and stir-fry for 5 to 7 minutes, or until golden brown. Stir in the remaining 1 cup water. Add the skillet's contents to the dal, along with the kidney beans, 1 tablespoon cilantro, and salt.

4. Continue simmering, covered, stirring occasionally, for 10 to 15 minutes to blend the flavors. Fold in the yogurt and sprinkle with the remaining cilantro.

Serves 8

Kashmiri Chana
Garbanzo Beans with Mushrooms

꙳ I often make this dish with shittake mushrooms, and in-season fresh morels. Each mushroom variety yields a different flavor, so use the kind that suits your palate and your pocketbook. Please refrain from using canned button mushrooms.

꙳ Fenugreek leaves impart a pleasant bitterness to the sauce, but if they are unavailable, you can eliminate them from the recipe. Dried leaves, known as kasoori méthi, are commonly found in stores that sell Indian groceries, but if seasonal fresh leaves are available, buy them in a heartbeat. To crumble dried leaves, rub them between your fingertips to release their earthy aroma.

꙳ Mango powder provides a natural tartness to the sauce, but you can substitute freshly squeezed lime or lemon juice.

Hema Malini emerged from behind the tall pine tree nestled on a plateau between two snow-capped mountains. Her left arm held on to a tree limb while her right arm swung toward the ocean-blue sky. Her saffron saree pullow buoyed against the chilly Kashmiri breeze briefly exposing her dough-smooth midriff. She mouthed to Lata Mangeshkar's melodious nightingale voice professing her love for Dharmendar, the ruggedly handsome, bushy-eyebrowed, debonair actor who eyed her with a smoldering passion. He reached over to kiss her as she gently turned her ruby-red lips away from him, appeasing the Indian Film Censor Board's taboo of projecting an on-screen kiss.

This is a hackneyed scene in many a Hindi movie, a product of the mass-producing studios of Bollywood, Mumbai's silver screen industry. The beautiful hills, valleys, and snow-kissed grounds of Kashmir make their way into almost every film, offering a stunning background for transporting the economically impoverished moviegoer into a faraway land that he or she may never experience in person. Kashmir is also home to the Himalayan Mountains, rising in majestic splendor, their cool, crisp, snowmelt perfuming the much-prized basmati rice. This part of the country is also blessed with mushrooms, a fungus rarely consumed outside its provincial boundaries. Kabuli chana (garbanzo beans), a Kashmiri staple, when combined with mushrooms yields a dish that is musk-strong, bold, and sensuously complex, much like Kashmir.

1 medium onion, coarsely chopped
1 tablespoon coarsely chopped gingerroot
10 medium cloves garlic
2 tablespoons Ghee (page 204) or vegetable oil
1 teaspoon cumin seed
2 tablespoons finely chopped fresh fenugreek leaves or 1 tablespoon dried, crumbled (see note)
1 tablespoon amchur (mango powder) (see note)
1 tablespoon Garam Masaala (page 206)

1 teaspoon salt
¼ teaspoon grated nutmeg
1½ cups water
8 ounces fresh button mushrooms
2 cans (15 ounces each) garbanzo beans, rinsed and drained
2 tablespoons finely chopped fresh cilantro
2 to 3 fresh Thai, cayenne, or serrano chilies, slit open lengthwise
1 medium lime, cut into wedges

1. In a food processor, finely mince the onion, gingerroot, and garlic.
2. In a 3-quart saucepan, heat the ghee over medium-high heat. Add the cumin seed and sizzle for 20 to 30 seconds. Add the onion mixture and stir-fry for 2 to 4 minutes, or until golden brown.
3. Add the fenugreek leaves, amchur, garam masaala, salt, nutmeg, and ½ cup water. Lower the heat and simmer, stirring occasionally, for 3 to 5 minutes, or until the water evaporates and a thin film of oil starts to form on the sauce's surface.
4. Stir in the mushrooms, garbanzo beans, and remaining 1 cup water. Bring to a boil over medium-high heat. Lower the heat and simmer, covered, stirring occasionally, for 15 minutes to blend the flavors.
5. Sprinkle with cilantro and chilies. Serve with lime wedges.

Serves 6

I love a bowl of steamed basmati rice with this dish, along with a basket of Aloo Naan (page 188) for a quiet weekend dinner. I always eat the chilies along with mouthfuls of steamed rice to lessen their potency. If they don't appeal to your adventurous spirit, do not eat them.

SHUNDAL
Black-Eyed Peas with Coconut and Jaggery

In supermarkets, black-eyed peas can be found three ways: cooked in cans, partially cooked and frozen; and dried peas next to the rice and other legumes. Rinse and drain canned peas before use. Cook frozen peas according to package's directions. Sort dried peas (1 cup dried will yield 3 cups cooked), for stones and other foreign objects; bring them to boil in a large pot of water, skimming off foam that floats to the surface, and simmer, covered, stirring occasionally, for about 30 minutes, or until tender. Drain.

Serve this deliciously easy delicacy as a snack with a piping hot cup of Adrak Chai (page 43) or even a mug of comforting coffee.

Once each year, during the October festival of Navratri that extends for nine nights, the three women who stood through thick and thin beside their well-known consorts Brahma the creator, Vishnu the preserver, and Shiva the destroyer, are worshipped. They are, respectively, Saraswati (the goddess of learning), Lakshmi (the goddess of wealth and prosperity), and Parvati (the mountain goddess of virtuosity and beauty).

The large rusty tin suitcase was wrapped in an old bedsheet in the loft above the bathroom. Being the youngest and the shortest, I was made to climb into the crawl-space and drag the cloth-covered metal to the loft's edge, where I could lower it into the waiting arms of my two older brothers, Ravi and Bhaskar. I knew exactly what it contained, but I still found great pleasure in opening the lid and unveiling individual newspaper-wrapped ceramic statues of all shapes and sizes. These were the gollu bommais, doll figurines of gods and goddesses that were to be displayed in the room where we kept our regularly worshiped religious icons. Lali fashioned five steps from old suitcases and draped them with old sarees. The statues were displayed neatly on the steps, the three goddesses occupying pivotal spots on the first landing.

Each evening, as the bindi-like sun set against the western horizon, the symbol of marriage on each goddess's forehead shone with brilliance against the dancing flame of the oil lamp that rested on the floor. Silver trays brimming with betel nuts and their leaves, bunches of baby bananas, small wreaths of jasmine, hardened dried roots of turmeric, and coconuts smeared with sandalwood paste perfumed the room along with glowing rose-scented incense sticks. The women in the neighborhood were invited for a darshan (viewing), and they came into the room, leaving their slippers at the doorstep. They all sat cross-legged on the floor, heads covered with their saree's pullow, facing the statues, as Lali burned pieces of camphor on a flat brass spoon held in her right hand. In her left hand was a silver bell, and she waved the flame in a circular motion, encompassing the goddesses while melodiously ringing the bell. After invoking the goddesses' blessings, she offered the flame to the gathered women, who held their hands over it briefly and touched their eyes, accepting the sanctions.

After brief conversation, they left with offerings from the silver tray and warm bundles of banana leaf–wrapped black-eyed peas smothered with freshly shredded coconut, jaggery, and menthol-like cardamom.

4 cups freshly cooked black-eyed
 peas or 2 cans (15 ounces each),
 rinsed and drained (see note)
2 cups water
1 cup freshly shredded coconut
 (page 6)

¼ cup coarsely chopped gur
 (jaggery) or firmly packed dark
 brown sugar
¼ teaspoon cardamom seed
 (removed from pods), ground

1. In a 2-quart saucepan, bring the peas and water to boil; drain.
2. Add the remaining ingredients and stir well to dissolve the gur.

Serves 6

Cauliflower Kootu
Cauliflower Stew with Yellow Split Peas

Kootus are stews that combine lentils and vegetables. Feel free to vary your mixture to suit your taste—my preference is this specific legume-vegetable blend.

Fresh karhi leaves offer an aroma that is fresh and unique, different from their dried form. These leaves are found in abundance in the produce section of your favorite Indian grocery store or mail-order sources that specialize in Indian groceries.

Her heart pounded with the beat of a pestle crushing chilies in a mortar as she approached the pasty-skinned, noodle-mustached customs officer at London's Heathrow Airport. Her lime-green dupatta lay silky smooth over her left shoulder. She lifted its front edge and carefully dabbed pearls of sweat above her lipsticked lips. Upon command she leaned forward and grabbed the diminutive key that dangled amid a cluster of others from her 22-karat gold necklace. She inserted it into the lock and popped it open. The dark green canvas suitcase's lid breathed a sigh of relief. As soon as the lid flew open, the officer's nostrils flared, breathing in the unmistakable light citrus scent of fresh karhi leaves that had recently been sun-dried by a mother's need to provide her American-educated son the basic ingredient that forms the heart and soul of southern Indian cooking.

"Madam," he hissed intensely, with Raj-like authority, "do you have karhi leaves in here?" Her right eyebrow arched with silent grace as she bit her lower lip, weighing the risk of saying no. "Yes," she replied as she pulled a zip-lock bag filled with arid, olive-green leaves and handed it to the officer. Lali felt defeated by her inability to bring to her brother their mother's dried treasure that promised Tamilian home cooking the way it should be done. I, on the other hand, was thrilled to have my beloved sister safe in my arms in a land that was my home, a country that was far from my birthplace, a tundra-like city called Minneapolis where vegetation was covered by icy snow, and karhi leaves were miserably absent.

1 cup chana dal (yellow split peas), sorted and rinsed

4 cups water

2 cups small cauliflower florets

1 teaspoon salt

¼ teaspoon ground turmeric

1 cup freshly shredded coconut (page 6)

1 teaspoon black peppercorns

1 teaspoon cumin seed

2 tablespoons Ghee (page 204) or vegetable oil

1 teaspoon black mustard seed

1 tablespoon urad dal (split and hulled black lentils), sorted

15 to 20 fresh karhi leaves

1. In a 3-quart saucepan, bring the dal and water to a boil over medium-high heat. Skim off any foam that forms on its surface. Lower the heat to

medium and simmer, partially covered, stirring occasionally, for 10 minutes, or until the dal is partially cooked.

2. Stir in the cauliflower, salt, and turmeric and continue simmering covered, stirring occasionally, for 15 minutes, or until the cauliflower and dal are fork-tender.

3. Meanwhile, grind the coconut, peppercorns, and cumin in a blender until smooth. Stir the paste into the cauliflower-dal mixture.

4. In a small skillet, heat the ghee over medium-high heat; add the mustard seed. When it starts to pop, cover the skillet until all the seed has popped. Immediately add the urad dal and stir-fry for 30 seconds or until golden brown. Remove the skillet from the heat and splutter the karhi leaves in the hot ghee. Pour the mixture into the cauliflower-dal and simmer, covered, for 5 minutes to blend the flavors.

Serves 6

MOLAGHU RASAM
Pepper Soup with Tamarind

❧ Use chana dal (yellow split peas) for a variation, especially when you have no toovar dal in your pantry. Skip the karhi leaves if they are unavailable, since there is no alternative for this recipe.

❧ I have made this recipe with ½ cup lemon juice instead of tamarind, for a simple and clear tart flavor. For a sweeter acidic influence, I have used fresh pineapple instead of tomatoes and have marveled at the result.

❧ This makes a simple lunch or dinner when accompanied by bowls of steamed rice. I have also served it as a second-course soup for elegant multiple-course dinners, acquainting my guests with the true "mulligatawny."

The evening meal in Amma's kitchen had four guarantees: the family ate together; shaadum (rice) was a must; some type of a sambhar (stew) or a rasam (soup) made an appearance; and the meal always culminated with yogurt or buttermilk. My favorite part was invariably the rasam, watery thin, tart, and nose-tinglingly spicy. I inhaled it as is in a small katori (bowl) or more often, I consumed it over a mound of perfectly cooked white rice. The fingers of my right hand, moving with the synchronized speed of an assembly line worker, emptied the thali (platter) in no time, often skipping the buttermilk course in favor of a second helping of comforting rasam.

Rasam has often been called molaghu tanni (pepper water). When the first Englishman was served this southern staple, he fell head over heels in love with this thin broth, but his clipped English tongue could not twirl the right way to enunciate the words. What came out sounded more like "mulligatawny," and so it stuck. It landed at the English table many reincarnations later, radically different from the original.

¼ cup toovar dal (split and hulled pigeon peas), sorted and rinsed

6 cups water

¼ teaspoon ground turmeric

Walnut-sized ball dried tamarind pulp or 1 tablespoon tamarind concentrate

1 medium tomato, cut into 1-inch cubes

3 tablespoons finely chopped fresh cilantro

1 teaspoon salt

¼ teaspoon hing (asafetida)

12 to 15 fresh karhi leaves

2 to 3 dried red Thai, cayenne, or serrano chilies

1 teaspoon cumin seed, ground

1 teaspoon black peppercorns, ground

1 tablespoon Ghee (page 204) or vegetable oil

1 teaspoon black mustard seed

1 teaspoon cumin seed

1. In a 1-quart saucepan, bring the toovar dal, 2 cups water, and turmeric to a boil over medium-high heat. Lower the heat and simmer, partially covered, for 15 to 20 minutes or the until dal is tender. Let cool. Transfer the dal to a blender or food processor and puree until smooth.

2. In a medium bowl, soak the tamarind in 4 cups water for about 5 minutes. Loosen up the tamarind pulp with your fingertips and continue soaking

for 10 to 15 minutes. Squeeze out and discard as much of the pulp as possible. Strain the liquid into a 2-quart saucepan, discarding any residual pulp and fibers left behind in the strainer. If using tamarind concentrate, dissolve it in 4 cups water. Stir in the remaining ingredients, except 1 tablespoon cilantro, ghee, and mustard and cumin seed.

3. Bring the mixture to a boil over medium-high heat. Lower the heat to medium and simmer, uncovered, for 30 minutes, or until the liquid is reduced by almost half.

4. Meanwhile, in a small skillet, heat the ghee over medium-high heat; add the mustard seed. When it starts to pop, cover the skillet until all the seed has popped. Stir in the cumin seed and sizzle for 10 to 15 seconds. Add to the pureed dal.

5. Add the dal mixture to the reduced tamarind water and reheat to a boil. Sprinkle with remaining cilantro.

Serves 6

SAMBHAR
Pigeon Pea Stew with Vegetables

Amma made this 365 days a year, with as many variations, making this staple my prime comfort food during the times I get terribly homesick. Because it freezes so well, I always make a double batch and freeze it in individual portions for up to 2 months.

❧ Try substituting chana dal for toovar dal for a richer, sweeter taste and texture. The flavors from tamarind and karhi leaves are intrinsic to this recipe's complexity. Using freshly squeezed lime or lemon juice (2 tablespoons) might provide the acidity but will definitely lack tamarind's intricacies. You are better off skipping the karhi leaves than substituting something else.

❧ Use any vegetables you like. Even though I have suggested some in this recipe, try potatoes, onions, fresh pumpkin, or even green beans for variations.

½ cup toovar dal (split and hulled pigeon peas), sorted and rinsed

5 cups water

¼ teaspoon ground turmeric

1 teaspoon tamarind concentrate

1 medium green pepper, seeded and cut into 1-inch cubes

1 medium carrot, peeled and thinly sliced crosswise

1 medium tomato, cut into 1-inch cubes

3 tablespoons finely chopped fresh cilantro

2 teaspoons Sambhar Masaala (page 208)

1 teaspoon salt

20 fresh karhi leaves

1 tablespoon Ghee (page 204) or vegetable oil

1 tablespoon chana dal (yellow split peas), sorted

½ teaspoon fenugreek seed

4 dried red Thai, cayenne, or serrano chilies

1 teaspoon black mustard seed

½ teaspoon hing (asafetida)

1. In a 1-quart saucepan, bring the toovar dal, 2 cups water, and turmeric to a boil over medium-high heat, skimming off any foam that forms on its surface. Lower the heat and simmer, partially covered, for 15 to 20 minutes, or until the dal is tender. Allow the dal to cool, then puree in a blender or food processor until smooth.

2. In a medium bowl, dissolve the tamarind in 3 cups water. Stir in the pepper, carrot, tomato, 2 tablespoons cilantro, sambhar masaala, salt, and 15 karhi leaves.

3. In a 2-quart saucepan, heat the ghee over medium-high heat. Add the chana dal, fenugreek, and 2 red chilies. Stir-fry for about 1 minute, or until the dal turns golden brown and the chilies slightly blacken. Remove the spice mixture with a slotted spoon and let cool. Grind in a spice grinder until the texture is like finely ground black pepper; add to the tamarind water.

4. In the same saucepan, reheat the ghee over medium-high heat; add the mustard seed. When it starts to pop, cover the pan until all the seed has popped. Immediately add the remaining dried chilies and hing; sizzle for 5 seconds.

5. Pour in the tamarind water and bring to boil. Lower the heat to medium and simmer, uncovered, stirring occasionally, for 15 minutes, or until the vegetables are fork-tender. Stir in the pureed dal and bring to a boil. Sprinkle with remaining cilantro and karhi leaves.

Serves 6

MENDIA KOZHUMBU
Onions in Tamarind-Fenugreek Sauce

❧ Dried tamarind pulp is available in Indian and other Asian grocery stores in brick form. Being a purist, I have always found its flavor more complex than that of the convenient tamarind concentrate. If you do use the concentrate, dissolve 1 teaspoon of the paste in 3 cups of water and proceed as directed.

❧ For variations, use eggplant or sweet potatoes instead of the onion. Sweet potatoes take longer to cook, so adjust the simmering time accordingly.

While I was a child, Akka, my grandmother, had us four young ones—Mathangi (my sister), Bhaskar and Ravi (my brothers), and me—sit cross-legged on the terrazzo kitchen floor in a semicircle facing her. She sat in a similar fashion, nimble for her eighty years, behind a thali (platter) mounded with steamed white rice and a big stainless steel katori (bowl) of mendia kozhumbu. She took a walnut-sized ball of rice and made a little dimple in its center with her stubby thumb, dunked it into the kozhumbu bowl, and hand-fed us in turn. This combination always tasted better when it was laced with her unconditional love. She kept our mouths opened wide with her wit and acid tongue as she regaled us with stories of Chandamama (the maternal Uncle Moon) and his tricks at making Surya, the sun god, disappear every single evening in order to woo the stars and make them shine with embarrassed glow. The stories trailed off as her platter became empty and our bellies grew full with tamarind and love.

This is peasant food at its bare-bones simplest. Amma often made this at the end of the month, when our rationed legumes ran out and we had to wait a few more days before the next paycheck. A small handful of chana dal was all she needed for that protein influence and nutty flavor. We always ate it served over steamed white rice and pieces of airily crisp pappadums (lentil wafers). I often resort to this combination during my "down-and-out" homesick days.

Walnut-sized ball dried tamarind pulp or 1 teaspoon tamarind concentrate (see note)

3 cups warm water

1 teaspoon salt

½ teaspoon ground turmeric

2 tablespoons vegetable oil

1 teaspoon black mustard seed

¼ cup chana dal (yellow split peas), sorted

1 medium onion, cut into ½-inch cubes

2 teaspoons Sambhar Masaala (page 208)

½ teaspoon hing (asafetida)

12 to 15 fresh karhi leaves

1. In a medium bowl, soak the tamarind in water for about 5 minutes. Loosen the tamarind pulp with your fingertips. Continue soaking for 10 to 15 minutes. Squeeze out and discard as much of the pulp as possible. Strain the liquid into a separate bowl, discarding any residual pulp and

fibers left behind in the strainer. If using tamarind concentrate, dissolve it in 3 cups water. Add the salt and turmeric.

2. In a 2-quart saucepan, heat the oil over medium-high heat; add the mustard seed. When it starts to pop, cover the pan until all the seed has popped. Immediately add the chana dal and stir-fry for 30 seconds or until golden brown.

3. Add the onion and stir-fry for 2 minutes until translucent. Stir in the sambhar masaala, hing, and karhi leaves and continue stir-frying for 1 minute.

4. Immediately add the tamarind mixture; reduce the heat to medium, and simmer, uncovered, for 12 to 15 minutes, stirring occasionally, until one-quarter of the liquid has evaporated.

Serves 4

Yezhai Kariha Kootu
Seven-Vegetable Curry with Jaggery

The perfect consort to Tiruvaadrai Kali (page 174), this very rich and satisfying stew is made once a year in my mother's kitchen. I never ate anything else the days Amma and Lali made this combination.

The two pumpkins in this vegetable medley, one commonly found around Halloween in the United States and the white summer variety found in Indian grocery stores, provide a visual and scrumptious balance to this stew. If unavailable, use a combination of any winter (preferably orange-colored) and summer (white-colored) squash.

½ cup toovar dal (split and hulled pigeon peas), sorted and rinsed

4 cups water

½ teaspoon tamarind concentrate

1 medium potato, peeled and cut into 1-inch cubes

1 medium plantain, peeled and cut into 1-inch thick slices

1 cup 1-inch-cubed pumpkin

1 cup 1-inch-cubed white pumpkin

1 small sweet potato, peeled and cut into 1-inch cubes

½ cup freshly shelled or frozen green peas

½ cup fresh (½-inch pieces) or frozen cut green beans

½ teaspoon ground turmeric

2 teaspoons Sambhar Masaala (page 208)

2 tablespoons Ghee (page 204) or vegetable oil

1 teaspoon black mustard seed

1 tablespoon urad dal (split and hulled black lentils), sorted

¼ teaspoon hing (asafetida)

15 to 20 fresh karhi leaves

2 tablespoons coarsely chopped gur (jaggery) or tightly packed dark brown sugar

1½ teaspoons salt

1. In a 1-quart saucepan, bring the toovar dal and 2 cups water to a boil over medium-high heat, skimming off any foam that forms on its surface. Lower the heat and simmer, partially covered, for 15 to 20 minutes, or until the dal is tender. Let cool, then puree in a blender or food processor until smooth. Stir in the tamarind concentrate until dissolved.

2. In a large stockpot or Dutch oven, bring the seven vegetables, turmeric, and 2 cups water to a boil over medium-high heat. Lower the heat and simmer, covered, stirring occasionally, for 8 to 10 minutes, or until the vegetables are fork-tender. Stir in the sambhar masaala.

3. Meanwhile, in a 6-inch skillet, heat the ghee over medium-high heat; add the mustard seed. When it starts to pop, cover the skillet until all the seed

has popped. Immediately add the urad dal and stir-fry for 30 seconds or until golden brown. Sizzle the hing in oil for 5 seconds and splutter karhi leaves for 1 to 2 seconds.

4. Scrape the skillet's contents into the stockpot with vegetables along with gur, salt, and pureed toovar dal mixture. Simmer for 5 minutes to blend the flavors.

Serves 6

CHANA DAL USLI
Steamed Yellow Split Peas with Green Beans

This fairly dry green bean–yellow split pea blend makes a nutritious side dish for any weekday meal. You can use 2 tablespoons finely chopped fresh cilantro as an alternative to karhi leaves.

1 cup chana dal (yellow split peas)

3 to 4 dried red Thai, cayenne, or serrano chilies

2 tablespoons coarsely chopped fresh karhi leaves

1½ teaspoons salt

½ teaspoon hing (asafetida)

2 tablespoons vegetable oil

1 teaspoon black mustard seed

1 tablespoon urad dal (split and hulled black lentils), sorted

½ pound green beans, trimmed and cut crosswise into ½-inch-thick pieces

¼ teaspoon ground turmeric

1. In a medium bowl, cover the dal with water. With your fingers, gently wash the grains for 10 to 20 seconds; drain. Repeat 5 or 6 times until the water is clear. Add the chilies. Cover the dal with warm water and soak at room temperature for at least 1 to 2 hours, or overnight (about 8 hours); drain.

2. In a food processor, grind the dal and chilies until smooth. The batter will be fairly thick and feel slightly gritty. Transfer the batter to a bowl and fold in the karhi leaves, 1 teaspoon salt, and hing.

3. Generously grease a steamer pan and spread the batter to form a patty about 1 inch thick. Steam for about 20 minutes, or until a knife inserted through its center comes out clean. Remove the patty and let cool. Crumble the patty into pieces no larger than tiny pebbles.

4. In a wok or 12-inch skillet, heat the vegetable oil over medium-high heat; add the mustard seed. When it begins to pop, cover the skillet. As soon as the seed finishes popping, add the urad dal and stir-fry for 30 seconds, or until golden brown.

5. Stir in the green beans, turmeric, and ½ teaspoon salt. Lower the heat and cook, covered, stirring occasionally, for 8 to 10 minutes until the beans are fork-tender.

6. Add the crumbled dal mixture and stir-fry for 1 to 2 minutes until warm.

Serves 6

Sevai, Idlis, aur Kozhakuttais
Noodles, Cakes, and Dumplings

Sevai
Fresh Rice Noodles

Puli Sevai
Rice Noodles with Tamarind

Maangai Sevai
Rice Noodles with Unripe Mango

Sevai Uppuma
Noodle Kedgeree

Mor Kozhambu Sevai
Buttermilk Curry with Rice Noodles

Thénga Sevai
Fresh Rice Noodles with Toasted Coconut

Sev
Garbanzo Bean Flour Noodles with Cayenne
Pepper

Idlis
Steamed Rice-Lentil Cakes

Kaancheepuram Idlis
Steamed Rice-Lentil Cakes with Cashews

Mrs. Pandian's Thidupu Idlis
Steamed Rice-Lentil Cakes with Bananas

Rava Idlis
Semolina Steamed Cakes

Warrupoo Kozhakuttais
Steamed Dumplings with Lentils

Pooranam Kozhakuttais
Steamed Dumplings with Coconut

SEVAI
Fresh Rice Noodles

It is truly a labor of love to make delicate strands of fresh sevai, rice noodles that are so tender they fall apart in your mouth. No pasta machines in this neck of the woods to expedite the process. When I asked Amma to make sevai in a hurry, I still had to endure her detailed explanation. "First I need to soak uncooked rice for a few hours and then grind it into a very fine batter. Then I have to cook the batter in a vanaali (wok) with oil and make sure all the water is evaporated. The dough cannot be sticky," she warned. "I have to let that cool for a few hours. Then I have to steam the dough for a half hour in my idli paanai (a special mold to make steamed cakes). While it is still hot, I have to push it through my sevai nari (noodle press), and only then you can have sevai." I rolled my eyes at the process, knowing full well that I had to appease myself with something else that evening. "No sevai tonight," I muttered under my breath. I knew that if I kept pushing and begging, maybe tomorrow I could feast on the delectable noodles.

I sit back and think of the laborious process my mother and all those million Tamilian women go through even to this day in making sevai. I realize, with sadness, that this is an endeavor not to be undertaken regularly in my hectic American kitchen. Dried rice noodles are now available at grocery stores all across this country. There are specialty stores that also carry fresh rice noodles with a consistency and flavor quite similar to the "real deal." As Amma grudgingly said on a recent visit to Minneapolis, "Thévalay" (not bad). It was not enough—I wanted her to utter, "rhumba" (very tasty). I promised myself to come up with an easier version of her noodle-making method, thus freeing those poor steam-ridden, noodle-making women in southern Indian home kitchens!

❧ My version of noodles is relatively quick to make, unlike Amma's laborious process. The Indian sevai nari (noodle press), available in brass, wood, or stainless steel at any Indian grocery store, is usually cylindrical in shape, about 4 inches long and 3 inches wide. The bottom of the press has four removable plate molds with variously shaped perforations. Use the mold with the tiniest holes to extrude these spaghetti-thin noodles.

❧ Take extra care not to handle the noodles when they are freshly extruded, as they may stick together and turn gummy. Allow them to cool before using them. At this point, they can be covered and refrigerated for up to two days. Often, they are cut up into smaller pieces (about 1 inch in length) to make them easier to pick up with the fingers—which is how we Indians usually eat. Makes it easier to slurp that last bit of noodle left behind on the banana leaf!

1¼ cups rice flour	1¼ cups warm water
1 teaspoon salt	2 tablespoons vegetable oil

1. In a medium bowl, combine the rice flour and salt. Whisk in the water a few tablespoons at a time until the batter has a thin crepe-batter consistency.
2. Add the oil and batter to a cold wok or nonstick skillet. Heat the batter over medium heat, stirring constantly, for 2 to 3 minutes, or until it thickens, starts to leave the sides of the pan, and comes together into a ball to

form soft dough. It should feel silky smooth but not sticky to the touch. Remove the dough and let cool for 2 to 3 minutes. Divide the dough into two equal portions; shape each portion into a ½-inch-thick disk.

3. Place the dough disks in a lightly greased steamer and steam for 10 minutes. Turn off the heat and keep the steamer covered so the dough stays warm.

4. Squeeze one dough disk through a noodle press (use the noodle mold plate with the smallest round holes) onto a plate in a single layer; repeat with the remaining dough disk.

5. Cool the noodles completely before handling them.

Makes about 1 pound

If you do not want to make your own noodles, use fresh (store-bought) rice noodles or dried noodles instead. Avoid overcooking rice noodles or they will become mushy. To cook fresh (store-bought) rice noodles, bring a pot of water to a boil. With a sharp knife or kitchen shears, cut the long noodles into approximately 2-inch strips and drop them into the boiling water. Immediately drain the noodles into a colander and rinse with cold water to stop the cooking. The cold water also helps wash away some of the starchiness. When it comes time to rewarm the noodles, briefly toss them into a bowl of warm water and drain. Add to seasonings. If you are using dried noodles, follow the cooking instructions on the package and use the chill-rewarm method described above.

Making Sevai

Puli Sevai
Rice Noodles with Tamarind

When I first offered a class on the noodles of southern India, a student questioned the authenticity of the recipes. "You are merely addressing the growing trend of noodles in this country and bastardizing the flavors," she blurted out defiantly. I was briefly taken aback but admitted that my mother would be tickled pink to realize that she had been a trendy cook for the bulk of her seventy-seven years, catering to the burgeoning demands of the American palate for noodles. Rice noodles have long been made in southern Indian homes but may not be familiar to Indians with other regional roots.

1 pound Sevai (page 118, or see note)

¼ cup unrefined sesame or vegetable oil

1 teaspoon black mustard seed

2 tablespoons urad dal (split and hulled black lentils), sorted

1 teaspoon cumin seed, roasted and ground

2 tablespoons finely chopped dried tamarind, roasted and ground (see note)

2 tablespoons finely chopped fresh cilantro

4 to 6 fresh Thai, cayenne, or serrano chilies, coarsely chopped

12 to 15 fresh karhi leaves

1 teaspoon salt

1. Place the noodles in medium bowl.
2. In 6-inch skillet, heat the oil over medium-high heat; add the mustard seed. When it starts to pop, cover the skillet. As soon as the seed finishes popping, immediately add the urad dal. Cook for 30 seconds to 1 minute, stirring constantly, until the lentils turn golden brown. Stir in the remaining ingredients.
3. Pour the skillet's contents over the noodles and toss gently.

Serves 6

Sidebar notes:

Dried tamarind is sold in "bricks" in Indian grocery stores and by mail order. They are either seedless or with some seed. Discard any seed from the pulp before use. To roast tamarind, place it in a dry skillet over medium-high heat and cook 3 to 4 minutes, stirring constantly, until dry and blackish brown in color. Remove the tamarind from the skillet and let cool (it will turn brittle). Grind it in a spice grinder until it has the texture of finely ground black pepper.

Unrefined sesame oil is widely available in natural food stores and in the health food or ethnic section of supermarkets. The sesame seed is not toasted, resulting in a deliciously light, crisp flavor.

When stir-fried in hot oil, the urad dal will retain its crunchiness and offer a sharp textural contrast to the soft noodles.

MAANGAI SEVAI
Rice Noodles with Unripe Mango

I go wild for the combination of buttery-soft rice noodles and slightly crunchy, tart unripe mangoes. Even though this recipe makes enough for four, I can usually finish it all in one big slurp!

1 pound Sevai (page 118)

2 tablespoons vegetable oil

1 teaspoon black mustard seed

2 tablespoons raw cashews, coarsely chopped

1 tablespoon urad dal (split and hulled black lentils), sorted

¼ teaspoon hing (asafetida)

1 medium unripe, green mango, peeled, seeded, and cut into ¼-inch cubes

1 tablespoon finely chopped fresh cilantro

1 teaspoon Sambhar Masaala (page 208)

1 teaspoon salt

15 to 20 fresh karhi leaves

1. Place the noodles in a medium bowl.
2. In a 10-inch skillet, heat the oil over medium-high heat; add the mustard seed. When it starts to pop, cover the skillet. As soon as the seed finishes popping, immediately add the cashews and urad dal. Cook for 30 seconds to 1 minute, stirring constantly, until the cashews and dal turn golden brown.
3. Stir in the remaining ingredients and cook, stirring occasionally, for 3 to 5 minutes, or until the mango warms through.
4. Spoon the mango mixture over the noodles and toss to coat.

Serves 4

SEVAI UPPUMA
Noodle Kedgeree

Any Indian grocery store stocks broken-up pieces of dried vermicelli noodles. You may also find them at your regular supermarket along with Italian dried pasta.

I love these noodles for a Sunday morning treat along with a cup of piping-hot Adrak Chai (page 43) and Thénga Chutney (page 226). Even when served alone, these are incredibly habit-forming.

The Brahmin cook vigorously stirred what seemed like a monumental load of hair-thin noodles in a gargantuan kadhai with a paddle-like spoon. He was the head chef orchestrating the meals—breakfast, lunch, afternoon snack, and dinner for two days, for 300 guests—for my brother Shankar's wedding. No wonder he kept wiping his brow with a ragged red handkerchief every two minutes. No countertops or preparation tables, only large portable gas burners on the bare concrete floor. His crew of 30 worked around the clock, cutting, grinding, frying, stewing, stir-frying, and blending. One cook's lonesome task was to grate hundreds of coconuts—a staple at south Indian weddings. The breakfast crowd was about to swoop down and sit cross-legged on the floor under the dining tent with their banana leaves placed in front of them, sprinkled with water and wiped squeaky clean by their right hands. Piping-hot medu vadaas—doughnut-shaped black lentil fritters studded with peppercorns, gingerroot, and chilies fried crispy brown—made their debut, followed by nutty-hot coconut chutney. I was more eager for the vermicelli noodles spiked with roasted cashews and mustard seed, the ones that the head chef kept referring to as thedir sevai, literally translated as "sudden noodles." Noodles in Tamilian kitchens, I knew from experience, took hours to make, but these were store-bought dried strands that were prepared and cooked in mere minutes. The first bite convinced me that they were indeed capable of producing intense, long-cooking flavors ever so suddenly.

5 tablespoons vegetable oil

2 cups broken-up dried vermicelli noodles (about 1-inch pieces)

1 teaspoon black mustard seed

¼ cup raw cashews, coarsely chopped

2 tablespoons urad dal (split and hulled black lentils), sorted

1 to 2 dried red Thai, cayenne, or serrano chilies

3 cups water

1 teaspoon salt

¼ teaspoon ground turmeric

2 tablespoons finely chopped fresh cilantro

2 to 4 fresh Thai, cayenne, or serrano chilies, finely chopped

1. In a wok or 3-quart saucepan, heat 3 tablespoons vegetable oil over medium-high heat. Add the noodles and stir-fry for 2 to 3 minutes until golden brown. Transfer the noodles to a plate.

2. In the same wok, heat 2 tablespoons oil over medium-high heat; add the mustard seed. When it starts to pop, cover the pan until all the seed has popped. Immediately add the cashews, urad dal, and dried chilies and stir-fry for 30 seconds or until the nuts and lentils are golden brown and the chilies slightly blacken.

3. Stir in the water, salt, and turmeric; bring to a boil. Add the noodles and continue cooking, stirring occasionally, for 5 to 7 minutes, or until all the water is absorbed by the noodles.

4. Fold in cilantro and fresh chilies.

Serves 4

Mor Kozhambu Sevai
Buttermilk Curry with Rice Noodles

Amma made buttermilk curry once a month, but her rice noodles graced our table maybe once in three months. Whenever the two incidents coincided, I was ecstatic because I cherished the spicy curry over a big bowl of fresh, soothing rice noodles. This makes for an easy lunch, especially when you use store-bought noodles (a bowl of steamed rice also works well as a substitute).

3 cups buttermilk

1½ cups water

2 tablespoons vegetable oil

2 tablespoons long-grain rice

1 teaspoon cumin seed

2 to 3 dried red Thai, cayenne, or serrano chilies

½ cup freshly shredded coconut (page 6)

1 teaspoon black mustard seed

12 to 15 fresh karhi leaves

1 pound Sevai (page 118)

1. In a medium bowl, whisk together the buttermilk and 1 cup water.
2. In a 6-inch skillet, heat 1 tablespoon oil over medium-high heat. Stir-fry the rice, cumin, and chilies for 1 to 2 minutes, or until the rice turns golden brown and the chilies slightly black. Transfer the skillet's contents to a blender with ½ cup water and coconut; puree until smooth. Add the paste to the buttermilk.
3. In a 2-quart saucepan, heat 1 tablespoon oil; add the mustard seed. When it begins to pop, cover the pan. As soon as the seed finishes popping, splutter the karhi leaves in the hot oil. Pour in the buttermilk mixture. Lower the heat and cook gently, uncovered, for 5 to 7 minutes until warm.
4. Divide the sevai into 4 individual serving bowls. Pour the warmed buttermilk equally over the noodles and serve immediately.

Serves 4

THÉNGA SEVAI
Fresh Rice Noodles with Toasted Coconut

This is often taken on picnics and long train journeys in southern India because it tastes divine when served at room temperature.

2 tablespoons urad dal (split and hulled black lentils), sorted

2 tablespoons chana dal (yellow split peas), sorted

4 dried red Thai, cayenne, or serrano chilies

2 tablespoons Ghee (page 204) or vegetable oil

1 teaspoon black mustard seed

1 tablespoon whole raw cashews, coarsely chopped

1 tablespoon dry-roasted unsalted peanuts, coarsely chopped

1 cup freshly shredded coconut (page 6)

1 tablespoon finely chopped fresh cilantro

12 to 15 fresh karhi leaves

1 teaspoon salt

1 pound Sevai (page 118)

✤ If you are using store-bought dried rice noodles, cook them according to package instructions. Take care not to overcook, or they will turn mushy and become unpalatable.

✤ Use an extra 2 tablespoons chana dal if urad dal is unavailable. Eliminate karhi leaves if none are on hand.

1. In a 10-inch skillet, place 1 tablespoon urad dal, 1 tablespoon chana dal, and 3 chilies. Heat over medium-high heat, shaking the pan occasionally, for 2 to 3 minutes, or until the dals are golden brown and the chilies slightly blacken. Transfer the roasted ingredients to a plate to cool, then grind in spice grinder until the mixture is the texture of finely ground black pepper.

2. In the same skillet, heat the ghee over medium-high heat; add the mustard seed. When it begins to pop, cover the skillet. As soon as the seed finishes popping, add 1 tablespoon urad dal, 1 tablespoon chana dal, 1 dried chili, cashews, and peanuts. Stir-fry for 30 seconds to 1 minute, or until the dal and nuts turn golden brown.

3. Stir in the coconut, cilantro, and karhi leaves and cook, stirring constantly, for 2 to 4 minutes, or until the coconut is golden brown.

4. In a large bowl, combine the coconut mixture, dal-chilies blend, salt, and sevai. Toss gently.

Serves 4

Sev
Garbanzo Bean Flour Noodles with Cayenne Pepper

I could not sleep any longer. Excitement rippled through my eight-year-old body. The fan blades whirred melodiously above while the alarm clock ticked on with an incessant beat. The fluorescent green illuminated the clock's hands positioned at 3:15—45 minutes more before it woke everyone else with its shrilling presence. This was not just any morning—this was the day when Lakshmi, the goddess of wealth, made her appearance in our home. Her Midas-like golden touch was revered in every Hindu home, making Diwali's celebration more memorable. Our hoard of fire-crackers rested in four neat piles on the terrazzo floor next to the plank of wood that housed Lakshmi's statue. The newly tailored shirts and trousers faced her clay figure next to the colorful stack of sarees. They all waited in pious subservience to be blessed before covering our bodies.

On schedule, the alarm broke the comforting scratches of the nightly crickets. Lali jumped out of bed, a Pavlovian response reminiscent of her nights at the hospital during her residency. I rushed to the porcelain sink to brush my teeth. Soon the rest of the household stirred into sleep-laden action, needing to get the religious ceremonies finished before Surya, the sun god, poked his red-hot body from under the blanketed horizon that chilly November morning. Akka, our grandmother, lined up us four young ones and massaged our scalps, hands, and feet with coconut oil. Her greasy hands smoothed her own smoky-gray hair, which kept cascading onto her seventy-year-old shoulders. We took turns entering the bathroom to wash off our oiled bodies with rust-colored arrapu podi, the earth-smelling powder that effectively washed away coconut oil. Amma and Lali could barely keep up with the demands of heating water on the two kerosene-fueled stoves to warm the iciness of the wintry morning water. Soon we stepped into our clothes, blessed by Lakshmi, whose presence was invoked by Appa, playing the dual role of our father and family priest.

We grabbed our packages of anars, cone-shaped flowerpots that burst with star-like brilliance when we lit their wicks with our red-tipped, jasmine-scented agarbattis (incense sticks). The Elephant brand, green-papered firecrackers, short like cigarette butts, awoke the neighborhood, the noise worsened by the furious barking of the stray dogs that were rudely disturbed from their deep slumber. Soon the sun graced the morning sky and our supply of firecrackers diminished with the disappearing moon. By now our stomachs growled in anticipation of Amma's freshly steamed idlis, golden-brown, doughnut-shaped vadaas, and nutty-pungent coconut chutney.

Once breakfast was under our belts, the next Diwali routine warranted our com-

plete attention: The weeklong preparation of mysore pak (ghee-laden roasted gar-
banzo bean flour bars), crunchy sev (fried noodles perked up with ground red pep-
per), and terrati paal (clumps of reduced milk solids flavored with jaggery) filled
round stainless steel thalis that were to be taken as gifts to neighbors, friends, and
relatives. I volunteered to bring them to the neighbors who historically were extra-
kind to me, slipping me an extra mithai to appease my sweet tooth while I waited for
them to replenish my now-emptied thali with goodies from their kitchens. Whenever
Amma replenished the thalis with sev, I always whispered to her to be slightly more
frugal with those delectably crunchy fried noodles, as I enjoyed the leftovers for days
to come.

2 cups garbanzo bean flour

2 tablespoons rice flour

1 teaspoon ground red pepper
  (cayenne)

1 teaspoon salt

½ teaspoon hing (asafetida)

2 tablespoons unsalted butter

About ⅓ cup warm water

Vegetable oil for deep-frying

1. In a medium bowl, combine the garbanzo bean flour, rice flour, cayenne, salt, and hing. Cut in the butter with a pastry cutter; or using the palms of your hands, rub the flour mixture and butter until the mixture looks like coarse breadcrumbs.

2. Make a small well in the center of the flour and pour half of the water in it. With your fingers, combine the ingredients to form dough. Add additional water, 2 tablespoons at a time, until the dough comes together in a ball. Knead 2 to 3 minutes or until the dough is soft and smooth. Cover with plastic wrap and set aside for 10 to 15 minutes. (You can refrigerate dough at this point, covered, up to 24 hours; bring it back to room temperature before proceeding.) Divide the dough into 2 equal portions.

3. In a wok or 3-quart saucepan, heat the vegetable oil (about 2 to 3 inches deep) over medium heat until a thermometer registers 350°.

4. Push one portion of the dough through a noodle press (use the mold plate with the larger round holes) directly into the hot oil. Fry for 2 to 3 minutes, turning once or twice, until the noodles are golden brown. Drain on paper towels. Repeat with the remaining dough.

5. Store the noodles in an airtight container or zip-lock plastic bag at room temperature for up to 2 months.

Makes about 12 ounces

Idlis
Steamed Rice-Lentil Cakes

Idlis are one of the signature dishes in southern Indian homes all across the world. A must for breakfast, they are also eaten at lunch and dinner as they provide valuable nutrients to the predominantly vegetarian population in southern India.

1 cup uncooked long-grain rice	About 2 cups warm water for
1 cup uncooked parboiled	grinding
(converted) rice	1 tablespoon salt
½ cup urad dal (split and hulled	¼ teaspoon baking soda
black lentils), sorted	Vegetable oil for greasing pan

1. Place the two varieties of rice in a medium bowl and cover with water. With your fingers, gently wash the grains for 30 seconds until the water becomes cloudy; drain. Repeat 5 or 6 times until the water is clear. Cover with warm water and soak at room temperature for at least 4 to 5 hours, or overnight; drain.

2. In a separate bowl, use the same procedure to rinse and soak the urad dal.

3. In a blender, puree ½ cup warm water and half the rice, scraping the sides of the container, until smooth. Transfer to a large bowl. Repeat with the remaining rice.

4. Grind the dal with ¼ cup water until smooth; add to the rice batter. Fold in the salt and ¾ cup water, or more as needed to make slightly thick pancake-consistency batter.

5. In a gas oven with a lit pilot light, slightly warm electric oven, or proofing unit, keep the bowl tightly covered with plastic wrap for 24 hours, or until the batter ferments and acquires sourdough-like smell. Stir in the baking soda.

6. Lightly grease the muffin tin with vegetable oil. Half fill the molds with batter and place them in the baking dish. Pour boiling water into the baking dish about 1 inch deep. Cover the entire baking pan tightly with aluminum foil and set on a burner over medium heat. Steam for 20 to 25 minutes, or until a toothpick or cake tester stuck in the idlis comes out clean. Remove the muffin tin from the water bath and let it cool for at

---

❧ I never squander the more expensive (and wonderful) basmati rice for this recipe, since it is ground up into a batter. Save it for another dish. Parboiled (converted) rice lightens the batter for a softer, fluffier, idli. While in India idlis are often made with only parboiled rice (and urad dal), I prefer to make them here in my Minneapolis home with a combination of white long-grain and parboiled rice, which results in a better texture. If parboiled rice is unavailable, use only uncooked long-grain rice.

❧ Soak and grind the rice and dal separately. Grinding them together will result in a slightly grainy texture that is unacceptable to the idli connoisseur.

❧ The fermentation of idli batter is crucial to a fluffy product. Fermented batter should smell slightly sour and nutty, with a few bubbles formed on the surface. The batter will rise by an inch or two under warmer

least 5 minutes. Slide the idlis out with a butter knife. Repeat with the remaining batter.

If you are using an idli pan, grease the individual disks and fill them three-quarters with batter. Stack them (there are usually 4 plates with 4 disks on each plate) around the idli stand, placing the small metal rod between each plate to separate them. Set the contraption in a stockpot containing about ½ inch of hot water. Cover and steam on medium-high heat for 20 to 25 minutes, or until a toothpick or cake tester stuck in the idlis comes out clean. Remove the idli stand from the stockpot and let it cool for at least 5 minutes. Slide the idlis out with a butter knife. Repeat with the remaining batter.

Makes about 40 idlis 2½ inches round
(a few less if using muffin tins).
Serves 10

conditions. Mothers-in-law are known to be catty in describing their son's wives in the not-so-glorified words, "The only good thing about my Raja's ardhangini [other half] is that her hot-headedness flows into her hands and so when she mixes the batter using her hands, they ferment faster. That's why her idlis are so fluffy." It is true that using hands to mix the batter does generate added heat essential for the fermentation.

ঞ If you do not have an idli pan, you can use a muffin tin with cups roughly 2¾ × 1⅛ inches set in a larger baking dish.

ঞ Idlis freeze well for up to 2 months and can be rewarmed in a microwave. Place the frozen idlis in microwave-safe dish and steam, covered, on high for 2 to 3 minutes.

ঞ Idlis back in India are a must with Thénga Chutney (page 226) and Sambhar (page 110). For a quick snack I often devour them with ghee-smothered Molagha Podi (page 212) along with a bowl of cool, plain yogurt.

Kaancheepuram Idlis
Steamed Rice-Lentil Cakes with Cashews

☙ If karhi leaves are unavailable, use finely chopped fresh cilantro instead, for a different flavor.

☙ Refer to the note with Idlis (page 128) for additional information.

Shortly after I turned eighteen, my Akka (grandmother), who lived with us almost all her life, passed away. Appa, her son and our dad, had succumbed to a malignant brain tumor two years earlier. My sister Lali gathered us four siblings for a month's journey to Chidambaram, their place of birth along the southeastern coast of India.

The train ride was slow and long. The steam engine puffed its way through the lush green valleys and quiet villages. The dark-chocolate-brown hard benches in our second-class compartment glistened with our night sweat. The pillow under my head and the two sheets of thin fabric did nothing to diminish its hardness. Mathangi, the younger of my two sisters, reminded me to eat more idlis to cover "my bony ass." In the hot morning sun we came to a screeching halt at a small station where the smell of fresh-brewed coffee being hawked by young men and little boys wafted through the window's steel bars.

"Coffee, coffee," yelled the man in a thin dhoti (a long "skirt," usually white, that drops to the ankles) carrying six stainless steel tumblers of a dark brew without spilling a drop. His Tamilian accent was thick and it sounded like, "Copy, copy." I heard my stomach roar and looked hungrily at Lali, the keeper of the purse. Grabbing the five-rupee bill in my sweaty palm, I rushed toward the man selling kaancheepuram idlis. These were special idlis, not often made by Amma, steamed with raw cashews, black pepper, and karhi leaves, from Kaancheepuram, the region known for beautiful hand-woven silk sarees with gold threads worn by Indian women on special occasions. Steamed in banana leaves, these soft, fluffy cakes were accompanied by fresh coconut chutney. I have never forgotten them.

1 cup uncooked long-grain rice

1 cup uncooked parboiled (converted) rice

½ cup urad dal (split and hulled black lentils), sorted

About 2 cups warm water for grinding

1 tablespoon salt

¼ teaspoon baking soda

½ cup coarsely chopped raw cashews

¼ cup coarsely chopped fresh karhi leaves

1 teaspoon coarsely cracked black peppercorns

Vegetable oil for greasing pan

1. Place the two varieties of rice in a medium bowl and cover with water. With your fingers, gently wash the grains for 30 seconds until the water

becomes cloudy; drain. Repeat 5 or 6 times until the water is clear. Cover with warm water and soak at room temperature for at least 4 to 5 hours, or overnight; drain.

2. In a separate bowl, use the same procedure to rinse and soak the urad dal.

3. In a blender, puree ½ cup warm water and half the rice, scraping the sides of the container, until smooth. Transfer to a large bowl. Repeat with the remaining rice.

4. Grind the dal with ¼ cup water until smooth; add to rice batter. Fold in the salt and ¾ cup water, or more as needed to make slightly thick pancake-consistency batter.

5. In a gas oven with a lit pilot light, slightly warm electric oven, or proofing unit, keep the bowl tightly covered with plastic wrap for 24 hours, or until the batter ferments and acquires sourdough-like smell. Stir in the baking soda, cashews, karhi leaves, and peppercorns.

6. Lightly grease the muffin tin with vegetable oil. Half fill the molds with batter and place them in the baking dish. Pour boiling water into the baking dish about 1 inch deep. Cover the entire baking pan tightly with aluminum foil and set on a burner over medium heat. Steam for 20 to 25 minutes, or until a toothpick or cake tester stuck in the idlis comes out clean. Remove the muffin tin from the water bath and let it cool for at least 5 minutes. Slide the idlis out with a butter knife. Repeat with the remaining batter.

   If you are using an idli pan, grease the individual disks and fill them three-quarters with batter. Stack them (there are usually 4 plates with 4 disks on each plate) around the idli stand, placing the small metal rod between each plate to separate them. Set the contraption in a stockpot containing about ½ inch of hot water. Cover and steam on medium-high heat for 20 to 25 minutes, or until a toothpick or cake tester stuck in the idlis comes out clean. Remove the idli stand from the stockpot and let cool for at least 5 minutes. Slide the idlis out with a butter knife. Repeat with the remaining batter.

Makes about 40 idlis 2½ inches round
(a few less if using muffin tins).
Serves 10

Mrs. Pandian's Thidupu Idlis
Steamed Rice-Lentil Cakes with Bananas

🪔 Use bananas that are quite overripe, like the ones you reserve for making banana bread. You can freeze them for up to 2 months for future use.

🪔 See Idlis (page 128) for more information.

The green bean–thick fingers of my right hand folded snugly into my sister's left hand as I grabbed on to the marble banisters with my other hand. My feet desperately tried to keep up with Mathangi's steps as we climbed the stairs to Mrs. Pandian's home school. Her husband and my Appa were colleagues at the Indian Navy, our families separated by two floors in the eight-floor high-rise apartments in the posh neighborhood of Napean Sea Road, across from the Arabian Sea.

Mrs. Pandian looked down at me with warm eyes and led me into her similar-looking living room, where I encountered four other neighbors, all now part of her preschool classroom. Soon the air was filled with her sweet rendition of "Baa Baa Black Sheep" mixed in with our painfully banal voices trying to keep up with her words. The hours faded into the early afternoon after what seemed endless repetitions of the English alphabet interspersed with Humpty Dumpty and hundreds of blackbirds that for some ungodly reason were being baked in a pie. It was time for a treat of freshly squeezed lemonade and coconut-sweetened biscuits before we were all shipped back to our own apartments.

This ritual continued four times a week and I grew accustomed to her gentle voice and maternal company. The Pandians' Tamilian Christian kitchen often generated aromas I was unfamiliar with: strong fishy odors of pomfrets fried in chili-spiked oil, freshly shredded coconut pounded with garlic and tempered with roasted mustard seed. Their Christmas meals, I remember, were peppered with Western delicacies of fruitcakes and custard gelatin puddings, while their Tamilian heritage peeked its head through the idlis and dosas more familiar in my Amma's Brahmin kitchen. But what struck me as odd was the presence of banana sweetness in her steamed rice-lentil cakes, a far cry from my Amma's savory, sourdough-tasting cakes. Soon I started making umpteen requests for their appearance beyond Jesus' day of birth, and Mrs. Pandian always obliged, her sugariness permeating the fermented batter to honeyed fluffiness.

1 cup uncooked long-grain rice

1 cup uncooked parboiled (converted) rice

½ cup urad dal (split and hulled black lentils), sorted

About 2 cups warm water for grinding

2 tablespoons sugar

¼ teaspoon baking soda

2 medium overripe bananas, mashed

Vegetable oil for greasing pan

1. Place the two varieties of rice in a medium bowl and cover with water. With your fingers, gently wash the grains for 30 seconds until the water becomes cloudy; drain. Repeat 5 or 6 times until the water is clear. Cover with warm water and soak at room temperature for at least 4 to 5 hours, or overnight; drain.

2. In a separate bowl, use the same procedure to rinse and soak the urad dal.

3. In a blender, puree ½ cup warm water and half the rice, scraping the sides of the container, until smooth. Transfer to a large bowl. Repeat with the remaining rice.

4. Grind the dal with ¼ cup water until smooth; add to rice batter. Fold in the sugar and ¾ cup water, or more as needed to make slightly thick pancake-consistency batter.

5. In a gas oven with a lit pilot light, slightly warm electric oven, or proofing unit, keep the bowl tightly covered with plastic wrap for 24 hours, or until the batter ferments and acquires sourdough-like smell. Stir in the baking soda and bananas.

6. Lightly grease the muffin tin with vegetable oil. Half fill the molds with batter and place them in the baking dish. Pour boiling water into the baking dish about 1 inch deep. Cover the entire baking pan tightly with aluminum foil and set on a burner over medium heat. Steam for 20 to 25 minutes, or until a toothpick or cake tester stuck in the idlis comes out clean. Remove the muffin tin from the water bath and let cool for at least 5 minutes. Slide the idlis out with a butter knife. Repeat with the remaining batter.

    If you are using an idli pan, grease the individual disks and fill them three-quarters with batter. Stack them (there are usually 4 plates with 4 disks on each plate) around the idli stand, placing the small metal rod between each plate to separate them; set the contraption in a stockpot containing about ½ inch of hot water. Cover and steam on medium-high heat for 20 to 25 minutes, or until a toothpick or cake tester stuck in the idlis comes out clean. Remove the idli stand from the stockpot and let cool for at least 5 minutes. Slide the idlis out with a butter knife. Repeat with the remaining batter.

Makes about 40 idlis 2½ inches round
(a few less if using muffin tins).
Serves 10

Rava Idlis
Semolina Steamed Cakes

Cream of wheat, also known as sooji or rava in Indian grocery stores, is available in its non-instant form in all supermarkets. The instant variety, used in American kitchens at the breakfast table, will not work in this recipe.

This batter can be made up to a month ahead and frozen.

For variety, I often fold thinly sliced green chilies into the batter before steaming the dumplings. A bowl of yogurt offers delicious comfort to the palate and soul alike.

See Idlis (page 128) for more information.

We all sat in near blackness in our dining room in the Mumbai suburb of Andheri (a name derived, ironically, from andher, meaning "darkness"). It was the early 1970s and India had declared war on its neighbor Pakistan. Once dusk settled in against the horizon, Mumbai's lights were forbidden to be turned on. Blackouts were essential to be invisible to the "other side," should any Pakistani bomber planes pass over India's skies. All the windows in our apartment were covered with black blotting paper, and our only light source was a single oil lamp sitting on the terrazzo floor. The light fluttered with the grace of a bharatanatyam dancer, casting shadows on the walls. We spoke in hushed voices, fearing that the bombers could hear us from their high-altitude mission.

In this frightened atmosphere we broke up pieces of rava idlis and dipped them in stainless steel katoris filled with shallot-enhanced pigeon pea stew. Rice, previously a staple in our Tamilian kitchen, was a rare commodity during the war. Rains were unusually scarce that year, and the cultivated meager grains were reserved for the soldiers in this ridiculous battle between neighbors agitated by religious zealots on both sides. Our government-rationed quota of rice was reserved for upcoming religious functions, and suddenly sooji (cream of wheat) and laapsi (cracked wheat husk) invaded our kitchen like cockroaches. After weeks of their coarse, grainy texture we longed for the soft, cushiony comfort of fluffy white mounds of steamed rice. But we comforted ourselves with these rava idlis instead, hoping for the expedient culmination of this ever-present, holy hatred.

1 cup urad dal (split and hulled black lentils), sorted
About 2 cups warm water for grinding

2 cups uncooked cream of wheat
1 tablespoon salt
¼ teaspoon baking soda
Vegetable oil for greasing pan

1. In a medium bowl, place the dal and cover with water. With your fingers, gently wash the dal for 30 seconds until the water becomes cloudy; drain. Repeat 5 or 6 times until the water is clear. Cover with warm water and soak at room temperature for at least 3 to 5 hours, or overnight; drain.
2. In a blender, puree ½ cup warm water and the dal; grind until smooth.

Add ¼ cup water toward the end of the grinding to create a smooth, fluffy batter. Transfer to large bowl.

3. Line a steamer basket with a clean dish towel (similar to a flour sack). Spread the cream of wheat on the towel and steam for about 15 minutes. Add the steamed wheat to the urad dal batter.

4. Fold in the salt and 1¼ cups water, or more as needed to make slightly thick pancake-consistency batter.

5. In a gas oven with lit pilot light, slightly warm electric oven, or proofing unit, keep the bowl tightly covered with plastic wrap for 24 hours, or until the batter ferments and acquires sourdough-like smell. Stir in the baking soda.

6. Lightly grease the muffin tin with vegetable oil. Half fill the molds with batter and place them in the baking dish. Pour boiling water into the baking dish about 1 inch deep. Cover the entire baking pan tightly with aluminum foil and set on a burner over medium heat. Steam for 20 to 25 minutes, or until a toothpick or cake tester stuck in the idlis comes out clean. Remove the muffin tin from the water bath and let cool for at least 5 minutes. Slide the idlis out with a butter knife. Repeat with remaining batter.

If you are using an idli pan, grease the individual disks and fill them three-quarters with batter. Stack them (there are usually 4 plates with 4 disks on each plate) around the idli stand, placing the small metal rod between each plate to separate them; set the contraption in a stockpot containing about ½ inch of hot water. Cover and steam on medium-high heat for 20 to 25 minutes, or until a toothpick or cake tester stuck in the idlis comes out clean. Remove the idli stand from the stockpot and let cool for at least 5 minutes. Slide the idlis out with a butter knife. Repeat with remaining batter.

Makes about 40 idlis 2½ inches round
(a few less if using muffin cups).
Serves 10

WARRUPOO KOZHAKUTTAIS
Steamed Dumplings with Lentils

🌿 These dumplings can be made up to 3 days ahead and resteamed or reheated. Leftover dumplings will keep in the freezer for a month.

🌿 It is important to stir the batter constantly, to prevent lumps from forming. If lumps get into the dough, smooth wrappers are next to impossible.

🌿 When tasted alone, the filling is spicy and slightly salty. This flavor will be tempered by the rice wrapper, and the combination will be perfectly balanced.

🌿 Make sure you have ample water in the steamer pan. You may have to add water between batches to prevent the pan from drying out.

Shiva had a temper as gargantuan as his persona, but that was to be expected from the god who destroys all evil. If you invoke his ire, be ready to be turned into stone. But if you appeal to his compassion through major sacrifices, sit back and reap the fruits lavished upon you. Shiva spent long periods of time on Mount Kailasha, his heavenly retreat where he performed penance in a solitary world away from his wife, Parvati, and their newly conceived child, Ganesh.

Parvati never got used to being alone without her husband but feared his wrath should she stoke his burning anger. She now spent her postpartum days showering attention on their beautiful, chubby baby boy. Her maternal love nurtured his body and soul and soon he grew into a vibrantly healthy young boy.

One morning, as was his routine, Ganesh stood guard outside his mother's door, with a sword in one hand, as she bathed in milk, honey, and fresh petals of rose and jasmine. Her strict instructions not to allow anyone entrance into her private chambers rang in his ears. The morning rays of Surya, the god of sun, filtered through the doorway. Within moments the room darkened and Ganesh looked up to see an unkempt old fakir in a white dhoti standing barefoot with a stick in one hand. He was about to march through the door into Parvati's private quarters when Ganesh stood in his way, brandishing his sword. The aged man was Shiva, his father, but Ganesh had never seen him since his birth. Shiva too did not recognize his son, and soon his annoyance filled the chambers like blinding smoke. He bellowed to Ganesh to step aside, but the boy refused to budge. Shiva yanked the sword from his little hands and, with the sharpness of its blade that swished through the air with metallic splendor, severed Ganesh's head in one clean motion.

The commotion brought Parvati running to the door and she shrieked in disbelief at what her husband had done. "You have killed your son with your own anger," she sobbed. "Now how can I continue to live?" Shiva's wrath dissipated as swiftly as icy cold water on a burning ember. He fell to his knees and wept for his son. He promised Parvati that he would bring back Ganesh by planting on his empty shoulders the first living creature's head that would walked by their home. Just then the earth shook and Shiva poked his head out the door to see what caused the tremor. A baby elephant had strayed away from his heard and was thundering by. As promised, Shiva ran to the elephant and, with the same sword that had made his son lifeless, rendered the elephant headless with one stroke. He gathered the head and planted it on his firstborn's shoulders. Soon Ganesh's body stirred into life, and he awoke to find his mother and father showering blessings on him, whispering his name,

"Gajanan Ganesh," the elephant-headed celestial being about to be worshiped by millions as the bestower of happiness and the eliminator of sorrow.

On Ganesh Chaturthi, the day of his birth, Amma always made his favorite: delicately wrapped shells of rice flour housing two different kinds of filling, one with red chili–spiked lentils, the other a sweet combination of fresh coconut, jaggery, and freshly ground cardamom (page 139). She always shaped the savory dumplings into boats, while the sweet ones were round, to differentiate them when they were sealed. Steamed with pearly beads of water clinging to their satin skins, they lay on banana leaves in front of Ganesh's statue as he sat on his throne, a dumpling in his left hand, right hand facing me in raised blessing, and his mascot, the furry rodent who lay by his feet, nibbling on a modak (dumpling). Once the kozhakuttais were blessed, they easily slid down our throats and into our hungry bellies, the spicy ones first followed by their sweetly innocent kin.

FILLING

½ cup urad dal (split and hulled black lentils), sorted
2 to 3 fresh Thai, cayenne, or serrano chilies
4 to 5 dried red Thai, cayenne, or serrano chilies
2 tablespoons finely chopped fresh karhi leaves
1½ teaspoons salt
¼ teaspoon hing (asafetida)

WRAPPERS

1½ cups rice flour
¼ teaspoon salt
1½ cups warm tap water
6 tablespoons vegetable oil
Additional oil for shaping

TO MAKE FILLING

1. In a medium bowl, cover the dal with water. With your fingers, gently wash the dal for 30 seconds until the water is cloudy; drain. Repeat 5 or 6 times until the water is clear. Cover with warm water and soak at room temperature for at least 2 to 3 hours, or overnight; drain.

2. In a food processor, grind the dal and chilies until smooth. Transfer to a medium bowl and fold in the remaining ingredients for filling.

3. Lightly grease a steamer pan and spread the filling to form a patty about 1 inch thick. Steam for about 20 to 25 minutes, or until a knife inserted through its center comes out clean. Remove the patty from the steamer

pan and cool for about 10 minutes. Crumble the patty into small pieces the size of tiny pebbles.

TO MAKE WRAPPERS

1. Combine the rice flour and salt in a medium bowl. Whisk in water a few tablespoons at a time until the batter has a thin crepe consistency.
2. Stir in 3 tablespoons oil. Put 3 tablespoons oil and batter into a cold wok or nonstick skillet. Heat the batter over medium heat, stirring constantly, for 2 to 3 minutes, or until the batter thickens, starts to leave the sides of the pan, and comes together into a ball to form soft dough. It should feel silky smooth but not sticky. Transfer the dough to a plate and spread it to cool for 5 to 8 minutes.
3. Divide the dough into 20 equal portions and shape each portion into a smooth ball. Grease your palms well with oil. Place a ball in the palm of one hand. With the fingers of the other hand, press and shape ball into a flat circle, 3 inches in diameter.
4. Place a scant tablespoon of filling in the center of a wrapper. Fold one edge over the filling and bring it toward the other edge; press the edges together to seal the dumpling. Repeat with remaining balls and filling.
5. Lightly grease a steamer pan. Line the dumplings (without overcrowding) and steam for 10 minutes. Repeat with the remaining dumplings.

Makes 20 dumplings. Serves 5

Pooranam Kozhakuttais
Steamed Dumplings with Coconut

Filling

1 cup freshly shredded coconut
   (page 6)
½ cup coarsely chopped gur
   (jaggery) or tightly packed dark
   brown sugar
½ teaspoon cardamom seed
   (removed from pods), ground

Wrappers

1½ cups rice flour
¼ teaspoon salt
1½ cups warm tap water
6 tablespoons vegetable oil
Additional oil for shaping

> These dumplings can be made up to 3 days ahead and resteamed or reheated. Leftover dumplings will keep in the freezer for a month.

> Stir the batter constantly, to prevent lumps from forming. If lumps get into the dough, smooth wrappers are next to impossible.

> Make sure you have ample water in the steamer pan. You may have to add water between batches to prevent the pan from drying out.

TO MAKE FILLING

1. In a 1-quart saucepan, heat the coconut and jaggery over medium heat, stirring occasionally, for 5 to 7 minutes, or until the jaggery dissolves.
2. Stir in the cardamom. Transfer the filling to a plate and let cool.

TO MAKE WRAPPERS

1. Combine the rice flour and salt in a medium bowl. Whisk in water a few tablespoons at a time until the batter has a thin crepe consistency.
2. Stir in 3 tablespoons oil. Put 3 tablespoons oil and batter into a cold wok or nonstick skillet. Heat the batter over medium heat, stirring constantly, for 2 to 3 minutes, or until the batter thickens and comes together into a ball to form soft dough. It should feel silky smooth but not sticky. Transfer the dough to a plate and spread it to cool for 5 to 8 minutes.
3. Divide the dough into 20 equal portions, and shape each portion into a smooth ball. Grease your palms well with oil. Place a ball in the palm of one hand. With the fingers of the other hand, press and shape ball into a flat circle, 3 inches in diameter.
4. Place a scant teaspoon of filling in the center of a wrapper. Gather up the sides of the wrapper. Bring them toward center to cover filling. Pinch the gathered edges together to seal shut. Repeat with remaining ingredients.
5. Lightly grease a steamer pan. Line the dumplings (without overcrowding) and steam for 10 minutes. Repeat with the remaining dumplings.

Makes 20 dumplings. Serves 5

Murghi, Gosht, Aur Meen
(Poultry, Meat, and Fish)

Bhetki Maach
Ginger-Fennel-Marinated Pan-Fried Fish Fillets

Meen Curry
Fish Fillets Poached in Coconut Milk

Maharashtrian-Style Muchee
Spicy Fish with Coconut

Tandoori Muchee
Marinated Grilled Fish

Chingri Maach Malai Curry
Shrimp with Cream and Fennel

Chettinad Jhinga
Shrimp with Chilies and Peppercorns

Mumbai Jhinga
Vegetable-Crusted Shrimp

Prawns Vindaloo
Shrimp Poached in Coconut Milk–Vinegar Sauce

Gosht Masaaledar
Spicy Lamb Chops

Badam Gosht
Lamb with Almonds

Murghi Korma
Chicken in Saffron-Almond Sauce

Bhetki Maach
Ginger-Fennel-Marinated Pan-Fried Fish Fillets

This teatime savory from West Bengal, home state to Calcutta, exemplifies that community's love affair with fish and seafood, bountiful gifts from the Bay of Bengal. It is a testimony to the simplicity of Bengali cooking that somehow produces such complex-tasting results.

1 cup coarsely chopped onion
¼ cup white vinegar
1 tablespoon coarsely chopped
  gingerroot
1 teaspoon fennel seed
1 teaspoon salt
4 pollack, cod, halibut, or monkfish
  fillets (6 ounces each), skin
  removed

1 cup plain breadcrumbs
1 teaspoon ground red pepper
  (cayenne)
¼ cup vegetable oil
1 large egg, slightly beaten

1. In a blender, puree the onion, vinegar, gingerroot, fennel, and salt until smooth. Pour the marinade over the fish fillets and coat them well. Refrigerate, covered, for 3 to 4 hours.
2. On a plate, combine the breadcrumbs and cayenne.
3. In a 12-inch skillet, heat the oil over medium heat. Dip the fillets (along with any marinade that clings to its surface) in the egg and coat with breadcrumbs. Fry each side for 4 to 5 minutes until the fillets are golden brown and start to flake easily with fork.
4. Drain on paper towels and serve immediately.

Serves 4

MEEN CURRY
Fish Fillets Poached in Coconut Milk

The coastal town of Kanyakumari is home to a vibrant fishing community, whose cuisine reflects the ocean's gifts of seafood fortified with coconut, chilies, karhi leaves, and black mustard seed—mainstays of southern Indian cooking. On a recent trip to the town, I watched bare-chested, dark-skinned men maneuver their canoes on the choppy waters that reflected the colors of the rising sun. They reeled in nets brimming with sparkling gifts from the ocean—fishes, crabs, and giant prawns, and they returned to shore, careful not to crash their canoes against the jagged rocks that lined Kanyakumari's shoreline.

Looming over the gigantic rocks at India's southernmost tip is a temple dedicated to the goddess Kanyakumari: kanya means "bride," and kumari means "virgin." The temple rests on the town's beach, speckled with unusually colored sand and seashells, overlooking the three merging oceans that hug India's coasts: the Arabian Sea, the Indian Ocean, and the Bay of Bengal. Tourists from around the world come to see the legendary sunrises and sunsets and the three distinct colors of the choppy waters. I was equally fascinated by the fable of Kanyakumari, the unmarried virgin bride, whose statue overlooked the oceans across the temple's now-barred windows.

Two asuras, wielding their demonic rage on India's inhabitants, threatened invasion once they crossed the turbulent oceans. Shiva, the destroyer of evil, was quickly summoned to offer a solution to head off the attack. He determined that only virgins could destroy the asuras' powers, and so he created two women, Kali and Kanyakumari, virgin goddesses who embodied his spirit and acumen in guarding the country along its eastern and southern coasts, respectively. Once they achieved their purpose, Kali returned to her heavenly abode, but Kanyakumari made penances to implore Shiva to let her remain at the southernmost tip of India.

Meanwhile, her vitality and beauty drew the attention of a god fashioned from the images of Brahma (the creator), Vishnu (the preserver), and Shiva (the destroyer), who resided nearby at another temple. He approached Shiva for her hand, not knowing Kanyakumari needed to maintain her virginity for fear of losing her goddess powers. Since he did not wish to be the bearer of bad news, Shiva gave permission for the marriage to take place, but said nothing about Kanyakumari's need to remain a virgin for fear of losing her goddess powers.

The festivities began with the lagnam muhuratam, time of marriage, set at midnight. Kanyakumari was fully adorned from head to toe in all her bridal glory, her hands and feet laced with henna, gold and diamond jewelry shining against her turmeric-stained body, her lush hair braided with hand-sewn strings of jasmine and rose. Her bindi stood out bright red as the morning sun between her black kaajal-laced eyes, offering a backdrop to the glowing diamond that hung from the parting of her forest thick hair. As her bridegroom left his temple in good time so as not to miss the muhuratam, Shiva unleashed his trusted sidekick, the cunningly devious Narada, disguised as a rooster on the unsuspecting groom. Narada crowed the false arrival of Surya the god of sun, leading the groom to believe that he had missed the auspicious midnight hour. With great disappointment, he turned around and returned to his abode.

Kanyakumari pined for her groom, her patience dissipating at midnight, displaced by anger and fury. She turned all the food and offerings for the wedding into multicolored sand and stones, and stayed at the temple, now transformed into a marbled body, dressed as a bride, her diamond shining a beacon bright across the window grate to unsuspecting fishermen returning to land in their canoes on moonless nights, causing them to crash against the jagged rocks of the tricolored sea. The window was eventually boarded shut, protecting the men from her hatred.

3 tablespoons vegetable oil

2 dried red Thai, cayenne, or serrano chilies

1 tablespoon chana dal (yellow split peas), sorted

1 tablespoon coriander seed

6 large cloves garlic, finely chopped

1 teaspoon salt

4 marlin, mahimahi, or swordfish fillets (6 ounces each), skin removed

1 teaspoon black mustard seed

1 can (14 ounces) coconut milk

20 to 25 fresh karhi leaves

1 cup finely chopped tomatoes

1. In a 12-inch skillet, heat 1 tablespoon oil over medium-high heat. Add the chilies, dal, and coriander seed and stir-fry for 1 to 2 minutes until the chilies slightly blacken, the dal turns golden brown, and the coriander seed is reddish brown and aromatic. Remove the mixture with a slotted spoon and cool for 2 to 4 minutes. Grind the mixture in a spice grinder until it has the texture of finely ground black pepper.

2. Combine the ground spice blend, garlic, and salt in small bowl. Divide the mixture into 4 portions and rub one portion on both sides of each fish fillet. Refrigerate, covered, for at least 1 hour or overnight.

3. Heat 2 tablespoons oil in the same skillet; add mustard seed. When it starts to pop, cover the skillet until all the seed has popped. Add the fillets and sear them on each side for 1 to 2 minutes until partially brown.

4. Pour in the coconut milk and karhi leaves. Lower the heat and simmer, covered, turning the fillets once or twice, for 5 to 7 minutes until almost cooked.
5. Stir in the tomatoes and continue simmering, uncovered, for about 2 minutes, or until the tomatoes are warm and the fish flakes easily with a fork.
6. Transfer the fillets to a serving platter and spoon sauce over them.

Serves 4

MAHARASHTRIAN-STYLE MUCHEE
Spicy Fish with Coconut

The Marathi-speaking community in and around Mumbai loves fish, especially since it is available in abundance from the Arabian Sea. This robustly flavored combination of spices highlights the area's natural bounty.

½ cup coarsely chopped onions

4 tablespoons coarsely chopped fresh cilantro

1 tablespoon coarsely chopped gingerroot

1 teaspoon tamarind concentrate or 1 tablespoon freshly squeezed lime juice

1 teaspoon salt

8 medium cloves garlic

4 to 6 fresh Thai, cayenne, or serrano chilies

4 halibut, mahimahi, or swordfish fillets (6 ounces each), skin removed

2 tablespoons vegetable oil

½ cup freshly shredded coconut (page 6)

1. In a food processor, finely mince the onions, 2 tablespoons cilantro, gingerroot, tamarind, salt, garlic, and chilies.
2. Rub the fish fillets on both sides with the onion mixture. Refrigerate for at least 30 minutes but not more than 8 hours.
3. In a 10-inch skillet, heat the oil over medium heat. Add the fish fillets including any marinade. Cook for 3 to 5 minutes, or until the underside is dark brown. Flip the fillets and top with coconut. Cook for 3 to 5 minutes until the underside is dark brown and the fish flakes easily with a fork. Sprinkle with remaining cilantro.

Serves 4

TANDOORI MUCHEE
Marinated Grilled Fish

For a quick weekday dinner on a hot summer day, this recipe comes to the rescue like every Hindi film hero who charges in to rescue the heroine from the grip of an evil villain just before she is stripped of her virtue. They inevitably fall in love, as you will with this heroic dish.

1 small onion, coarsely chopped
8 medium cloves garlic
2 tablespoons coarsely chopped
  gingerroot
¼ cup plain yogurt
2 tablespoons finely chopped fresh
  cilantro
1 tablespoon Garam Masaala
  (page 206)

1 teaspoon salt
½ teaspoon ground red pepper
  (cayenne)
½ teaspoon red food coloring
4 swordfish, pollack, cod, halibut, or
  monkfish fillets (6 ounces each),
  skin removed
Vegetable oil for brushing

1. In a food processor, finely mince the onion, garlic, and gingerroot.
2. In a medium bowl, combine the onion mixture with the remaining ingredients except fillets and oil.
3. Coat the fillets well with the marinade and refrigerate, covered, for 1 to 4 hours.
4. Brush a grill rack with vegetable oil. Heat coals or gas grill for direct heat. Grill the fish, uncovered, 5 to 6 inches from medium heat for 8 to 10 minutes, turning once, until the fish flakes easily with a fork.
   To broil: Place the fish on a lightly oiled rack in the broiler pan. Broil 2 to 3 inches from the heat for 10 to 12 minutes, turning occasionally, until the fish flakes easily with a fork.

Serves 4

CHINGRI MAACH MALAI CURRY
Shrimp with Cream and Fennel

- For a variation, use scallops instead of shrimp (or a combination of the two). For the vegetarian at the table, substitute slices of Paneer (page 210) for the shrimp. Fry the marinated paneer slices for the same amount of time as you would shrimp.

- Ground black mustard seed yields a required bitterness to the dish, but you can substitute yellow mustard seed.

- To pound dried chilies, place them in a mortar and pound 5 to 6 times with a pestle until the chilies break down into smaller pieces and some of their seed is released. You can also place them between sheets of plastic wrap and mash them with a rolling pin.

Rekha Ganguly was an indomitable presence even at five feet tall, her mustard-oil-massaged hair cascading past her waist as it dried with reckless abandon under the Calcutta sun. Her shidoor glowed in red brilliance on her forehead between her doe-like eyes. She bent down to turn the spicy-sharp cayenne chilies yet one more time to ensure even drying as they lay on her old green-saffron saree. Her shaka and paula, white conch shell and mineral red bangles, reminders of her marital status, jingled with the twist of each pepper. The purple-black pullow draped over her left shoulder and around her slender neck was weighted down with her house keys resting against her right bosom. She had just been married to Amritalal Mukherjee, fifteen years her senior, her first wedding, his second, much to her family's dismay.

Rekha's quiet demeanor was a stark contrast to Amritalal's boisterous, commanding presence punctuated by hearty guffaws. He was the life of the party, while she was the winsome beauty in the background tending to their guests' gastronomical needs. Her prowess in cooking fish and seafood, staples in the community's diet, was matched by none. The truth of the matter was the guests came not for Amritalal's wild stories but to indulge in Rekha's succulent shrimp bathed in creamy coconut milk and perked up by strong chilies and pungent ground mustard. The curry was as sweet as her honeyed daughter Mithu, my good friend, who was a harmonious blend of unassuming Ganguly and spicy Mukherjee.

1 pound uncooked shrimp (about 16 to 20), peeled and deveined

4 medium cloves garlic, finely chopped

2 dried red Thai, cayenne, or serrano chilies, pounded (see note)

1 teaspoon fennel seed, ground

1 teaspoon salt

½ teaspoon black mustard seed, ground

¼ teaspoon cardamom seed (removed from pods), ground

2 tablespoons mustard oil or vegetable oil

½ cup coconut milk

1 tablespoon finely chopped fresh cilantro

1. In a medium bowl, thoroughly combine all the ingredients except oil, coconut milk, and cilantro. Refrigerate, covered, for at least 1 hour or overnight.

2. In a 10-inch skillet, heat the oil over medium-high heat. Arrange the shrimp in a single layer. Cook for 1 to 2 minutes until the underside is salmon-pink. Turn the shrimp and cook 1 to 2 minutes.

3. Reduce the heat to simmer. Stir in the coconut milk and cook for 1 to 2 minutes until warm. Sprinkle with cilantro.

Serves 4

CHETTINAD JHINGA
Shrimp with Chilies and Peppercorns

I usually serve this dish with Shorakai Curry (page 88) and steamed basmati rice for a quick weekday dinner. The shrimp is fairly spicy and so rice (or bread) is essential for absorbing the heat from the various chilies and peppercorns. I always like to serve a "wet" curry to complement a dish like this one, which has no sauce—since balancing flavors and textures is a hallmark of Indian cuisine.

The Chettiars of the deep south state of Tamil Nadu (Chennai, previously known as Madras, is its most recognized city) are known for their business acumen and adventurous spirit that increased their presence in faraway places like Singapore, Malaysia, and Myanmar. Numerous caricatures and statues depict Chettiars with characteristic potbellies as symbols of success and wealth. The cuisine from this community became known as Chettinad and is marked by a preference for hot and spicy chilies, peppercorns, and sesame oil.

1 pound uncooked shrimp (about 16 to 20), tail on, peeled, and deveined
¾ teaspoon salt
1 tablespoon chana dal (yellow split peas), sorted
1 to 2 dried red Thai, cayenne, or serrano chilies
¼ teaspoon black peppercorns
½ teaspoon tamarind concentrate

2 tablespoons water
1 tablespoon finely chopped fresh cilantro
12 to 15 fresh karhi leaves, finely chopped
1 to 2 fresh Thai, cayenne, or serrano chilies, finely chopped
2 tablespoons unrefined sesame oil or vegetable oil
1 teaspoon black mustard seed

1. In a medium bowl, combine the shrimp and salt.
2. In a preheated 10-inch skillet over medium heat, roast the dal, dried chilies, and peppercorns, shaking the pan occasionally, for 2 to 3 minutes or until the dal turns reddish-brown and the chilies slightly blacken. Remove from the skillet and let cool. In a blender or spice grinder, grind the mixture until it is the texture of finely ground black pepper. Add to shrimp.
3. Dissolve the tamarind in water. Add to shrimp.
4. Add the cilantro, karhi leaves, and fresh chilies to shrimp and mix well. Refrigerate for at least 30 minutes or up to 8 hours to blend the flavors.
5. In the same skillet, heat the sesame oil over medium heat; add the mustard seed. When it begins to pop, cover the skillet. As soon as the seed finishes popping, arrange the shrimp in a single layer and cook for 1 to 2 minutes until the underside is salmon-pink. Turn the shrimp and cook 1 to 2 minutes. Serve immediately.

Serves 4

Mumbai Jhinga
Vegetable-Crusted Shrimp

Every morning off the coast of the Arabian Sea, the fishing community of Mumbai, known as the kohlis, haul to the shore bountiful treasures of giant shrimp in large fishing nets. Some of these are laid out on the beaches of Versova in suburban Mumbai to dry under the hot sun, while the rest of the loot is brought to the fish markets around the bustling city. Some of the street vendors roll them in uncooked cream of wheat, smother them in minced vegetables, and cook them on large griddles, barely able to contain them from the growing throngs of hungry customers. You'll soon see why.

4 medium cloves garlic

1 medium carrot, peeled and coarsely chopped

1 small onion, coarsely chopped

3 to 5 fresh Thai, cayenne, or serrano chilies

2 tablespoons coarsely chopped fresh cilantro

1 pound uncooked shrimp (about 16 to 20), tail on, peeled, deveined, and butterflied (see note)

Juice of 1 medium lime

1 cup uncooked cream of wheat or plain breadcrumbs

¼ cup vegetable oil

1. In a food processor, finely mince the garlic, carrot, onion, chilies, and cilantro.
2. In a medium bowl, combine the minced vegetable mixture and shrimp; fold in lime juice.
3. Completely coat each shrimp with cream of wheat.
4. In a 12-inch skillet, heat the oil over medium-high heat. Arrange the shrimp in a single layer without overcrowding. Cook the shrimp, turning occasionally, for 4 to 6 minutes or until crusty brown and the tail is salmon-pink. Drain on paper towels.

Serves 4

⁂ These are delicious as a first course when served with Kishmish Chutney (page 224). Shrimp is at its succulent best when cooked to order. Make sure you do not overcook them or they will become rubbery.

⁂ To butterfly shrimp, make a cut about ¼ inch deep along the back from the head to the start of the tail, taking care not to cut all the way through. Gently pry open the back and flatten it on a cutting board.

PRAWNS VINDALOO
Shrimp Poached in Coconut Milk–Vinegar Sauce

Vindaloo sauces are often associated with peppery hotness, when in reality the term refers only to their vinegar content. In this dish, the vinegar's pungent, nose-tingling aroma is well balanced by the coconut milk's smoothness, making the sauce a wonderfully rustic bed for the plump, succulent shrimp. Because vindaloo dishes are very "saucy," I always serve them with steamed white rice, which does a wonderful job of mopping up every last flavorful drop.

Since Aunty Lobo always appeased me with potatoes instead of shrimp, I recommend you do the same for the vegetarian at your dinner table. Try cubes of pork, chicken, or even beef if you have shellfish-averse eaters. You will have to adjust your cooking time since each of these cooks at a different pace.

I was the shortest boy in seventh grade. Lali always said I would grow tall "all in due time." Once she ruled out all medical reasons for my shortcomings, she couldn't resist chiding me about my "horrible eating habits"—"Arré, you never drink your milk!" I didn't mind leading the class during morning assembly (shortest in front with the tallest bringing up the rear) because the popular school athlete, Desmond, with his starched white shirt covering skin the color of black mustard seed, chiseled square jaw, and long gray trousers (full pants, we called them in India) with polished black shoes, was just behind.

He lived in Mahim and I in Andheri, suburban stops along our daily train ride to school that took an hour and a half—on a good day. We became close friends, thrown together by shortness, me the quiet, shy one, and he the boisterous, outgoing athlete. I hung onto every escapade he shared with me and was easily regaled by his silly antics. His Catholic background with roots embedded in Goa, the beach-kissed state just south of Mumbai, was equally enthralling. His mother, Aunty Lobo (we always addressed our elders not related by blood as "Uncle" or "Aunty," as a sign of respect), who always wore European outfits, was a woman who embodied, to me, the beauty of her home state.

She spoke longingly of the plump cashews wrapped in brown paper-like skin that hung precariously at the end of the reddish-brown cashew apple fruit permeating tall, musky cashew trees. Her eyes glistened with childhood memories of the crunch of delicate seashells against the hot white sands of the Arabian Sea's beaches. She fashioned the sign of the cross in midair whenever she talked about the Basilica of Bom Jesus, the splendid Jesuit church that housed its patron, Saint Xavier. She explained why his partially opened casket was paraded every few years: "to share with the world the miracle that was the saint whose body barely deteriorated after decades of spiritual release from this material world."

But most of all, I was drawn to her cooking, which was perfumed with the ingredients of Portuguese ancestry. Aromas of vinegar, garlic, chilies, coconut milk, and roasted cashews smothered every story she wove while we ate. I always left feeling completely satiated by her warmth, love, and the plateful of steamed rice mounded with her potato vindaloo, a vegetarian alternative to her famous prawn vindaloo, cooked specially for me.

½ cup coarsely chopped onions

2 tablespoons raw cashews

1 tablespoon coarsely chopped
gingerroot

1 teaspoon cumin seed

4 large cloves garlic

2 to 3 fresh Thai, cayenne, or
serrano chilies

2 tablespoons vegetable oil

1 cup coconut milk

¼ cup white vinegar

1 teaspoon Garam Masaala
(page 206)

1 teaspoon salt

1 pound uncooked shrimp (about
16 to 20), peeled and deveined

1 tablespoon finely chopped fresh
cilantro

1. In a food processor, finely mince the onions, cashews, gingerroot, cumin, garlic, and chilies.
2. In a 2-quart saucepan, heat the oil over medium-high heat. Stir-fry the onion mixture for 3 to 5 minutes until golden brown.
3. Stir in the remaining ingredients except cilantro. Cook for 3 to 5 minutes, stirring occasionally, until the shrimp is reddish-orange in color and the sauce is slightly thickened. Sprinkle with cilantro.

Serves 4

GOSHT MASAALEDAR
Spicy Lamb Chops

"If you give us your old clothes or money, the eclipse will go away," bellowed the ragged-looking beggars from our building's courtyard. We watched from our sixth-floor balcony as some of our old clothes sailed in the air and landed in a limbless heap on the concrete ground. The beggars ran from one piece of clothing to the next, stuffing them into large gunnysacks hanging from their shoulders. The sun was partially hidden behind the moon, playing peekaboo with the world below. We had to wait for Surya the sun god's game to end before we could break from our daylong fast.

Across the building's courtyard, a construction crew worked in shadowed glory on a half-erected cement high-rise. A group of men gathered, checkered lungis around their waists, a harmonious chanting rising up toward the darkening sky. A mature goat stood in their circle tied to a metal post, a tear-shaped red spot anointing his forehead while a small garland of marigold blossoms rested between his two horns, blissfully unaware of his sacrificial role. The sharp, dagger-like khukari's blade glistened against the smoldering embers of the open pit fire. A bleat hung in the air as it sliced through the goat's jugular vein, the life force draining into a metal bucket. A few deft strokes separated the meat from the skin, and soon hunks of flesh lay in garlic-and-clove-perfumed marinade.

During this ceremonial ritual, I watched Shakuntala, our second-floor neighbor, run into our courtyard, her sky-blue dupatta trailing over her left shoulder. She was a twenty-two-year-old beauty with shoulder-length hair the color of black mustard seed and eyes as shockingly wide as the goat's. Only hers were brimming with love-torn tears, angry at her parents' refusal to grant permission to marry her chosen soul mate. She handed her black purse and kolhapuri chappals to a neighbor as she ran barefoot into the building. While my questioning mind pondered the unfolding scene below, a fleeting object whizzed from above and landed in a bone-warped mass on bare concrete in a sickening, stomach-wrenching thud, with synchronous irony to the goat's silenced bleat. Shakuntala lay in a grotesque pile; her dupatta for one last time billowed in the wind and covered her twisted face. The crowds gathered down below as the goat meat across the street swathed in an aromatic poultice of yogurt and freshly ground spices hung between two poles over the hot pit.

The offerings of discarded old clothes, unfulfilled human desires, and betrayed animal innocence did indeed lift the eclipse from darkness that shed harsh light in my pre-teenage mind on the mysteries of life and death.

½ cup plain yogurt

½ cup raw cashews

1 tablespoon coarsely chopped
gingerroot

8 medium cloves garlic

1 teaspoon cardamom seed (removed
from pods)

½ teaspoon black peppercorns

2 three-inch cinnamon sticks, broken
into smaller pieces

2 tablespoons finely chopped fresh
cilantro

1 teaspoon salt

4 bone-in leg of lamb steaks or loin
chops (6 to 8 ounces each)

1. In a blender puree all the ingredients except the cilantro, salt, and lamb
   until smooth.
2. Transfer the marinade to a medium bowl and fold in the cilantro and salt.
   Rub the lamb well with the marinade and refrigerate, covered, for at least
   1 hour or overnight.
3. Heat coals or a gas grill for indirect heat. Remove the lamb steaks from
   the marinade, reserving the liquid. Grill the lamb, covered, 4 to 5 inches
   from medium heat for 10 to 15 minutes, brushing occasionally with
   reserved marinade, turning steaks once or twice, until the lamb is pink
   when cut.

Serves 4

BADAM GOSHT
Lamb with Almonds

You can substitute chicken, turkey, or even seafood. The cooking time will vary accordingly.

Almonds are prized nuts that were introduced to India by the Middle Eastern traders from Kabul, Afghanistan. Their Islamic religion made its way into the northern regions of India and so did their architectural influences, evident in the beautiful monuments, the Taj Mahal being the finest example of them all. Mature goat is a delicacy among the Muslim community, and for special occasions the tough meat is simmered for hours with aromatic spices, garlic, onions, and an abundance of pureed almonds over low flame. This is a variation on the theme.

½ cup coarsely chopped red onion
4 medium cloves garlic
½ teaspoon black peppercorns
6 whole cloves
2 tablespoons vegetable oil
1 teaspoon cumin seed
½ cup blanched almonds, ground

1 pound boneless lamb, cut into 1-inch cubes
½ cup half-and-half
1 teaspoon Garam Masaala (page 206)
1 teaspoon salt
2 tablespoons finely chopped fresh cilantro

1. In a food processor, finely mince the onion, garlic, peppercorns, and cloves.
2. In a 12-inch skillet, heat the oil over medium-high heat. Add the cumin seed and sizzle for 10 to 15 seconds. Add the minced onion mixture and stir-fry for about 5 minutes, or until golden brown.
3. Stir in the ground almonds and cook for 2 to 3 minutes, stirring occasionally, until golden brown.
4. Add the lamb and cook for 18 to 20 minutes, stirring occasionally, until all the water released from the lamb evaporates.
5. Stir in the half-and-half, garam masaala, and salt. Lower the heat and simmer, covered, stirring occasionally, for about 20 minutes, or until the lamb is fork-tender. Sprinkle with cilantro.

Serves 4

Murghi Korma
Chicken in Saffron-Almond Sauce

Every north Indian home has its own version of korma, richly complex nut-based sauces. The kormas in restaurants often incorporate tomatoes, but I prefer to leave the acid out to showcase the purity of the almonds, saffron, and cream.

½ teaspoon saffron threads

½ cup heavy (whipping) cream, slightly warm

1¼ pounds boneless, skinless chicken breasts, cut crosswise into 1-inch-thick strips

2 tablespoons finely chopped fresh cilantro

1 teaspoon salt

½ teaspoon ground red pepper (cayenne)

½ cup blanched almond slivers

¼ cup water

1 teaspoon Garam Masaala (page 206)

2 tablespoons Ghee (page 204) or vegetable oil

2 tablespoons finely chopped gingerroot

5 large cloves garlic, finely chopped

1. In a large bowl, steep the saffron in heavy cream for 1 to 2 minutes.
2. Add the chicken, cilantro, salt, and red pepper. Refrigerate for at least 30 minutes but no more than 8 hours.
3. In a blender, puree the almonds, water, and Garam Masaala until smooth.
4. In a 10-inch skillet, heat the ghee over medium-high heat. Add the gingerroot and garlic. Stir-fry for 2 to 3 minutes, or until golden brown.
5. Stir in the chicken mixture and cook, uncovered, stirring occasionally, for 12 to 15 minutes, or until partially cooked.
6. Mix in the almond paste and simmer, covered, stirring occasionally, for 8 to 10 minutes, or until the chicken is no longer pink in the center.

Serves 4

Maa Annapurna
A Tribute to the Rice Goddess

Shaadum
Steamed Rice

Subzi Pulao
Basmati Rice with Vegetables

Tamatar Shaadum
Tomato Rice Pilaf

Paruppu Shaadum
Rice with Pigeon Peas and Clarified Butter

Mrs. Sharma's Kichidi
Rice and Split Green Lentil Porridge

Chana Pulao
Basmati Rice with Garbanzo Beans

Tayyar Shaadum
Basmati Rice with Yogurt

Thénga Shaadum
Basmati Rice with Toasted Coconut

Tiruvaadrai Kali
Cracked Rice Pilaf with Jaggery

Zarda Pulao
Basmati Rice with Saffron and Rose Petals

Zeera Chaawal
Cumin-Scented Basmati Rice

Arshi Uppama
Cracked Rice "Polenta" with Onion

SHAADUM
Steamed Rice

There are several ways to make steamed rice: in a covered pan with just enough water to be absorbed by the kernels, in a large pot of water not unlike cooking pasta, in a rice cooker, or in a pressure cooker. If you are using a tender grain like basmati (the variety that is grown at the foothills of the Himalayan Mountains), I do not recommend using a rice cooker or pressure cooker. The intense heat these appliances generate overcooks it to yield a gummy product.

It was that time of the week. The servant had swept and mopped the floors around the house, then headed for the bathroom. She soaked the soiled clothes in a red bucket filled with soapy water. She grabbed the baseball-bat-like stick and thrashed the soaped fabrics with a rhythmic beat. Soon they made their way into a white plastic bucket filled with clean water for rinsing. Each fabric was twisted dry, except for the cotton sarees that lay, beaten clean, in a twisted pile on the bathroom's white-tiled floor.

Meanwhile Amma was in the kitchen heating up a large stainless steel pot of water on a kerosene-fueled stove. She threw in a bowl ful of long-grain rice from a newer crop sold by the rice vendor who came to our door once a week with a large gunnysack trailing heavily over her left shoulder. The fresher the crop, the starchier the rice, I later found out, and this was important for her impending chore. The water came to a second boil and the rice kernels rose to the top with each rising bubble, puffing up with heated pride. The cooked grains clouded the water sticky-white with a slotted spoon, Amma scooped out a few grains, squishing one between her thumb and forefinger to test its doneness. She was pleased to see it give in with no residual hardness. She placed a tight-fitting lid on the pot and lifted it off the stove. She placed the pot on its side, holding it by its lip with its lid slightly pulled back, at the sink's edge as a large bowl in the sink collected the starchy liquid. Sure, it would have been easier with a colander placed in the bowl, but she didn't have one.

She grabbed the starch-filled water and shuffled to the bathroom. She dunked the sarees, one at a time, coating each with the rice starch and letting it soak through. They rested fifteen minutes and then were lightly rinsed and wrung dry by hand. Akka awoke from her nap and grabbed the sarees that now lay in a bucket waiting to be dried. She hung them out under the hot sun on the clotheslines pulled taut between two hooks nailed from each end of the balcony's wooden ledge. Once dry, the sarees were picked up by the ironing vendor. They came back into our home the same day, all starched and neatly pressed, smelling like hot, steamed, nutty rice.

METHOD 1

1 cup uncooked basmati or long-grain rice

1½ cups cold water

1. In a 2-quart saucepan, cover the rice with water. With your fingers, gently swish grains until the water becomes cloudy; drain. Repeat 3 or 4 times until the water appears almost clear. Cover with 1½ cups cold water and soak for 20 to 30 minutes.
2. Bring the rice and water to a boil over medium-high heat. Cook, uncovered, stirring once or twice for 5 to 6 minutes or until most of the liquid has evaporated. Cover the pan and simmer at the lowest heat possible for 5 minutes. Turn off the burner and let the pan sit for 5 minutes. Fluff the rice with a fork or spoon to release steam.

METHOD 2

| 1 cup uncooked basmati or long-grain rice | 8 cups water |

1. In a 2-quart saucepan, cover the rice with water. With your fingers, gently swish the grains until the water becomes cloudy; drain. Repeat 3 or 4 times until the water appears almost clear.
2. Bring 8 cups water to a boil. Add the rice. Return to a boil and cook, uncovered, for 5 to 7 minutes until the rice is tender. Drain and rinse the rice under cold water to prevent overcooking.

Serves 4

SUBZI PULAO
Basmati Rice with Vegetables

I often serve this rice as is, or with a bowl of plain yogurt. For presentation and flavor, I never remove the whole spices but do caution my guests against eating the cardamom pods, cloves, cinnamon sticks, and bay leaf.

I adored Sundays at home, especially the early morning hours before the day fell prey to the tuneless cacophony of Mumbai's street life: the jingle of bicycle bells, the rickshaw drivers' snappy expletives hurled at two-legged and four-legged ruminators, the harried vendors' parched voices hawking mangoes, rice, and dripping pomfrets still twitching for the comfort of their oceanic bed. Before the sun arose from its slumber, the cotton-clad, white-sareed women and men in their starched dumpling-white kurtas quietly formed a procession, gathering disciples along the way; their hushed voices paid homage to Surya, the sun god. Their barefoot steps unscathed by the hot tarred roads anointed the day set aside for respite; a break from the harshness of life that is India, an occasion to reacquaint your harried soul with the simple pleasures of family, food, and friends.

The gentle chants of these Jain monks, with the occasional "ting" of their brass cymbals, floated into my sleep and shook me awake from my deep teenage repose. The Sunday Times of India had already made its way around the household. Lali, who often worked six days a week at the clinic and was always an early riser, had finished the paper along with her tumbler of warm whole milk sweetened with just a hint of cane sugar. My stainless steel tumbler waited patiently for me, filled with milk flavored with Cadbury's Drinking Chocolate—the only trick that would get me to choke it down.

I would stumble out of my cot and make my way to the porcelain sink to brush my teeth. Pretty soon the conversation around the breakfast table would lead us to our favorite weekly game: guessing which relative or friend would drop by unannounced in the afternoon and just happen to stay around for dinner. Lali, in addition to being our family's medical practitioner, was the champion of cooking north Indian foods in our southern kitchen. Every Sunday evening she made vegetable pulao with basmati rice (a rare, expensive appearance in our middle-income home), tempering it with the northern flavors of cinnamon sticks and bay leaves, and combining it with mustard seed, the quintessential darling child of southern cooking, Sambhar Masaala (page 208), and fresh seasonal vegetables. My eyes always popped open with glee when fresh green peas at their juiciest plumpness were added to the aromatic mix.

No matter which favorite friend or pesky relative showed up, the smile on his or her face after a few mouthfuls of the pulao with plain yogurt that was still warm from its cultured humid day, was reason enough to treasure the true meaning of Sunday.

1 cup uncooked basmati or long-grain rice
2 tablespoons Ghee (page 204) or vegetable oil
1 teaspoon black mustard seed
1 teaspoon cumin seed
6 whole cloves
6 green or white cardamom pods
2 three-inch cinnamon sticks
1 fresh or dried bay leaf

½ cup finely chopped red onion
3 medium carrots, peeled and cut crosswise into ¼-inch slices
1 medium potato, peeled and cut into ¼-inch cubes
2 teaspoons Sambhar Masaala (page 208)
2 cups water
1 cup frozen green peas
1 teaspoon salt

1. In a small bowl, cover the rice with water. With your fingers, gently swish the grains until the water becomes cloudy; drain. Repeat 3 or 4 times until the water appears almost clear. Cover with cold water and soak for 20 to 30 minutes; drain.

2. In a 2-quart saucepan, heat the oil over medium-high heat; add mustard seed. When it starts to pop, cover the pan until all the seed has popped. Immediately add the cumin, cloves, cardamom, cinnamon, and bay leaf. Sizzle for 20 to 30 seconds. Add the onion and stir-fry for 1 to 2 minutes, or until golden brown.

3. Stir in the carrots, potato, sambhar masaala, and ½ cup water. Bring to a boil. Cover and steam for 3 to 4 minutes, or until the water evaporates. Add the rice, remaining 1½ cups water, peas, and salt.

4. Bring to a boil and cook, uncovered, stirring once or twice, for 4 to 5 minutes, or until almost all the water has evaporated. Lower the heat as much as possible and cook, covered, for 5 minutes. Turn off the burner and let the pan sit for 8 to 10 minutes.

5. Fluff the rice with a fork or spoon to release the steam.

Serves 6

TAMATAR SHAADUM
Tomato Rice Pilaf

It was almost the end of the month and the plastic vegetable bin looked pretty bare. Paychecks filtered into the house only once a month. Another week before Amma could send one of us to the open-air market. She scratched her head in puzzlement, the kudumai (bun) at the back of her head moving in synchronous motion, wondering what to do to perk up steamed rice. I had lamented the absence of any flavors in "plain old boring shaadum" once too often. There was one lonesome tomato in the basket. What's a mother to do?

She squatted on the kitchen's bare tile floor and opened up the armamanai, resting her left thigh on the floor cleaver's wood board. With a few deft strokes set to music by her gold bangles clanking in harmony, she diced the tomato with the armamanai's sharp blade. Within minutes, the rice was done, seasoned with the only available tomato, spiked with her very own sambhar masaala, fresh karhi leaves, and roasted black mustard seed—the epitome of down-home cooking southern Indian style. I had an extra helping, licking the fingers on my right hand, savoring every last grain as if it were my last.

꽃 Fresh karhi leaves impart a delicate flavor to the rice. The unmistakable sweetly citric aroma holds no comparison to any other herb. Use 2 tablespoons freshly chopped cilantro as an alternative, although it really is not a substitute for beautifully mysterious fresh karhi leaves.

꽃 Use yellow split peas for a slightly different variation and nuttiness if you don't have split and hulled black lentils on hand.

꽃 Try any other vegetable, such as finely chopped spinach, onions, or even eggplant.

1 cup uncooked basmati or long-grain rice	1 large tomato, finely chopped
2 tablespoons vegetable oil	1 teaspoon Sambhar Masaala (page 208)
1 teaspoon black mustard seed	1½ cups cold water
1 tablespoon urad dal (split and hulled black lentils), sorted	1 teaspoon salt
	15 fresh karhi leaves

1. In a small bowl, cover the rice with water. With your fingers, gently swish the grains until the water becomes cloudy; drain. Repeat 3 or 4 times until the water appears almost clear. Cover with cold water and soak for 20 to 30 minutes; drain.

2. In a 2-quart saucepan, heat the oil over medium-high heat; add the mustard seed. When it starts to pop, cover the pan until all the seed has popped. Immediately add the urad dal and stir-fry for 30 seconds or until golden brown.

3. Stir in the tomato and sambhar masaala. Cook for 2 to 3 minutes, until the tomato softens.

4. Stir in the rice, water, salt, and karhi leaves. Bring to a boil and cook, uncovered, stirring once or twice, for 5 to 6 minutes or until most of the liquid has evaporated. Lower the heat as far as possible, and cook, covered, for 5 minutes. Turn off the burner and let the pan sit for 5 minutes. Fluff the rice with a spoon or fork to release the steam.

Serves 4

PARUPPU SHAADUM
Rice with Pigeon Peas and Clarified Butter

Every Indian baby, for many generations, has started his or her adventure into the world of solid foods with this easy-to-digest, very nutritious combination of pigeon peas and rice drizzled with clarified butter. I too was inducted this way by Akka's loving hands as she lay me on her lap and fed me this familiar food, cooing and humming to me as I stared at her gentle face, wrinkled with years of maternal experience.

PARUPPU
(PUREED PIGEON PEAS)

1 cup toovar dal (split and
   hulled pigeon peas), sorted
   and rinsed
4 cups water
1 teaspoon salt
½ teaspoon ground turmeric

SHAADUM
(STEAMED RICE)

1 cup uncooked basmati or long-
   grain rice
1½ cups cold water
Ghee (page 204) for drizzling
Coarsely cracked black peppercorns
   (optional)

TO MAKE PARUPPU

In a 1-quart saucepan, bring the toovar dal and water to a boil over medium-high heat, skimming off any foam that forms on its surface. Lower the heat and simmer, partially covered, for 20 to 25 minutes, or until the dal is tender. Let cool. Puree in a blender with the salt and turmeric until smooth.

TO MAKE SHAADUM

1. In a 2-quart saucepan, cover the rice with water. With your fingers, gently swish the grains until the water becomes cloudy; drain. Repeat 3 or 4 times until the water appears almost clear. Cover with 1½ cups cold water and soak for 20 to 30 minutes.

2. Bring the rice and water to a boil over medium-high heat. Cook, uncovered, stirring once or twice, for 5 to 6 minutes or until most of the liquid has evaporated. Lower the heat as far as possible and cook, covered, for

5 minutes. Turn off the burner and let the pan sit for 5 minutes. Fluff the rice with a fork or spoon to release the steam.

TO SERVE
Divide the rice into 6 individual serving bowls. Ladle the pureed lentils over the rice. Drizzle each mound with ghee and sprinkle with black pepper.

Serves 6

MRS. SHARMA'S KICHIDI
Rice and Split Green Lentil Porridge

❧ Kichidis are soothingly simple porridges usually eaten when convalescing from an illness. The easily digestible grains, when "washed down" with plain yogurt, make for a comforting meal.

❧ If onions, chilies, and tomatoes bother your stomach, leave them out. The humble cumin seed and ghee are equally satisfying on their own.

Mrs. Sharma was far more imposing in height than her almost six-foot-tall son Anil. She always wore a white stonewashed cotton saree, a sign of unwavering respect usually reserved for widows but in this case meant to honor her departed mother. Sharma Aunty loved to tell stories; her gift for weaving tight-knit plots in a soothing, soft-spoken tone always made us sit closer to her with rapt attention. With mouths agape (except when chewing rice-lentil porridge dipped in a katori filled with sweetly cultured yogurt), we listened to yet another tale of Akbar and Birbal, the well-known Moghul emperor and his wise, never-to-be-outwitted sidekick and trusted adviser.

Birbal listened patiently to the poor Brahmin's predicament. The Brahmin, with teeth still chattering from the previous night's bone-chilling waters of the lake, recounted how he was promised one hundred rupees for spending the night in the icy bed. He had managed to survive the frigidity by cozy thoughts of his children's soon-to-be-filled bellies with the help of this small fortune. He called upon Rama for strength, hands folded in pious servitude, looking toward a lighted oil lamp two hundred feet away for the only flicker in an otherwise charcoal-black night. His prayers helped him make it to the crack of dawn, when he emerged from the lake with frozen, shriveled skin but a warmed heart for the hope of a hot meal that would feed his hungry babies.

The court ministers marveled at the Brahmin's fortitude and quizzed him at length on his successful survival. But once they heard that he had made it through with the "warmth" from the flickering light two hundred feet away, they refused him his meager prize. "You cheated us, you insolent man," they fumed. "You heated yourself with the oil lamp two hundred feet away." His earnest pleadings fell on deaf ears even when he insisted on presenting his case to the usually fair-minded emperor, Akbar.

Birbal stroked his beard as he listened to the Brahmin's misery. It was time to teach the cruel ministers and Akbar a lesson. He invited them to a simple dinner of kichidi in the palatial courtyard. With help from the Brahmin, he lit a small fire from dried twigs. He fashioned a supporting structure fifty feet high from which dangled a large earthenware pot filled with rice, lentils, and gold-yellow turmeric. The crowds gathered and waited with growing impatience for the humble, delicately spiced porridge. Akbar's anger rose along with the wisps of smoke from the pitiful twig fire as he demanded explanation for Birbal's obvious stupidity in trying to cook a pot of kichidi fifty feet away with such a weak flame. "Jahanpana," he said with respect, "if a flickering light two hundred feet away could warm a Brahmin standing in waist-high icy-cold water, why can't I cook this kichidi only fifty feet away?" Akbar realized his folly, duly reprimanded his ministers, and ordered them to pay the Brahmin five times what was promised to him. Birbal once again prevailed!

Sharma Aunty ladled yet another helping of her kichidi onto our plates as we marveled at Birbal's sharp mind and Aunty's mercifully quick-cooking kichidi.

1 cup uncooked basmati or long-grain rice
½ cup mung dal (split and hulled green lentils), sorted
4 cups cold water
1 teaspoon ground turmeric
2 tablespoons Ghee (page 204) or melted butter
1 teaspoon cumin seed
1 large red onion, halved and thinly sliced

2 to 4 fresh Thai, cayenne, or serrano chilies, slit open lengthwise
1 cup diced tomato
2 tablespoons finely chopped fresh cilantro
1 teaspoon salt
¼ teaspoon black peppercorns, coarsely cracked

1. In a 2-quart saucepan, cover the rice and dal with water. With your fingers, gently swish the grains until the water becomes cloudy; drain. Repeat 3 or 4 times until the water appears almost clear. Add 4 cups cold water and ½ teaspoon turmeric and bring to a boil over medium-high heat. Skim off any lentil suds that float to the top. Lower the heat to medium and simmer, partially covered, for 10 minutes, or until most of the water has evaporated. Cover the pan and continue simmering for about 5 minutes. Turn off the burner and let the pan sit for 5 to 10 minutes.
2. Meanwhile, in a 12-inch skillet, heat the ghee over medium-high heat. Add the cumin seed and sizzle for 10 to 15 seconds. Add the onion and chilies and stir-fry for 4 to 6 minutes until the onions turn caramel brown.
3. Stir in the remaining ingredients and cook for 1 to 2 minutes, stirring occasionally, until the tomato softens. Blend thoroughly into the rice-lentil mixture.

Serves 6

Chana Pulao
Basmati Rice with Garbanzo Beans

For a simple dinner, I often sit down in the peaceful cushioned comfort of my favorite rocking chair with a large plateful of chana pulao and plain yogurt. Heaven could not be better than this!

1 cup uncooked basmati or long-grain rice

2 tablespoons Ghee (page 204) or vegetable oil

1 teaspoon cumin seed

6 whole cloves

4 black, green, or white cardamom pods

2 three-inch cinnamon sticks

1 fresh or dried bay leaf

1 small onion, cut in half lengthwise and thinly sliced

2 large cloves garlic, finely chopped

4 to 6 fresh Thai, cayenne, or serrano chilies, finely chopped

2 cups cold water

½ cup finely chopped tomato

2 tablespoons finely chopped fresh cilantro

1 teaspoon salt

1 can (15 ounces) garbanzo beans, rinsed and drained

¼ cup finely chopped fresh mint leaves

1. In a small bowl, cover the rice with water. With your fingers, gently swish the grains until the water becomes cloudy; drain. Repeat 3 or 4 times until the water appears almost clear. Cover the rice with cold water and soak for 20 to 30 minutes; drain.

2. In a 2-quart saucepan, heat the oil over medium-high heat. Add the cumin, cloves, cardamom, cinnamon, and bay leaf; sizzle for 20 to 30 seconds. Add the onion, garlic, and chilies; stir-fry for 1 to 2 minutes, or until the onion and garlic are golden brown.

3. Stir in the rice and remaining ingredients except mint. Bring to a boil and cook, uncovered, stirring once or twice, for 4 to 5 minutes, or until almost all the water has evaporated. Lower the heat as far as possible and cook, covered, for 5 minutes. Turn off the burner and let the pan sit for 8 to 10 minutes.

4. Fluff the rice with a fork or spoon to release the steam. Sprinkle with mint.

Serves 4

Tayyar Shaadum
Basmati Rice with Yogurt

"You will not leave the table unless you eat some tayyar shaadum or drink some buttermilk," scolded Lali. I never knew why my dairy intake was such a big issue with her. I always discarded and filed that reproach under "being a big sister." Years later she explained to me that since south Indian foods were fortified with an abundance of chilies, calming yogurt or buttermilk was essential in coating the digestive tract for easy absorption.

1 cup uncooked basmati or long-grain rice

1½ cups cold water

1 tablespoon vegetable oil

1 teaspoon black mustard seed

1 tablespoon chana dal (yellow split peas), sorted

1 piece gingerroot (about 2 inches long and ¼ inch thick), cut into thin slivers

2 to 4 fresh Thai, cayenne, or serrano chilies, cut crosswise into ¼-inch slices

15 to 20 fresh karhi leaves

2 cups plain yogurt, whisked

1 tablespoon finely chopped fresh cilantro

1 teaspoon salt

1. In a 2-quart saucepan, cover the rice with water. With your fingers, gently swish the grains until the water becomes cloudy; drain. Repeat 3 or 4 times until the water appears almost clear. Cover with 1½ cups cold water and soak for 20 to 30 minutes.
2. Bring the rice and water to a boil over medium-high heat. Cook, uncovered, stirring once or twice, for 5 to 6 minutes or until most of the liquid has evaporated. Lower the heat as far as possible and cook, covered, for 5 minutes. Turn off the burner and let the pan sit for 5 minutes.
3. Meanwhile, in a 6-inch skillet, heat the oil over medium-high heat; add the mustard seed. Cover when it begins to pop. As soon as the seed finishes popping, add the chana dal and stir-fry for about 30 seconds, or until the dal turns golden brown. Stir in the gingerroot and stir-fry for 30 seconds, or until golden brown. Remove from heat and splutter the chilies and karhi leaves in the hot oil-seed mixture for about 5 seconds.
4. Add the contents of the skillet and the remaining ingredients to the cooked rice. Stir well.

Serves 6

THÉNGA SHAADUM
Basmati Rice with Toasted Coconut

⚘ I find this dish comforting with a bowl of cool, plain yogurt. Throw in some Katarikai Thuviyal (page 222), and I am in seventh heaven. Give me some fried pappadums (lentil wafers) in addition, and I will be indebted to you for years to come!

⚘ Use an extra 2 tablespoons chana dal if urad dal is unavailable. You can eliminate the karhi leaves if they are unavailable.

In southern India, rice crops are harvested between December and January. This grain, a gift from Annapurna, the rice goddess, is cherished in many forms. At the end of the harvest season, festivals celebrate the myriad uses of rice. One such event, called Kanu, prepares your stomach by not feeding it anything from dawn. At dusk, large stockpots are filled with water and brought to a vigorous boil. Husked white rice is cooked in large quantities. The tender rice is strained and divided into three portions. One part is seasoned with freshly shredded coconut, the second is tossed with a tamarind-chili sauce, and the third is mellowed with creamy yogurt and fresh karhi leaves. The seasoned preparations are then wrapped in banana leaves. Families gather together in open fields to devour their packets, remembering to thank the goddess who made it all possible. This is my favorite of the three treasures of that celebration.

1 cup uncooked basmati or long-grain rice

1½ cups cold water

2 tablespoons urad dal (split and hulled black lentils), sorted

2 tablespoons chana dal (yellow split peas), sorted

4 dried red Thai, cayenne, or serrano chilies

2 tablespoons Ghee (page 204) or vegetable oil

1 teaspoon black mustard seed

1 tablespoon whole raw cashews, coarsely chopped

1 tablespoon dry-roasted unsalted peanuts, coarsely chopped

1 cup freshly shredded coconut (page 6)

1 tablespoon finely chopped fresh cilantro

12 to 15 fresh karhi leaves

1 teaspoon salt

1. In a 2-quart saucepan, cover the rice with water. With your fingers, gently swish the grains until the water becomes cloudy; drain. Repeat 3 or 4 times until the water appears almost clear. Cover with 1½ cups cold water and soak for 20 to 30 minutes.

2. Bring the rice and water to a boil over medium-high heat. Cook, uncovered, stirring once or twice, for 5 to 6 minutes, or until most of the liquid has evaporated. Lower the heat as far as possible and cook, covered, for 5 minutes. Turn off the burner and let the pan sit for 5 minutes.

❧ Dahi Batata Pooris (Crispy Hollowed Breads with Mung Beans) as found at a street vendor's cart, page 20

❧ BELOW LEFT: Dahi Batata Poori, page 20

❧ BELOW: Sev Batata Poori (Crispy Flat Bread with Potato, Mango, and Noodles), page 21

✥ Yezhai Kariha Kootu (Seven-Vegetable Curry with Jaggery), page 114, served with Méthi Naan (Grilled Breads with Fenugreek and Garlic), page 191

❧ ABOVE LEFT: Warrupoo Kozhakuttais (Steamed Dumplings with Lentils), page 136

❧ ABOVE: Kaancheepuram Idlis (Steamed Rice-Lentil Cakes with Cashews), page 130

❧ Sevai (Fresh Rice Noodles), page 118

- Chana Bhatura (Garbanzo Bean Stew with Puffy Bread), page 39; Maharashtrian-Style Muchee (Spicy Fish with Coconut), page 146; Vendakkai Bhaaji (Stuffed Fresh Okra), page 68; Muri (Puffed Rice with Fennel and Cucumber), page 55; Mirchi Pakoras (Batter-Dipped Chilies), page 50; Dal Maharani (Black Lentils with Kidney Beans), page 101
- Falooda Kulfi (Cellophane Noodles with Rose Syrup and Ice Cream), page 42

Chettinad Jhinga (Shrimp with Chilies and Peppercorns), page 150, served over Tamatar Shaadum (Tomato Rice Pilaf), page 164

❧ Gosht Masaaledar (Spicy Lamb Chops), page 154, served with Zarda Pulao (Basmati Rice with Saffron and Rose Petals), page 176

Masaala Dosai (Rice-Lentil Crepes with Spiced Potato Filling), page 196, and Thénga Chutney (Coconut Chutney with Garlic), page 226

BELOW LEFT: Subzi Uttapam (Vegetable-Studded Rice-Lentil Pancakes), page 201

BELOW: Rava Pooris (Puffy Cream of Wheat Breads), page 194

❦ ABOVE LEFT: Garam Masaala ("Warm" Spice Blend), page 206

❦ ABOVE: Asian eggplants and red onions, typically used in Indian cuisine

❦ Karuvapillai Thuviyal (Fresh Karhi Leaves Chutney), page 218; Limboo Urughai (Lemon Pickles), page 217

3. Meanwhile, in a 10-inch skillet, place 1 tablespoon urad dal, 1 table-spoon chana dal, and 3 chilies. Heat over medium-high heat, shaking the pan occasionally, for 2 to 3 minutes, or until the dals are golden brown and the chilies slightly blackened. Transfer the roasted ingredients to a plate and cool for 3 to 5 minutes. Grind in a spice grinder until the mixture is the texture of finely ground black pepper.

4. In the same skillet, heat the ghee over medium-high heat; add the mustard seed. When it begins to pop, cover the skillet. As soon as the seed finishes popping, add 1 tablespoon urad dal, 1 tablespoon chana dal, 1 dried chili, cashews, and peanuts. Stir-fry for 30 seconds to 1 minute, or until the dal and nuts turn golden brown.

5. Stir in the coconut, cilantro, and karhi leaves and cook, stirring constantly, for 2 to 4 minutes, or until the coconut is golden brown.

6. Add the coconut mixture, dal-chili blend, and salt to the cooked rice. Mix well.

Serves 4

Tiruvaadrai Kali
Cracked Rice Pilaf with Jaggery

This is traditionally served with Yezhai Kariha Kootu (page 114), but if time is of the essence, feel free to serve any of the other quick-prep curries in this book.

One of the two biggest events at the Nataraja temple in Chidambaram, my grand-mother and father's hometown, is the festival of Tiruvaadrai, a ten-day celebration beginning December 15 that brings out the temple's five main deities in colorful pro-cessions and large, hand-pulled jeweled chariots. The center of attraction is Nataraja himself, the best-known reincarnation of Shiva, with his striking Ananda Tandam pose, the Dance of Bliss, whose gold-adorned lifelike statue graces the town's streets amid hundreds of thousands of devotees from all over the world on the ninth day.

Very early on the tenth morning, under the shimmering rays of the full moon, we would witness the abhishekham, ritual anointing of his statue, performed with hon-eyed milk, water from the Ganges River, bananas mashed with raw cane sugar (gur), and luxuriously aromatic sandalwood paste. The sensually graceful flames emanat-ing from oil lamps, dancers in vibrant silk sarees emulating Nataraja's well-known dance through bharatanatyam, musicians with heart-pounding mridangams, and the scholarly dikshitars chanting Sanskrit verses always sent a chill down my bare, poonal thread–draped back. Wisps from rose incense sticks blended with cardamom-scented kali, the quintessential gruel of cracked rice and split and hulled green lentils sweetened with gur and freshly shredded coconut. The abhishekams ended and Nataraja was returned to his sanctuary within the temple's monumental, hand-carved stone walls. We rushed with the thousands of worshipers to the men doling out banana leaf–wrapped packets of kali and yezhai kariha kootu, our souls sati-ated with Nataraja's visit, our bodies thankful for this delectable and blessed combi-nation of kali and kootu.

1 cup uncooked long-grain rice
½ cup mung dal (split and hulled green lentils), sorted
3 cups water
¼ cup coarsely chopped gur (jaggery) or tightly packed dark brown sugar

1 cup freshly shredded coconut (page 6)
½ teaspoon cardamom seed (removed from pods), ground

1. In a 10-inch skillet, toast the rice over medium-high heat, stirring con-stantly, for 4 to 6 minutes, or until light brown and fragrant. Let cool. In a blender, grind it until it is the texture of kosher salt.

2. In a 2-quart saucepan, toast the mung dal over medium-high heat, stiring constantly, for 4 to 6 minutes or until golden brown and nutty smelling. Add the water and bring to a boil. Stir in the ground toasted rice and jaggery. Reheat to a boil and stir once or twice. Lower the heat and simmer, covered, for 10 to 12 minutes, or until the water is absorbed and the dal is cooked.
3. Stir in the coconut and cardamom.

Serves 6

ZARDA PULAO
Basmati Rice with Saffron and Rose Petals

Black cardamom pods have a strong smoky aroma and are widely available in Indian grocery stores. The pods are left whole and served still embedded in the rice as they continue to permeate the dish. Do not eat the pods since their powerful flavor will mask the delicate rose petals, saffron, and basmati rice and will linger in many subsequent mouthfuls.

Use rose petals that have not been sprayed with pesticides. Any color rose will suffice—I have often used a combination of different roses for a truly sensuous presentation.

Appa, my dad, had a penchant for growing roses on the balcony of our humble two-bedroom flat in the Mumbai suburb of Andheri. Appa's failing health prevented him from personally tending to his perfectly formed red, white, yellow, and pink roses, so he coaxed his sons daily to water them and care for them. He always admired his daughters when they left home with a rose pinned to their thick, long, charcoal-black hair. He loved to see the pictures of Rama, Laxman, Sita, and their humble Hanuman (the monkey god) all together on the family altar, adorned with rose petals from his "front yard."

My oldest sister, Lali, became the designated family vadiyaar (priest), a non-traditional role for an unmarried woman. She performed the daily morning pooja (prayer), sitting cross-legged on the terrazzo floor reading from the yellowed pages of the thick, hardbound, tattered copy of the Ramayana, while Appa and Akka (my grandmother) listened to the familiar Sanskrit words, repeating in mouthed silence, hands folded in pious servitude. The jasmine-scented agarbatti (incense) rose in perfumed wisps while the camphor burned in handheld brass lamps. The tinkling of the mani (bell) and the occasional ping of turmeric-stained uncooked rice showered on the icons accompanied Lali's fluent Sanskrit verses. I brought in fresh-cut roses, which she plucked, one petal at a time, and laid gently by Rama's feet.

When Appa passed away, the ritual continued, sweet-smelling red petals strewn next to his photo that rested by the gods he so fervently prayed to. The roses now came from a vendor across the street from our building since his own had withered away from neglect. I have always been drawn to roses, their sweet temperament reminding me of of Lali's poojas, and their thorns jabbing my guilt for letting Appa's fragrant blossoms languish.

1 cup uncooked basmati or long-grain rice
2 tablespoons Ghee (page 204) or vegetable oil
2 black, green, or white cardamom pods
¼ teaspoon saffron threads

1¼ cups cold water
¼ cup heavy (whipping) cream or half-and-half
2 teaspoons sugar
1 teaspoon salt
25 to 30 rose petals

1. In a small bowl, cover the rice with water. With your fingers, gently swish the grains until the water becomes cloudy; drain. Repeat 3 or 4 times until the water appears almost clear. Cover with cold water and soak for 20 to 30 minutes; drain.
2. In a 2-quart saucepan, heat the oil over medium-high heat. Add the rice, cardamom, and saffron. Gently stir-fry for 1 to 2 minutes to coat the rice with ghee.
3. Add the remaining ingredient except rose petals and bring to a boil. Cook, uncovered, stirring once or twice, for 4 to 5 minutes, or until almost all the water has evaporated. Lower the heat as far as possible, sprinkle rose petals on top (reserving about 5 petals for garnish), and cook, covered, for 5 minutes. Turn off the burner and let the pan sit for 8 to 10 minutes.
4. Fluff the rice with a fork or spoon to release the steam. Sprinkle with the remaining rose petals.

Serves 4

Appa

Zeera Chaawal
Cumin-Scented Basmati Rice

I always serve this rice as an accompaniment to more full-flavored curries and stir-fries. Even a piece of simply grilled fish served on a bed of zeera chaawal makes for a satisfying meal.

In this dish, the haunting sweetness of basmati rice is enhanced by the caramelized combination of stir-fried red onion and nutty cumin seed.

1 cup uncooked basmati or long-grain rice

1 tablespoon Ghee (page 204) or vegetable oil

1 teaspoon cumin seed

1 small red onion, cut in half lengthwise and thinly sliced

1½ cups cold water

1 teaspoon salt

1. In a small bowl, cover the rice with water. With your fingers, gently swish the grains until the water becomes cloudy; drain. Repeat 3 or 4 times until the water appears almost clear. Cover the rice with cold water and soak for 20 to 30 minutes; drain.

2. In a 2-quart saucepan, heat the oil over medium-high heat. Add the cumin seed and sizzle for 10 to 15 seconds. Add the onion and stir-fry for 2 to 3 minutes until golden brown.

3. Stir in the rice, water, and salt; bring to a boil. Cook, uncovered, stirring once or twice, for 4 to 5 minutes, or until almost all the water has evaporated. Lower the heat as far as possible and cook, covered, for 5 minutes. Turn off the burner and let the pan sit for 5 to 10 minutes. Fluff the rice with a fork or spoon to release the steam.

Serves 4

ARSHI UPPAMA
Cracked Rice "Polenta" with Onion

I always looked forward to Sunday mornings, when Amma prepared this for our leisurely breakfast. I especially enjoyed it with katoris filled with just-cultured plain yogurt that was still slightly warm and a heaping serving of Limboo Urughai (page 217).

1 cup uncooked long-grain rice

¼ cup toovar dal (split and hulled pigeon peas), sorted (see note)

2 tablespoons vegetable oil

1 teaspoon black mustard seed

1 tablespoon urad dal (split and hulled black lentils), sorted

1 tablespoon chana dal (yellow split peas), sorted

1 tablespoon raw cashews, coarsely chopped

2 to 3 dried red Thai, cayenne, or serrano chilies

1 cup finely chopped onion

4 cups water

2 tablespoons finely chopped fresh cilantro

2 teaspoons salt

¼ teaspoon ground turmeric

15 fresh karhi leaves

3 to 5 fresh Thai, cayenne, or serrano chilies, slit open lengthwise

❧ You can use chana dal (yellow split peas) instead of toovar dal. Toovar dal is widely available in Indian stores in two forms: oily and dry. These peas have an inherent sweetness that is especially tempting to bugs. The oil-coated variety prevents this fatal attraction and hence extends the peas' shelf life. For this recipe I prefer the non-oily ones since I don't have to wash off the grease and dry them before grinding.

❧ Toovar dal can be stored in a zip-lock bag in the refrigerator or freezer.

1. In a blender, grind the rice and toovar dal until mixture is the texture of kosher salt.
2. In a wok or 2-quart saucepan, heat the oil over medium-high heat; add the mustard seed. When it starts to pop, cover the skillet. As soon as the seed finishes popping, add the urad dal, chana dal, cashews, and dried chilies. Stir-fry for 30 seconds, or until the dal and cashews turn golden brown.
3. Add the onion and stir-fry for 2 to 4 minutes, or until the onion turns golden brown.
4. Stir in the ground rice-dal mixture and remaining ingredients. Bring to a boil, then lower the heat and simmer, covered, stirring occasionally, for 20 to 25 minutes, or until the polenta-like mixture is tender but still slightly nutty in texture.

Serves 4

Rotis

Breads, Pancakes, and Crepes

Rotlis
Whole Wheat Unleavened Breads

Paneer Paranthas
Griddle Breads Stuffed with Cheese and
Almonds

Gobhi Paranthas
Griddle Breads Stuffed with Spiced
Cauliflower

Aloo Naan
Grilled Bread with Spiced Potatoes

Méthi Naan
Grilled Breads with Fenugreek and Garlic

Bésan Palak Theplas
Garbanzo Bean Flour Crepes with Spinach

Makkai Ki Roti
Corn Griddle Bread

Rava Pooris
Puffy Cream of Wheat Breads

Pesarat
Mung Bean Crepes with Onions and
Tomatoes

Masaala Dosai
Rice-Lentil Crepes with Spiced Potato Filling

Rava Molagha Dosai
Cream of Wheat Crepes with Chilies

Subzi Uttapam
Vegetable-Studded Rice-Lentil Pancakes

ROTLIS
Whole Wheat Unleavened Breads

❧ Chappati flour, also called roti flour or atta, is widely available in Indian and Middle Eastern grocery stores. Natural food stores often stock this flour as well. It is made from a light whole wheat grain; the heavier whole wheat flour or all-purpose is not recommended as a substitute.

❧ These rotlis are often cooked in India over an open flame or hot charcoal. If you have a gas stove, you can create a similar effect. Cook the dough on one side as described in step 5, then flip the dough over and cook the other side directly on a burner over medium-high heat. Cook for 15 to 20 seconds, or until the dough puffs up. Brush one side with ghee; keep wrapped in aluminum foil.

I could not wait to see Pinank every morning at school. He was my best friend, a buddy who would stand by through thick and thin, and my cub partner during our pre-adolescent entrée into the world of Boy Scouts. Each day I weighed my chances of being invited to his home for lunch. I loved his mother's cooking—her Gujarati foods were a far cry from my daily barrage of dosai (crepes), idlis (steamed cakes), and shaadum (rice). Their Jain philosophies forbade the consumption of all types of meat, eggs, onions, and garlic (these bulbs were believed to incite passion, which stood in the way of attaining moksha, a spiritual release from the reincarnation cycle). Jains were strict believers in the principle of ahimsa (non-violence), made more worldly visible by India's most famous Jain—Mahatma Gandhi.

The Jesuit leaders of St. Xavier's Boys' Academy allowed us only thirty minutes for lunch. Luckily, Pinank's home was near the school, so a quick scale over the concrete wall and a sprint across the courtyard placed us into his dining room within seconds. His thali was patiently waiting on the table with three to four katoris, and my surprise appearance never drew even a raised eyebrow, since there was always plenty to go around. Mysteriously, my thali too appeared, along with stainless steel serving bowls filled with toovar nu dal (cumin-scented split and hulled pigeon peas), kadhi (silky smooth yogurt kissed with slivers of fresh Thai chilies and gingerroot), shaak (vegetables flavored with peanuts, turmeric, ground red pepper, and a hint of sugar), chaawal (steamed long-grain white rice), and achar (fiery hot seasonal vegetable pickle). I eagerly awaited the most important item, those delectable, tender whole wheat rounds of rotlis moistened with clarified butter. These rotlis, in my opinion, are the best; they cater to my taste of paper-thin unleavened breads. With fingers eagerly breaking pieces of rotlis, Pinank and I wrapped them around the various accompaniments, competing to see who could wolf down the most. There seemed to be an unending supply of them, always piping hot, fluffy, and laced with mounds of ghee-drenched love.

2 cups chappati flour
1 teaspoon salt
About ¾ cup warm water

Additional flour for rolling
Ghee (page 204) or melted butter for
   brushing

1. In a medium bowl combine the flour and salt; mix well. Make a small well in the center of the flour and pour half of the water in it.

2. With your fingers, combine the ingredients to form dough. Add additional water, 2 tablespoons at a time, until the dough comes together to form a ball. Knead for 2 to 3 minutes until the dough is soft and smooth. Brush with ghee and wrap the dough in plastic wrap. Set aside for 10 to 15 minutes.

3. Divide the dough into 12 equal portions. Shape each portion into a smooth round. Keep the remaining rounds covered while working with individual ones. Press each round into a ½-inch-thick patty between your palms. On a lightly floured surface, roll out the patty evenly into a 6-inch-diameter disk without tearing the dough.

4. Preheat a 10-inch skillet over medium heat. One at a time, cook the disks for 1 to 2 minutes until brown spots appear on the underside and the top side bubbles slightly. Flip once and cook for 1 to 2 minutes until brown spots appear. Brush the top side with ghee. Keep warm wrapped in aluminum foil.

Makes 12 rotlis. Serves 6

Kindergarten class in Mumbai. Raghavan Iyer is fourth from left in the top row.

PANEER PARANTHAS
Griddle Breads Stuffed with Cheese and Almonds

Paranthas were special-occasion breads in Amma's kitchen. The extra ghee they call for and the extra steps involved in making them ruled them out as an everyday selection in her economically constrained kitchen. My sister Lali, the adventuresome medic, with all her exposure to multi-regional foods experienced through her professional travels, brought this Moghalai specialty into greater rotation for us. We were grateful—you'll soon see why.

❧ Crumbled paneer resembles feta cheese in appearance. You can use feta as an alternative (use only 1 teaspoon salt, since feta is salty). Extra-firm tofu, drained, frozen, thawed, and crumbled, yields the same textural consistency as paneer.

❧ These paranthas can be fully cooked and frozen for a month. Rewarm them frozen, wrapped in foil, in a preheated 250° oven for 30 minutes.

❧ I often serve these paranthas for an elegant dinner. They always draw a collective "wow" from my guests once they sink their teeth in them.

DOUGH

3 cups chappati flour
1 teaspoon salt
2 tablespoons vegetable oil
About ¾ cup warm water

FILLING

1 cup crumbled Paneer (page 210)
½ cup finely chopped red onion
¼ cup blanched almonds, ground
¼ cup finely chopped fresh cilantro
2 teaspoons salt
1 teaspoon ground red pepper (cayenne)
1 teaspoon Garam Masaala (page 206)
Ghee (page 204) or melted butter for brushing

Additional chappati flour for dusting

TO MAKE DOUGH

1. In a medium bowl, combine the flour and salt. Add the oil and rub the flour between your fingers and palms for 1 minute until it has the texture of breadcrumbs. Make a small well in the center of the flour and pour half of the water in it.

2. With your fingers, combine the ingredients to form dough. Add additional water, 2 tablespoons at a time, until the dough comes together to form a ball. Knead for 2 to 3 minutes until the dough is soft and smooth. Brush with ghee and wrap the dough in plastic wrap. Set aside for 10 to 15 min-

utes. (You can refrigerate the dough at this point, covered, up to 24 hours. Bring it back to room temperature before proceeding.)

3. Divide the dough into 6 equal portions. Shape each portion into a ball. Set aside covered with plastic wrap.

TO MAKE FILLING

In a medium bowl, combine all the ingredients. Divide the filling into 6 portions, about 3 tablespoons each.

TO ASSEMBLE PARANTHAS

1. Place a dough round on a lightly floured surface. With your palm, flatten the dough into a disk. Using a rolling pin, roll out the dough into a 6-inch circle. Spoon a portion of the filling in the center. Gather the edges of the dough toward the center, twisting slightly to form a closed ball. Turn the ball seam side down, flatten it, and roll it evenly into a 7- to 8-inch disk (dust with flour if it's too sticky). Some of the filling will tear through the dough—that's okay.

2. Preheat a 10-inch skillet over medium heat. One at a time, cook the disks for 1 to 2 minutes, or until brown spots appear. Flip and cook the other side for 1 to 2 minutes, or until brown spots appear. Brush both sides with ghee and cook an additional 30 seconds to 1 minute on each side. Transfer to aluminum foil; wrap well to keep warm.

Makes 6 paranthas

GOBHI PARANTHAS
Griddle Breads Stuffed with Spiced Cauliflower

❧ Use any vegetable of your choice. If you are using frozen spinach, thaw and squeeze out all water before seasoning it. I have also made these with only onions and loved the results.

❧ These paranthas can be fully cooked and frozen for up to a month. Rewarm them frozen, wrapped in foil in a preheated 250° oven for 30 minutes.

❧ Paranthas are often eaten in India with pickle, vegetables, meat dishes, or raitas (yogurt-based accompaniments). For a quick lunch, I often devour them with a bowl of plain yogurt.

DOUGH

3 cups chappati flour
1 teaspoon salt
2 tablespoons vegetable oil
About ¾ cup warm water

FILLING

1 cup finely chopped cauliflower florets
¼ cup finely chopped onions
3 tablespoons finely chopped fresh cilantro
1 tablespoon finely chopped gingerroot
1 tablespoon amchur (mango powder)
1 teaspoon salt
3 to 4 fresh Thai, cayenne, or serrano chilies, finely chopped

Ghee (page 204) or melted butter for brushing

TO MAKE DOUGH

1. In a medium bowl, combine the flour and salt. Add the oil and rub the flour between your fingers and palms for 1 minute until it has the texture of breadcrumbs. Make a small well in the center of the flour and pour half of the water in it.

2. With your fingers, combine the ingredients to form dough. Add additional water, 2 tablespoons at a time, until the dough comes together to form a ball. Knead for 2 to 3 minutes until the dough is soft and smooth. Brush with the ghee and wrap the dough in plastic wrap. Set aside for 10 to 15 minutes. (You can refrigerate the dough at this point, covered, up to 24 hours. Bring it back to room temperature before proceeding.)

3. Divide the dough into 6 equal portions. Shape each portion into a ball; set aside covered with plastic wrap.

TO MAKE FILLING

In a medium bowl, combine all the ingredients. Divide the filling into 6 portions (about 2 to 3 tablespoons each).

TO ASSEMBLE PARANTHAS

1. Place a dough round on a lightly floured surface. With your palm, flatten the dough into a disk. Using a rolling pin, roll out the dough into a 6-inch circle. Spoon a portion of the filling in the center. Gather the edges of the dough and bring toward the center, twisting slightly to form a closed ball. Turn the ball seam side down, flatten it, and roll it evenly into a 7- to 8-inch disk. Some of the filling will tear through the dough—that's okay.
2. Preheat a 10-inch skillet over medium heat. One at a time, cook the disks for 1 to 2 minutes, or until brown spots appear. Flip and cook the other side for 1 to 2 minutes, or until brown spots appear. Brush both sides with ghee and cook for an additional 30 seconds to 1 minute on each side. Transfer to aluminum foil; wrap well to keep warm.

Makes 6 paranthas

Aloo Naan
Grilled Bread with Spiced Potatoes

❧ I prefer using white
potatoes for this recipe
since they are not as
waxy as the red ones.
This makes the dough
less sticky and easier
to handle.

❧ To parboil potatoes,
scrub them well. In a
1-quart saucepan,
cover the potatoes
with water and bring
to a boil over medium-
high heat. Lower the
heat and simmer,
partially covered, for 6
to 8 minutes until
partially cooked but
still firm. Cool.

❧ If you do not have a
pizza stone, use a
cookie sheet instead.

My initial encounter with a commercial tandoor during my first job as a north Indian restaurant chef was not love at first sight. The clay-lined oven encased in a stainless-steel shell sat atop a gargantuan gas burner, quietly smoldering, seething at almost 700°F, waiting to engulf me in its deepness. I approached gingerly, stepping up onto the metal step and peeking down into the hot abyss. I felt a searing blast slap my face but fought a strong desire to flee. I was, after all, going to master the tandoor, tame it into submission, make it conform to my commands, and produce those delicious naans and chickens that sent people into a culinary ecstasy.

I rolled up my chef's coat sleeves and reached for a dough round that lay on a large tray resting next to thirty other similar-looking soft white balls. I placed the dough round on the metal surface close to the tandoor's hot mouth. I pushed the dough with my trembling fingers, stretching it evenly to roughly 3 inches in diameter. I picked it up with one hand, and with both palms held up, fingers facing skyward, I started slapping the dough between my outstretched palms while gently stretching it with my thumbs. The slapping sound provided a false sense of being in control, but hey, I was grabbing at every straw on the way down into a hotness that felt like hell.

Soon the dough resembled the familiar tear-shaped naan I had eaten hundreds of times. I wet the top side of the dough and placed it on a rolled-up blue terrycloth pad. I bent down slightly and felt the dragon breath once again. I lowered my right hand along with the pad and dough resting on it with the tear-shaped end looking woefully at the glowing briquettes that lay on a grate atop the gas burners. I felt like someone had just blowtorched the hair off my right arm, and I quickly slapped the bundle onto the inner wall. I watched the dough bubble up and acquire those wonderful golden brown spots. With a long flat-edged skewer in my right hand and an L-shaped skewer in my left, I pried the naan away from the wall and caught the bread deftly, saving it from the pyre of briquettes. A brush of warm melted ghee on the naan brought a smirk to my face, and I stepped down onto the red quarry-stoned floor, feeling cocky and fearless. My satisfaction was short-lived as I realized that the demon tandoor had indeed singed off the hair on my right arm!

3 cups all-purpose flour

2 teaspoons salt

2 teaspoons baking powder

1 teaspoon Garam Masaala
 (page 206)

½ teaspoon baking soda

2 medium white potatoes, scrubbed,
 unpeeled, parboiled, and shredded
 (1 cup) (see note)

4 to 6 fresh Thai, cayenne, or
 serrano chilies, finely chopped

2 tablespoons finely chopped fresh
 cilantro

1 cup plain yogurt, whisked

Ghee (page 204) or melted butter for
 brushing

Additional flour for dusting

1. In a medium bowl, combine the flour, salt, baking powder, garam masaala, and baking soda. Stir in the potatoes, chilies, and cilantro. Add the yogurt and stir the mixture into a ball to form soft dough.

2. Knead the dough, dusting with flour if sticky, for 2 to 4 minutes until the dough is smooth. Brush with the ghee. Let the dough rest, covered, for 15 to 20 minutes.

3. Divide the dough into 4 equal parts. Shape each part into a patty (like a hamburger) and brush with ghee. Cover and set aside for 15 to 20 minutes.

4. Preheat a pizza stone on a rack in grill at high heat or on a lower rack in a 500° oven. With a rolling pin, roll out a dough round into a circle 7 to 8 inches in diameter or a tear shape ¼ inch thick. Place one piece at a time directly on the pizza stone and cook, covered, for 1 to 2 minutes until the underside is dark brown and crispy and the top side puffs up. Flip the bread and cook for 1 minute or until golden brown spots form. Remove from the stone; brush with ghee and keep warm in aluminum foil.

5. Cut each naan in half lengthwise. Serve as is for a delicious first course or with any good curry.

Serves 8

A chef making Naans

Méthi Naan
Grilled Breads with Fenugreek and Garlic

The flavors in this bread are synonymous with northern India and lend themselves well to the smoky confines of a classic tandoor—that clay-lined oven made popular by the thousands of north Indian restaurants in the United States. A preheated pizza stone in a charcoal or gas grill yields similar results. For a delectable lunch or a substantial appetizer, I often serve these along with Dal Maharani (page 101).

The flavor of fenugreek leaves is intrinsic to this recipe's success. If fresh leaves are not available in Indian grocery stores, dried ones, also called kasoori méthi, are an acceptable substitute.

3 cups all-purpose flour
2 teaspoons salt
2 teaspoons baking powder
½ teaspoon baking soda
¼ cup finely chopped fresh fenugreek leaves or 2 tablespoons dried
6 medium cloves garlic, finely chopped

4 to 6 fresh Thai, cayenne, or serrano chilies, finely chopped
About 1 cup warm water
Ghee (page 204) or melted butter for brushing
Additional flour for dusting

1. In a medium bowl, combine the flour, salt, baking powder, and baking soda. Stir in the fenugreek, garlic, and chilies. Add water a few table-spoons at a time and stir until the dough forms a ball.
2. Knead the dough, dusting with flour if too sticky, for 2 to 4 minutes until smooth. Brush with ghee. Let it rest, covered, for 15 to 20 minutes.
3. Divide the dough into 4 equal parts. Shape each part into a patty (like a hamburger) and brush with ghee. Cover and set aside for 15 to 20 minutes.
4. Preheat a pizza stone on a rack in grill at high heat or on a lower rack in a 500° oven. With a rolling pin, roll out a dough round into a circle 7 to 8 inches in diameter or a tear shape ¼ inch thick. Place one piece at a time directly on the pizza stone and cook, covered, for 1 to 2 minutes until the underside is dark brown and crispy and the top side puffs up. Flip the bread and cook for 1 minute or until golden brown spots form. Remove from the stone; brush with ghee and keep warm in aluminum foil.
5. Cut each naan in half lengthwise. Serve as is for a delicious first course or with any good curry.

Serves 8

Bésan Palak Theplas
Garbanzo Bean Flour Crepes with Spinach

These crepes have a remarkable resemblance to egg omelets, thanks to garbanzo bean flour. Since they are a cinch to make, they can be whipped up for breakfast even on a weekday.

- When salted, fresh spinach loses water. Drain off the residual water before adding spinach to crepes.

- If the skillet gets too hot, the batter will clump up as soon as it's poured, preventing an even spread. Lower the heat or wipe the skillet with a clean paper towel moistened with cold water before continuing.

- Because this flour has no gluten, reheating leftover crepes in a microwave will not cause toughness.

1 cup garbanzo bean flour
¼ cup rice flour
1½ teaspoons salt
¼ teaspoon ground turmeric
1 cup water

2 cups (4 ounces) firmly packed fresh spinach, finely chopped
1 teaspoon Sambhar Masaala (page 208)
6 teaspoons vegetable oil

1. In a medium bowl, combine the flours, 1 teaspoon salt, and turmeric. Stir in the water a few tablespoons at a time to form a smooth, crepelike batter.
2. In a separate medium bowl, combine the spinach, ½ teaspoon salt, and sambhar masaala.
3. Coat a 10-inch nonstick skillet with 1 teaspoon vegetable oil over medium heat. Pour in ¼ cup batter and tilt the skillet so that the batter spreads out evenly to form a circle roughly 6 inches in diameter. Spread about ¼ cup spinach on top of the crepe. Cook for about 2 minutes, or until the top side loses its glossy sheen and is an opaque yellow color. Flip the crepe and cook for 1 minute or until some of the spinach is crisp and brown. Repeat with the remaining batter and spinach. Keep the cooked crepes warm in aluminum foil.

Makes about 6 crepes

Makkai Ki Roti
Corn Griddle Bread

They are the hardworking wheat- and corn-growing farmers of India from the northern state of Haryana. They till the land from dawn until dusk, taking a break around noon, during the hottest part of the day. They sit on the ground by their cows, tractors, and other farm equipment, unraveling cloth sacks of warm corn griddle breads and homemade lemon pickle. A tall glass of earthenware-chilled buttermilk rounds out each farmer's simple lunch. Needless to say, these pack well!

1 cup yellow cornmeal
1 cup chappati flour
1 teaspoon salt
2 tablespoons Ghee (page 204) or
vegetable oil
1 small onion, coarsely
chopped

1 tablespoon coarsely chopped
gingerroot
4 to 6 fresh Thai, cayenne, or
serrano chilies
2 tablespoons finely chopped fresh
cilantro
About ½ cup warm water

1. In a medium bowl, combine the cornmeal, flour, and salt. Add the ghee and rub the flour between fingers and palms for 1 minute until it is the texture of breadcrumbs.
2. In a food processor, mince the onion, gingerroot, and chilies. Add to the flour along with the cilantro. Add water a few tablespoons at a time and, with your fingers, combine the ingredients until the dough comes together to form a stiff ball. Knead for 1 to 2 minutes. The dough should feel grainy and rather dry.
3. Divide the dough into 10 equal pieces. Shape each piece into a round. (While working with individual rounds, keep the remaining ones covered under plastic wrap or a slightly damp, clean dishcloth.) Press each dough round into a flat patty. With a rolling pin, gently roll out the patty into a circle roughly 4 to 5 inches in diameter and about ¼ inch thick. The dough will crack around the edges since it is fairly dry and grainy.
4. Preheat a 6-inch nonstick skillet over medium heat. With a spatula, place one dough round at a time in the skillet. Cook for 1 to 2 minutes until golden brown spots appear. Flip the dough and repeat. Brush ghee on both sides and fry each side for 10 to 20 seconds. Remove from the skillet and keep wrapped in aluminum foil.

Makes 10 breads

Rava Pooris
Puffy Cream of Wheat Breads

The milk in the dough provides a smoothness that counterbalances the heavier cream of wheat. If you are lactose intolerant, use water instead. Often, when I boil potatoes, I reserve the water for making dough, as it not only provides a delicate flavor but also makes it silky smooth.

Pooris are puffy breads that are ubiquitous in India, but this version threw me for a loop the first time I savored it at a friend's house in Mumbai. I speculated on the bread's grainy texture and queried his mother as to its ingredients. Cream of wheat was the unexpected component, which explained the slightly heavier texture of the dough when compared to the dough made from only chappati flour. Because the dough is heavier, the breads remain puffed for a longer time period, making them an ideal "do-ahead" food. Even though they can be cooked hours ahead, I prefer them deep-fried just minutes before serving. Piping hot pooris dipped in freshly pureed mango pulp is my idea of heaven on earth!

1½ cups chappati flour	2 tablespoons vegetable oil
1½ cup uncooked cream of wheat	About ½ cup milk, slightly warmed
1 teaspoon salt	Vegetable oil for deep-frying

1. In a medium bowl, thoroughly combine the flour, cream of wheat, and salt. Add the oil and rub the mixture between your fingers and palms for 1 minute until it has the texture of breadcrumbs. Make a small well in the center of the flour and pour ¼ cup milk in it.
2. With your fingers, combine the ingredients to form dough. Add additional milk, 2 tablespoons at a time, until the dough comes together in a ball. Knead for 2 to 3 minutes until the dough is soft and smooth. Brush the dough with ghee and wrap in plastic wrap. Set aside for 10 to 15 minutes. (You can refrigerate dough at this point, covered, up to 24 hours. Bring it back to room temperature before proceeding.)
3. Roll the dough into a 14-inch log and cut it into 16 equal portions. Shape each portion into a ball; set aside in plastic wrap.
4. In a wok or 3-quart saucepan, heat the vegetable oil (about 2 to 3 inches deep) over medium heat until a thermometer registers 375°.
5. With your palm, flatten each dough round into a patty. Keeping the remaining patties covered, evenly roll out one patty at a time with a rolling pin, to form a circle roughly 3 inches in diameter and ¼ inch thick. Slip the dough into the hot oil. With the back of a slotted spoon, gently and repeatedly submerge the dough until it puffs up. Flip once and brown for 10 seconds. Drain on paper towels.

Makes 16 pooris

PESARAT
Mung Bean Crepes with Onions and Tomatoes

These crepes are typical of cuisine from the state of Andhra Pradesh in southeastern India. These are not only scrumptious but nutritious too.

1 cup mung dal (split and hulled green lentils), sorted

½ cup uncooked parboiled (converted) rice

1½ cups water

4 to 6 fresh Thai, cayenne, or serrano chilies

1 medium tomato, finely chopped

1 small onion, finely chopped

1 tablespoon finely chopped fresh cilantro

1 teaspoon salt

¼ teaspoon hing (asafetida)

Vegetable oil for frying

1. In a medium bowl, cover the dal and rice with water. With your fingers, gently wash the grains for 30 seconds until the water becomes cloudy; drain. Repeat 5 or 6 times until the water is clear. Cover with warm water and soak at room temperature for at least 1 to 3 hours; drain.
2. In a blender puree ½ cup warm water, half the dal-rice mixture, and half the chilies, scraping the walls of the container, until smooth. Transfer to a large bowl. Repeat with the remaining mixture and chilies.
3. Fold in the remaining ½ cup water and remaining ingredients except oil.
4. In a 10-inch skillet, heat 1 teaspoon oil over low to medium heat. Pour in ¼ cup batter. With the bottom of a ladle, swirl the batter in a smooth circular motion to form a crepe roughly 6 to 7 inches in diameter. Cook for 1 to 2 minutes until golden brown and the top looks opaque. Flip the crepe and cook for 1 minute. Transfer to a plate. Repeat with the remaining batter.

Makes about 10 crepes

The pan will get hot between crepes. Batter poured into in a hot pan will immediately clump up, making it difficult to spread. Cool the pan before continuing by either removing it from the burner for 3 to 5 minutes or wiping it with a clean paper towel or dishcloth soaked in cold water.

Serve these crepes as is, with Thénga Chutney (page 226), or with Vendakkai Pachadi (page 214).

MASAALA DOSAI
Rice-Lentil Crepes with Spiced Potato Filling

- If the pan gets too hot between crepes, the batter will clump up as soon as it's poured, preventing an even spread. Lower the heat or wipe the skillet with a clean paper towel moistened with cold water before continuing.

- Dosais are traditionally served with Sambhar (page 110) and Thénga Chutney (page 226). I have also eaten them unaccompanied on many a harried occasion.

- Leftover batter can be refrigerated for a week, and if when frozen, it can bring you joy even two months later!

The journey was already excruciatingly long and it had just begun. This was the next morning of our overnight train trip to Madras to commence our month-long journey of the south as tribute to Akka and Appa who had recently passed away. True, our grandmother and father could not be physically present, but we all felt their spiritual presence providing extra warmth to the compartment's air. Lunch hour was fast approaching, the rumblings in my stomach providing a reminder every five minutes. I looked out the barred window as the boxcar rocked in a cradle-like motion while the train's wheels rattled on tracks over a bridge. The muddy water below shimmered under the sun's rays as three water buffaloes wallowed in siesta-like laziness. Fields of sunflowers appeared magically, close to the town of Guntakal, standing in erect subservience to Surya, the sun god, on bridal-red southern soil. "They are being harvested for their seeds, which will be turned into cooking oil," Lali remarked. A pang of hunger washed over me like yet another weather-beaten wave against calloused rocks along the banks of the Indian Ocean.

As the electric engine chugged onto the platform of Renigunta Junction, I saw throngs of people waiting to greet loved ones at the station. A little boy with tattered clothes held a baby monkey in his arms as he glided under the windows, one hand outstretched for money, while a taxidermist with coarse hair carried a sleeping baby on her back as she hawked stuffed squirrels. A vendor with his dhoti folded in half along his charcoal-black muscular thighs pushed a wooden cart filled with eggs and onions surrounding a gas-lit portable stove. A flat, round griddle rested atop the stove, with beaten eggs sizzling in oil. He served the prepared omelets folded with cilantro-flavored onions accompanied by slices of white bread and long, curvaceous green cayenne chilies. Another vendor dunked thick slices of plantains in garbanzo bean flour batter and fried them golden brown, offering them for sale on rectangular pieces of grease-stained newspaper. My eyes were drawn to a woman playing gofer to her husband who prepared, with the grace of a bharatanatyam dancer, lacy-thin, golden-crisp crepes stuffed with lime-kissed, chili-smothered potatoes. I knew this was what I needed to appease the cavernous hole in my belly—and seconds later his nose-ringed wife with her creased face handed me a masaala dosai rolled in a large square of banana leaf as she grabbed the two rupees from my right hand and scurried back to her husband.

I was amazed at the briskness of transactions that occurred on that platform within all of fifteen minutes while we waited for the train to switch to diesel. Shortly after we pulled away, another train pulled in, and its passengers took in the same, ongoing performance.

BATTER

1 cup uncooked long-grain rice
1 cup uncooked parboiled
  (converted) rice
1 teaspoon fenugreek seed
½ cup urad dal (split and hulled
  black lentils), sorted
About 2½ cups warm water for
  grinding
1 tablespoon salt

FILLING

4 medium potatoes, peeled, boiled,
  and coarsely mashed
2 tablespoons finely chopped fresh
  cilantro
1 teaspoon salt
¼ teaspoon ground turmeric
12 to 15 fresh karhi leaves
3 to 5 fresh Thai, cayenne, or
  serrano chilies, coarsely chopped
Juice of 1 medium lime
2 tablespoons vegetable oil
1 teaspoon black mustard seed
1 tablespoon urad dal (split and
  hulled black lentils), sorted

Additional vegetable oil for
  brushing

TO MAKE BATTER

1. In a medium bowl, cover both rices with water. With your fingers, gently wash the grains for 30 seconds until the water becomes cloudy; drain. Repeat 5 or 6 times until the water is clear. Add the fenugreek seed and cover the rice with warm water. Soak at room temperature for at least 4 to 5 hours, or overnight; drain.

2. In a separate medium bowl, use the same procedure to rinse and soak the urad dal.

3. In a blender puree ½ cup warm water and half the rice mixture, scraping the sides of the container, until smooth. Transfer to a large bowl; repeat with the remaining rice.

4. Grind the dal with ¼ cup water until smooth; add to rice batter. Fold in the salt and 1¼ cups water, or more as needed, to make slightly thin pancake-consistency batter.

5. In a gas oven with a lit pilot light, slightly warm electric oven, or proofing unit, keep the bowl tightly covered with plastic wrap for 24 hours, or until the batter ferments and acquires a sourdough-like smell.

TO MAKE FILLING

1. In a medium bowl, thoroughly mix the potatoes, cilantro, salt, turmeric, karhi leaves, chilies, and lime juice.
2. In a small skillet, heat 2 tablespoons oil over medium-high heat; add the mustard seed. When it begins to pop, cover the skillet. As soon as the seed finishes popping, add the urad dal. Stir-fry for 30 seconds, or until the dal is golden brown. Add the mixture to the potatoes and stir well. Divide into 10 equal portions.

TO MAKE CREPES

1. Coat and heat a 12-inch nonstick skillet with 1 teaspoon vegetable oil over medium heat. Ladle ½ cup batter and, with the bottom of the ladle, quickly and evenly spread the batter to form a paper-thin, unbroken circle roughly 8 inches in diameter. Cook for 2 to 3 minutes or until the top of the crepe is opaque and the bottom is golden brown and starts to curl up around the edges. Flip the crepe and brown for about 1 minute.
2. Transfer the crepe to a serving platter. Place one portion of filling in the center and fold the crepe in half to cover the filling. Serve immediately.
3. Repeat with the remaining batter and filling.

Makes 10 dosais

Rava Molagha Dosai
Cream of Wheat Crepes with Chilies

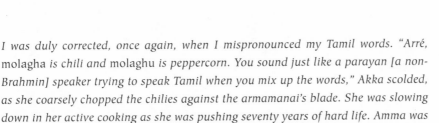

I was duly corrected, once again, when I mispronounced my Tamil words. "Arré, molagha is chili and molaghu is peppercorn. You sound just like a parayan [a non-Brahmin] speaker trying to speak Tamil when you mix up the words," Akka scolded, as she coarsely chopped the chilies against the armamanai's blade. She was slowing down in her active cooking as she was pushing seventy years of hard life. Amma was incapacitated with a short-term water-borne illness and Akka helped as much as she could in preparing the family's meals.

Her fingers, hampered by arthritis, took on the task of a wire whisk as they mixed the two flours into a batter that was lump-free, the consistency of slightly watered-down paint. She folded the chilies and coarsely pounded sea salt into the liquid. She placed her left hand on the floor as she raised her frail body off the ground from her lotuslike seated position. She groaned and invoked Rama three times as if Vishnu's well-known reincarnation would provide her fortitude and guidance in her tasks. She hobbled out of the kitchen as Lali took over and commenced her crepe-making chores.

I particularly enjoyed the dosais that night, as Akka's chilies sweetened my tongue with her unconditional love. The image of her gargantuan presence in that tiny boxcar of a kitchen was seared in my memory for life.

2 cups uncooked cream of wheat
¼ cup rice flour
2 teaspoons salt
1 teaspoon cumin seed
½ teaspoon baking powder
1 cup plain yogurt, whisked
2 cups water
½ cup finely chopped red onion
3 tablespoons finely chopped fresh
  cilantro

1 tablespoon finely chopped
  gingerroot
12 to 15 fresh karhi leaves, coarsely
  chopped
4 to 6 fresh Thai, cayenne, or
  serrano chilies, cut crosswise into
  thin slices
Vegetable oil for frying

> ❧ The batter will continue to thicken as it rests. Thin the batter with water to return it to the desired crepe batter–like consistency. The batter can be refrigerated for 4 days. Cooked crepes can be reheated in a microwave. I of course love the texture and flavor when "cooked to order."

> ❧ The pan will get hot between crepes. Batter poured in a hot pan will immediately clump up, making it difficult to spread. Cool the pan before continuing either by removing it from the burner for 3 to 5 minutes or wiping it with a clean paper towel or dishcloth soaked in cold water.

1. In a medium bowl, combine the cream of wheat, rice flour, salt, cumin, and baking powder. Whisk in the yogurt and 1 cup water, a few tablespoons at a time, until the batter is smooth but still fairly thick. Let the

batter rest at room temperature for about 30 minutes. Whisk in the remaining water, a few tablespoons at a time, until the batter is smooth and the consistency of thin crepe batter.

2. Fold in the remaining ingredients except the oil.

3. In a 10-inch non-stick skillet, heat 1 teaspoon oil over low to medium heat. Pour in ⅓ cup batter and with the bottom of the ladle, swirl the batter in a smooth circular motion to form a crepe roughly 6 to 7 inches in diameter. Cook for 1 to 2 minutes until the bottom is golden brown and the top looks opaque. Flip the crepe and cook for 1 minute. Transfer to a plate or aluminum foil. Repeat with the remaining batter.

Makes about 12 dosais

Subzi Uttapam
Vegetable-Studded Rice-Lentil Pancakes

I often find myself resorting to a stack of these uttapams on lazy Sunday mornings, along with a bowl of Sambhar (page 110). Leftover batter and filling will keep for 3 days in the refrigerator. The batter can be frozen for a month.

Batter

1 cup uncooked long-grain rice

1 cup uncooked parboiled (converted) rice

1 teaspoon fenugreek seed

½ cup urad dal (split and hulled black lentils), sorted

About 2 cups warm water for grinding

1 tablespoon salt

½ cup frozen green peas

2 tablespoons finely chopped fresh cilantro

2 tablespoons coarsely chopped fresh karhi leaves

½ teaspoon salt

3 to 5 fresh Thai, cayenne, or serrano chilies, finely chopped

Vegetable oil for brushing

Filling

1 cup finely chopped red onion

½ cup finely chopped carrot

If the pan gets too hot between uttapams, the batter will clump up as soon as it's poured, preventing an even spread. Lower the heat or wipe the skillet with a clean paper towel moistened with cold water before continuing.

TO MAKE BATTER

1. In a medium bowl, cover both varieties of rice with water. With your fingers, gently wash the grains for 30 seconds until the water becomes cloudy; drain. Repeat 5 or 6 times until the water is clear. Add the fenugreek seed and cover the rice with warm water. Soak at room temperature for at least 4 to 5 hours, or overnight; drain.

2. In a separate medium bowl, use the same procedure to rinse and soak the urad dal.

3. In a blender, puree ½ cup warm water and half the rice mixture, scraping the sides of the container, until smooth. Transfer to a large bowl; repeat with the remaining rice.

4. Grind the dal with ¼ cup water until smooth; add to the rice batter. Fold in the salt and ¾ cup water, or more as needed, to make slightly thick pancake-consistency batter.

5. In a gas oven with a lit pilot light, slightly warm electric oven, or proofing unit, keep the bowl tightly covered with plastic wrap for 24 hours or until the batter ferments and acquires sourdough-like smell.

TO MAKE FILLING

In medium bowl combine all ingredients except oil. Mix well.

TO MAKE UTTAPAMS

1. Coat and heat a 10-inch nonstick skillet with 1 teaspoon vegetable oil over medium heat. Ladle ½ cup batter and with the bottom of the ladle evenly spread the batter to form circle roughly 6 inches in diameter. Spread about 2 tablespoons filling on the pancake. Lower the heat and cook for 2 to 3 minutes or until the top is opaque, little holes appear on the surface, and the bottom is brown. Flip the pancake and brown for 2 to 3 minutes. Remove from the pan and keep warm wrapped in aluminum foil.

2. Repeat with the remaining batter and filling.

Makes 10 uttapams

Chutneys, Achars, Aur Masaalas
Relishes, Pickles, and Spice Blends

Ghee
Clarified Butter

Garam Masaala
"Warm" Spice Blend

Sambhar Masaala
Roasted Spice and Lentil Blend

Paneer
Whole Milk Cheese

Boondi Raita
Garbanzo Bean Flour Pearls Drenched with
Yogurt and Chilies

Molagha Podi
Red Pepper Powder

Vendakkai Pachadi
Yogurt with Okra

Kakadi Kosumalli
Cucumber-Lentil Salad

Kacchu Papaya Nu Salade
Unripe Papaya Salad with Chilies

Limboo Urughai
Lemon Pickle

Karuvapillai Thuviyal
Fresh Karhi Leaves Chutney

Maangai Urughai
Spicy Mango Pickle

Vengayam Thuviyal
Caramelized Onion Chutney

Katarikai Thuviyal
Roasted Eggplant Chutney

Mirchi Chutney
Roasted Chilies Condiment

Kishmish Chutney
Golden Raisin Relish

Tamatar Chutney
Tomato Relish with Coconut

Thénga Chutney
Coconut Chutney with Garlic

GHEE
Clarified Butter

❧ As I always warn my students, you cannot hurry perfection. You might be tempted to turn up the heat to expedite the process of melting butter and skimming milk solids. Fall into that trap and watch your butter burn. The milk solids lower the smoke point, the temperature at which fat starts to smoke. Higher heat will burn the solids before they can be eliminated from the butter. Once eliminated, the clarified butter (ghee) makes it possible to stir-fry ingredients at a higher smoke point.

❧ This is also India's way of extending the shelf life of butter by eliminating the milk solids that promote rancidity, and therefore removing the need to refrigerate. Refrigeration will further its life, while frozen ghee may outlive you.

Gopala, Shyam, Mohan, Govinda . . . A charmer with several names, he is best known as Krishna, the blue-blooded reincarnation of Vishnu, the preserver. He was born into royalty to parents who were imprisoned by the evil Kamsa, a demon who had usurped the throne in Mathura along the banks of the river Yamuna. Kamsa was warned that the imperial Devakai and her husband Vasudeva's eighth son would be the cause of his demise. So Kamsa made a visit each of the first six times Devakai delivered a child and quickly destroyed it. The seventh miraculously transferred to Vasudeva's other wife (men during those times had multiple wives), who bore the son to full term.

The eighth son was born in the still of the night under the shimmering light of a full moon that filtered through the bars of the humble prison. Vasudeva carried his son, destined to bring back order in the town of Mathura, in a wicker basket perched on his head through the suddenly unlocked door past the mysteriously drugged guards. When he reached the banks of the Yamuna, his qualms of crossing it quickly dissipated upon its parting, making his task of delivering the boy to safety an easy one. A cowherd in the town of Gokhul found the beautiful baby, and he and his wife raised the baby as their own, naming him Krishna amid great fanfare.

Stories of Krishna's antics spread quickly through the tight-knit community. Every inhabitant in town knew of his pre-destined celestial purpose: to kill Kamsa and bring back happiness, beauty, and order to life, things that were non-existent under the demon's regime. Krishna's beauty, lightheartedness, and mischievous demeanor gave every mother in town a joyous heartbreak. His penchant for milk, cream, and butter became well known. No dairy products could be left within reach for fear of being devoured within seconds. Whenever cream had to be collected to make butter, it was amassed in clay pots and strung up high between the loftiest treetops. Krishna coaxed his fellow cowherds to form a human pyramid, and he was found at its apex, gulping his dairy prize with great satisfaction.

In his adult life Krishna fulfilled his purpose and defeated Kamsa in a wrestling match, restoring all that was just and human to Mathura, his native land.

The process of churning fresh cream into butter is still widely practiced in homes all across India. Each morning, Amma skimmed cream from her saucepan filled with hot milk. She squatted on the floor with her deep pot and long-handled wooden beater. Within minutes white, silky-smooth butter separated and floated to the top, separating itself from the whey. Amma scooped handfuls of butter and placed them in a heavy-bottomed saucepan. I always happened to be there just in the nick of time to steal a few scoops, Krishna-style, its sweetness coating my tongue, the name "maakhan chor" (butter thief) ringing in my ears. Stainless steel tumblers collected buttermilk ready to be drunk in thirst-quenching gulps while the freshly churned butter melted on low heat and milk solids were skimmed and discarded. The clear fat, now turned into ghee, rested in a chipped orange porcelain jar, nutty and pure, waiting to bless every dish it would touch with its heavenly aroma and flavor.

❧ Ghee is available in ethnic grocery stores and supermarkets. Be ready to plunk down premium cash for this convenience if you do not have 15 to 20 minutes to spare to make your own.

1 pound unsalted butter

1. In a small saucepan, heat the butter over low heat until it is completely melted. Continue simmering on low heat, skimming off any milk solids that rise to the top, for 15 to 20 minutes until the remaining liquid is clear and light yellow.
2. Strain the liquid into a clean jar, leaving behind any dark brown residual solids that coat the bottom of pan. Store at room temperature for a few weeks or in the refrigerator for up to 6 months. The ghee will solidify.

Makes about ¾ cup

Garam Masaala
"Warm" Spice Blend

Garam masaala has many incarnations that feature prominently in every northern Indian home and restaurant. The blend can be a loose collection of whole spices like bay leaves, peppercorns, cinnamon sticks, and cumin; it can be ground; or it can be roasted for 2 to 3 minutes, cooled, and then ground. The contents of the blend vary among households, each cook creating his or her own aromatic signature.

If the cinnamon sticks are too thick, break them up into smaller pieces before using them. They will grind better and faster, without getting lodged in the blades of the blender.

"Do I have to eat this?" I asked, holding my pug-shaped nose with my thin, eight-year-old fingers. Lali's brow tightened and her eyes glazed over like fresh rain on an oil-slick road. She threatened me with the promise of a tight slap in front of Savitri Aunty, her colleague at work. I loved Savitri Aunty, whose small face was nearly covered by her soda-bottle-thick lenses held in square gray spectacle frames. She had a crackling voice that always sounded gargled and apologetic, not quite what I expected from a doctor. She smiled shyly and clucked, "Don't eat it if you don't like it. I won't mind."

Lali's smoldering look was more powerful than Savitri Aunty's permission to forgo the tasting, so I obliged Lali and grabbed a small piece of roti, gingerly dipping it in the brown, murky dal that was the object of my disdain. As if she could read my mind, Savitri Aunty explained that the color was from garam masaala, a blend of spices common to every north Indian kitchen. "Garam means warm—it will make you hot from the inside and protect you from this horrible rain," she stuttered, her eyes searching mine to gauge my reaction. The masaala offered a curious spicy sweetness to the dal as it coated my tongue. The more I chewed, the more I liked it, and my reluctant smile deepened my dimpled cheeks, which brought a squeal of delight to Savitri Aunty's shaky voice. Lali was at peace, once again proving that sister knows best.

1 teaspoon cumin seed

1 teaspoon coriander seed

1 teaspoon black peppercorns

1 teaspoon cardamom seed (removed from pods)

½ teaspoon fennel seed

15 whole cloves

3 three-inch cinnamon sticks, broken into pieces

1. In a small, heavy skillet, roast all the spices over medium-high heat for 2 to 3 minutes, stirring constantly, until the spices turn one shade darker, start to crackle, and become fragrant.
2. Transfer the roasted spices to a plate to cool for 3 to 5 minutes. Grind in a spice grinder until the mixture has the texture of finely ground black pepper.
3. Store in an airtight jar in a cool, dark place for up to a month.

Makes about ¼ cup

Spices on display at market in Mumbai

Sambhar Masaala
Roasted Spice and Lentil Blend

Each type of lentil imparts its own flavor to any dish and hence plays an important role. These three dals—chana, toovar, and urad—form the backbone of south Indian cooking and are widely available in ethnic stores that sell Indian groceries. You can always add more or less of a dal (or even leave one out) to tweak different flavors each time you make a batch of sambhar masaala.

Use adequate ventilation whenever you roast chilies, or the throat-burning aromas will to drive you away from the kitchen for a few minutes.

Oftentimes, when I hanker for flavors from my Amma's kitchen, I add a teaspoon of this aromatic blend to American dishes. It never fails to bring a satisfied smile to my face when I take that first bite of otherwise ho-hum macaroni and cheese. See how easy it is to bring worlds together in the kitchen?

The little sparrow mother, Rukmani, was beside herself. Her hungry offspring desperately needed some sambhar (sweet pigeon pea stew) to wet their whistles. She had no masaala (spice blend) left with which to flavor the earthy stew, a staple in her nest for nourishing her babies' tiny little bellies. Their incessant shrieking forced her to resort to the unthinkable—steal from Gopal, the stingy storekeeper squirrel who had shown no mercy when she had gone begging for some grains. "What's a poor mother to do?" she lamented.

She decided to seek out the services of Raja, the crafty crow who knew all the ins and outs of pilfering. She fluttered over to the tall banyan tree and knocked on his door. Raja opened it a crack and peered at her through his horn-rimmed glasses. "What do you want, you pesky little fool?" he cawed. She summoned up all her courage and chattered in an uneven voice, "Oh, kind soul, please help me. Show me how I can gather some chilies, coriander, and dals from Gopal to make sambhar masaala so that I can finish flavoring the sambhar and feed my starving babies." Raja could not care less about any little ones, especially those of Rukmani, a lowly sparrow. But he had always pined for her well-known sambhar, its aromas driving him wild with hunger each time he flew by her nest. She never gave him any to sample, and he yearned for its tart, hot, nutty flavors. The wheels in his pointed head spun with conniving speed, plotting to take advantage of her current predicament. "All right, then, I will show you what to do on the condition that you share with me half your sambhar. I am truly concerned for your useless—I mean, helpless—newborns and I will see what I can do, out of the goodness of my heart, of course."

He grabbed Rukmani by her wing and dragged her to a big black vat filled to the brim with light yellow vegetable oil. He ordered her to perch herself on the barrel's edge and dip her feathery behind in it. She was hesitant but frantic. She did just that and followed Raja to Gopal's store, which was surrounded by large gunnysacks filled with red hot chilies, light brown coriander seed, and all those beautifully colored lentils, beans, and peas. While storekeeper Gopal was busy haggling with Shakuni, the nosy owl, Raja the crow signaled Rukmani to go squat on the chilies. She was perplexed but obliged, and upon command, she lifted her body and flew off to her nest, a red chili trailing from her oiled rump.

She made numerous trips from the oil vat to the gunnysacks and eventually gathered enough to make her masaala. The stew that night was exceptionally good and the trickster Raja beamed with each beakful, admiring his own sharp and crafty *mind. The little sparrow darlings drifted into a peaceful slumber, their tummies full of nutritious sambhar, and their bodies warm under their Amma Rukmani's feathers, fortified by her maternal love.*

No matter how often Lali retold this fable, I never tired of it, loving every delicious detail from beginning to end. Lali always obliged my request to hear it again, her voice offering lulling comfort to my six-year-old ears.

½ cup dried red Thai, cayenne, or serrano chilies

1 tablespoon chana dal (yellow split peas), sorted

1 tablespoon toovar dal (split and hulled pigeon peas), sorted

1 tablespoon urad dal (split and hulled black lentils), sorted

1 teaspoon coriander seed

1 teaspoon fenugreek seed

1 teaspoon black peppercorns

1 teaspoon vegetable oil

½ teaspoon cumin seed

20 fresh karhi leaves

½ teaspoon ground turmeric

1. In a small bowl, combine all ingredients except turmeric to coat well with oil.
2. Preheat a small skillet over medium-high heat. Add the spice blend and roast, shaking pan occasionally or stirring, for 3 to 4 minutes, or until the chilies slightly blacken and the lentils turn golden brown. Transfer to a bowl or plate and cool for 5 to 7 minutes.
3. In a spice grinder or blender, grind the cooled spice blend until the mixture has the texture of finely ground black pepper. Stir in the turmeric. The mixture will keep in an airtight jar at room temperature in a cool, dark spot for 2 months.

Makes about ¾ cup

PANEER
Whole Milk Cheese

Paneer is quintessentially north Indian and makes its way into classic restaurant favorites like Palak Paneer (page 86) and mutter paneer (homemade cheese with peas). This cheese is similar in texture to farmer's cheese and is quite easy to make. When time is of the essence, I often substitute extra-firm tofu for similar results.

1 gallon whole milk   ⅓ cup white vinegar

1. In a large stockpot, bring the milk to a boil over medium-high heat, stirring occasionally to prevent scorching.
2. Stir in the vinegar and remove from heat. The milk will separate into clumps of soft white cheese and whey the color of diluted skim milk.
3. Line a colander with cheesecloth or a clean dishtowel (the flour sack variety). With a tea strainer, skim off the cheese from the whey and collect it in the cloth. Discard the whey. Fold the edges of cloth over the cheese to completely cover it. Flatten the wrapped cheese into a disk.
4. Place the cloth-wrapped cheese on an inverted high-sided round cake pan resting in the same colander. Place the colander in the sink. Fill a stockpot (or a similar heavy contraption) with water and place it directly on the cheese to weigh it down. The cheese will harden under the weight of the stockpot after about 2 to 3 hours.
5. Remove the hardened cheese disk from cloth and wrap it in plastic wrap or foil. It will keep in the refrigerator for 3 days.

Makes about 4 cups of ½-inch cubes

To fry paneer, cut the cheese carefully into ½-inch-thick slices, then cut each slice into ½-inch cubes. In a wok or 3-quart saucepan, heat vegetable oil about 2 to 3 inches deep over medium heat until a thermometer registers 350°. Gently add the paneer cubes and fry, turning occasionally, for 2 to 4 minutes or until golden brown. Drain on paper towels. You can freeze fried paneer as is in a freezer bag for a month, or store cubed paneer in the refrigerator in a bowl covered with water, changing the water daily, for a week.

Boondi Raita

Garbanzo Bean Flour Pearls Drenched with Yogurt and Chilies

Raitas are yogurt-based accompaniments often served to provide cool comfort to your palate from robust-flavored dishes. The yogurt also aids in digestion. Yogurt is always the key ingredient in a raita; what else you put in is entirely your choice. Fresh vegetables, fruits, herbs, and spices are among the wide range of alternatives.

2 cups plain yogurt, whisked
2 tablespoons finely chopped fresh cilantro
½ teaspoon salt
2 to 4 fresh Thai, cayenne, or serrano chilies, cut crosswise into ¼-inch thick slices

2 cups boondi (garbanzo bean flour pearls) (see note)
2 cups hot water

1. In a medium bowl, combine the yogurt, cilantro, salt, and chilies.
2. In a separate bowl, soak the boondi in hot water for about 5 minutes. Pick up handfuls of boondi, squeeze out all the water, and add to the yogurt.
3. Chill in the refrigerator at least 1 hour before serving. Can be made up to 4 days ahead.

Serves 8

⁂ Boondi is widely available either salted or spiced with red chilies in Indian grocery stores in the snack foods section. In India it is often eaten as a treat with a cup of hot tea, a glass of beer, or a shot of scotch (straight up). The savory pearls are made with garbanzo bean flour batter that is poured through a wide-holed sieve into hot oil and fried golden brown. If unavailable, you can make your own (page 232, steps 2 through 5).

⁂ For a similar textural experience, use a can of fried shoestring potatoes instead, available in the snack foods section of supermarkets next to the potato chips. Since these are quite salty, eliminate the salt from the recipe if you use them.

MOLAGHA PODI
Red Pepper Powder

Twice a week, Vishu tumbled out of bed, and, with eyes barely open, picked up the metal crate of empty milk bottles, walked down to the government-run milk booth and exchanged them for filled ones. Within minutes Lali woke up along with Amma, and the milk was soon boiling in tall saucepans on the propane stoves. Amma grabbed the stainless steel bowl of fermented idli batter from the refrigerator and sat on the floor with the idli stand in front of her. She coated the molds with oil and filled them with batter. She lowered the stand into a pressure cooker and placed the contraption on the free burner.

The cooker's whistle pierced my sleep, and I awoke as the sourdough-like smell of steaming idlis merged with sweet-perfumed milk and wafted through my open bedroom door. Amma slid the fluffy soft idlis onto a thali and reached for the orange-red porcelain jar filled with the fiery-tart molagha podi, which in my book made the idlis celestial: Sure, food should sing in your mouth, but this combination did the Shiva Tandam, a dance that was sensuous, robust, and truly melodious. Amma drizzled unrefined sesame oil in a bowl and mixed in some of the powder to form a wet chutney. Soon the idlis were enclosed in this red spicy blanket and packed away in a light pink tin lunchbox that was wrapped in a Bata Shoes plastic shopping bag.

At 10:15 A.M. twice a week, I opened my lunchbox to devour the savory idlis while I leaned against St. Francis Xavier's cold marble statue, but I also used the molagha podi–spiked idlis as barter tools in trading my friend's lunch whenever I desired something different.

2 tablespoons coarsely chopped dried tamarind (see note with Puli Sevai, page 120)

½ cup dried red Thai, cayenne, or serrano chilies

2 tablespoons sesame seed

1 tablespoon chana dal (yellow split peas), sorted

1 tablespoon urad dal (split and hulled black lentils), sorted

1 teaspoon vegetable oil

1 teaspoon salt

1. Heat a 10-inch skillet over medium-high heat. Toast the tamarind for 3 to 4 minutes, stirring constantly, until dry and blackish-brown in color. Let cool in a small bowl (it will turn brittle).

2. In a separate bowl, combine the remaining ingredients except salt. Toss well to coat with oil.
3. In the same skillet, roast the chili blend over medium-high heat, shaking the pan occasionally or stirring, for 3 to 4 minutes, or until the chilies slightly blacken and the lentils turn golden brown. Add to the toasted tamarind and let cool for 5 to 7 minutes.
4. In a spice grinder or blender, grind the cooled spice blend until the mixture has the texture of finely ground black pepper. Stir in the salt. The mixture will keep in an airtight jar at room temperature in a cool, dark spot for 2 months.

Makes about ¾ cup

VENDAKKAI PACHADI
Yogurt with Okra

I first sampled this unusual salad when it was plopped on my banana leaf's top right corner during my brother Shankar's wedding. Like many people, I thought okra was always slimy, so I gently prodded the slices bathed in the spiced yogurt to confirm my fears—and I was pleasantly surprised. I was blessed in having stumbled upon the most perfect marriage between ordinarily slick okra and soothing yogurt.

½ pound fresh okra
2 tablespoons Ghee (page 204) or
  vegetable oil
1 teaspoon black mustard seed
1 tablespoon urad dal (split and
  hulled black lentils), sorted
½ teaspoon hing (asafetida)
½ teaspoon ground turmeric

2 tablespoons finely chopped fresh
  cilantro
1 teaspoon salt
6 to 8 fresh Thai, cayenne, or
  serrano chilies, finely chopped
15 to 20 fresh karhi leaves
2 cups plain yogurt, whisked

1. Wash and dry the okra. Trim off the stem end (see note with Vendakkai Bhaaji, page 68). Slice the okra crosswise in ¼-inch-thick slices.
2. In a 10-inch skillet, heat the ghee over medium-high heat; add the mustard seed. When it begins to pop, cover the skillet. As soon as the seed finishes popping, add the urad dal and stir-fry for 30 seconds, or until the dal is golden brown.
3. Stir in the okra, hing, and turmeric. Lower the heat and cook, covered, stirring occasionally, for 8 to 10 minutes until the okra is fork-tender.
4. Add the remaining ingredients except yogurt. Remove from heat and let cool to room temperature. Fold the skillet's contents into the yogurt. Serve chilled or at room temperature. Will keep in the refrigerator for 3 days.

Serves 8

KAKADI KOSUMALLI
Cucumber-Lentil Salad

This dish is often served at south Indian weddings. I especially love the combination of cool, crunchy cucumbers and barely cooked lentils. Often the split and hulled lentils are soaked for 6 to 8 hours and added uncooked to the mix. I prefer partially cooking them for a nuttier, smoother flavor.

¼ cup mung dal (split and hulled green lentils), sorted and rinsed

1 cup water

2 medium cucumbers, peeled, cut lengthwise in half and seeded, and thinly sliced

½ cup freshly shredded coconut (page 6)

2 tablespoons finely chopped fresh cilantro

1 teaspoon salt

1 to 2 fresh Thai, cayenne, or serrano chilies, finely chopped

1 tablespoon vegetable oil

1 teaspoon black mustard seed

¼ teaspoon hing (asafetida)

15 to 20 fresh karhi leaves

❧ Take extra care not to overcook the lentils, since they turn mushy, a texture not suitable for this composed salad. Use yellow split peas for a firmer-textured grain.

❧ Skip the karhi leaves if they are unavailable.

1. In a 1-quart saucepan, bring the mung dal and water to a boil over medium-high heat. Lower the heat to medium and cook, uncovered, stirring occasionally and skimming off any foam that forms on top, for 8 to 10 minutes until the dal is barely cooked and still firm; drain.

2. In a medium bowl, combine the cucumbers, coconut, cilantro, salt, chilies, and dal.

3. In a small skillet, heat the oil over medium-high heat; add the mustard seed. When it begins to pop, cover the skillet. As soon as the seed finishes popping, remove the skillet from the heat. Add the hing and karhi leaves to the hot oil and splutter for 2 to 5 seconds. Pour the oil mixture into the cucumber; stir well. Serve chilled or at room temperature.

Serves 4

Kacchu Papaya Nu Salade
Unripe Papaya Salad with Chilies

Choose a papaya that is green, firm, and unripe. Peel it with a potato peeler or a paring knife. The flesh will be light green in color (unlike the orange red color when ripe). Slice the papaya lengthwise, and with a spoon scoop out and discard the pearl-like white seeds (which will turn a beautiful black color when ripe). Use the slicer blade attachment of a food processor to slice the papaya thin; a box grater's slicer surface will also suffice.

This is a specialty from Surat in northwestern India. I am always drawn to the scent of a green papaya enhanced by nutty mustard seed popped in hot oil. I often make a point of strolling through certain suburban districts in Mumbai on Sunday mornings when the allure of freshly fried papdis (wide strips of hand-pushed garbanzo bean flour dough) draws me to the line of customers who patiently await their turn to buy grease-stained, newspaper-wrapped packets of papdi and plastic bags filled with this mouth-watering salad accompaniment.

Back at home, I serve this as an appetizer with baskets of flame-roasted or fried papads (lentil wafers). Enjoy them on hot buttered toast for a quick lunch.

1 medium green (unripe) papaya, peeled, seeded, and thinly sliced (see note)
Juice of 1 large lime
2 tablespoons finely chopped fresh cilantro
1 teaspoon salt

1 teaspoon sugar
¼ teaspoon ground turmeric
3 to 4 fresh Thai, cayenne, or serrano chilies, slit open lengthwise
1 tablespoon vegetable oil
1 teaspoon black mustard seed
¼ teaspoon hing (asafetida)

1. In a medium bowl, combine the papaya, lime juice, cilantro, salt, sugar, turmeric, and chilies. Mix well.
2. In a small skillet, heat the oil over medium-high heat; add the mustard seed. When it begins to pop, cover the skillet. As soon as the seed finishes popping, add the hing and sizzle for 2 to 5 seconds. Pour the seed-oil mixture over the papaya and toss well to coat. Serve chilled or at room temperature.

Serves 4

LIMBOO URUGHAI
Lemon Pickle

This potent pickle packs a strong oomph in each bite. Use it sparingly with steamed rice or Rotlis (page 182), or as an accompaniment to any Indian meal. I especially enjoy it with Tayyar Shaadum (page 171), the culmination to many a Tamilian meal.

4 medium lemons, cut into 8 wedges each

2 tablespoons salt

2 tablespoons ground red pepper (cayenne)

1 teaspoon ground turmeric

2 tablespoons vegetable oil

1 teaspoon black mustard seed

½ teaspoon hing (asafetida)

1. Combine the lemons and salt in a glass jar with a lid. Refrigerate, shaking the jar occasionally, for about 2 to 3 weeks, or until the lemons are fork-tender.
2. Stir in the red pepper and turmeric.
3. In a small skillet, heat the oil over medium-high heat; add the mustard seed. When it starts to pop, cover until all the seed has popped. Remove from heat and add the hing. Pour the oil-seed mixture over the lemons. Stir well. Lemon pickle will keep refrigerated for 2 months.

Makes about 2 cups

Street vendor in Mumbai making Papdi (Fried Strips of Garbanzo Flour Dough) to be served with Unripe Papaya Salad (opposite)

Karuvapillai Thuviyal
Fresh Karhi Leaves Chutney

* Toast sesame seed in a small skillet over medium-high heat, shaking the pan occasionally, for 1 to 2 minutes, or until golden brown and fragrant.

* I love this chutney's underlying sweetness and often serve it with the spicy flavors of Pesarat (page 195).

When I was seventeen years old, Appa, my father, lost his battle with cancer. My grandmother had nursed him with all her love and care, and my sister Lali had assisted in the surgery that removed a tumor eight years earlier. But now, on a crisp Sunday in October, his frail body had finally succumbed to Yaman, the god of death.

The thirteen-day mourning process had begun. Akka, eighty-two and frail herself, sat on the terrazzo floor near Appa's body, mourning her son by the light of the oil lamp we now kept lit at all hours.

The vadiyaars (Brahamin priests) came daily, their rituals and Sanskrit verses giving meaning to our grief. The kitchen fires were lit after two days, and the women busied themselves by roasting and grinding spice blends for this solemn occasion. Yellow split peas and split and hulled black lentils were put away, and split and hulled green lentils took their place. Soon the air was filled with the sweetness of white sesame seeds toasted golden brown, pungent peppercorns, nutty roasted uncooked rice, and fresh karhi leaves. Turmeric, an everyday presence in our Tamilian kitchen and a symbol of Amma's marriage, was markedly absent. The dried root was used extensively in the ceremonies along with arid rice husks, sweet-smelling, sun-dried dung cakes, ghee, and sprigs of tulsi—aromatic sharp-edged leaves of holy basil.

On the twelfth day, Amma, my mother, was brought into the ceremonial circle. She sobbed in grief as my aunt wiped Amma's sun-like bindi, her deep red third eye, from her forehead. Her mangalsutra, a 24-karat-gold amulet that hung around her neck by a turmeric-stained thread that her husband had tied during their wedding, was taken off and handed over to the priest. Her bangles were removed, one at a time. She stood simply dressed in a plain-colored saree, alone and stripped of all wifely attire.

On the thirteenth day, Appa reached his destination, a soul completely free from earthly desires. We shared with family and friends a feast usually served at weddings and joyous occasions. After all, we were celebrating Appa's new beginning.

2 cups tightly packed fresh karhi
   leaves
½ cup water
2 tablespoons coarsely chopped
   gingerroot
1 tablespoon coarsely chopped gur
   (jaggery) or tightly packed dark
   brown sugar

1 tablespoon toasted sesame seed
   (see note)
1 teaspoon salt
½ teaspoon tamarind concentrate

In a blender puree all ingredients until smooth. Serve chilled or at room temperature as a condiment. It will keep in the refrigerator, covered, for 4 days and in the freezer for a month.

Makes about 1½ cups

Maangai Urughai
Spicy Mango Pickle

A sensuously tart seductress, she made my lips pucker in anticipation each time she came to the table, speckled with black mustard seed, covered in bridal-like turmeric, and hot with green chilies. I salivated as my fingers picked her up with morsels of unleavened, handkerchief-like bread. She never failed to amaze me with her ability to orchestrate Shiva's Ananda Tandam, the sensually blissful dance, with flavor. She would always be my one and only, even though she had more than a hundred other cousins, equally delicious. The love of my life, my maangai urughai!

1 large unripe mango (about 1½ pounds), peeled, pitted, and cut into ½-inch cubes
2 teaspoons salt
¼ teaspoon ground turmeric
10 fresh Thai, cayenne, or serrano chilies, coarsely chopped
¼ cup vegetable oil

1 tablespoon urad dal (split and hulled black lentils), sorted
½ teaspoon fenugreek seed
10 dried red Thai, cayenne, or serrano chilies
1 teaspoon black mustard seed
½ teaspoon hing (asafetida)

1. In a medium bowl, combine the mango, salt, turmeric, and fresh chilies.
2. In a small skillet, heat 1 teaspoon oil over medium-high heat. Add the urad dal, fenugreek, and dried chilies. Stir-fry for 1 to 2 minutes, or until the dal turns golden brown and the chilies slightly blacken. Remove from the skillet and cool for 3 to 5 minutes. Grind the mixture in a spice grinder or with a mortar and pestle until its texture is like finely ground black pepper. Add to the mangoes.
3. In the same skillet, heat the remaining oil over medium-high heat; add the mustard seed. When it starts to pop, cover until all the seed has popped. Remove the skillet from heat and add the hing. Pour the oil-seed mixture over the mangoes. Stir well and store in the refrigerator for up to a week.

Makes 3 cups

VENGAYAM THUVIYAL
Caramelized Onion Chutney

This incredibly complex-tasting chutney derives an essential sweetness from caramelized red onion. Serve this condiment with any of the breads in this book—or if you're a wake-up-in-the-middle-of-the-night-and-munch-in-the-light-of-the-open-refrigerator type, spread it on crackers for a light snack, or mix it with leftover steamed rice drizzled with plain yogurt for guilt-free pleasure.

2 tablespoons vegetable oil
1 tablespoon urad dal (split and
  hulled black lentils), sorted
2 to 3 dried red Thai, cayenne, or
  serrano chilies

1 large red onion, halved lengthwise
  and thinly sliced
1 teaspoon salt
½ cup water
½ teaspoon tamarind concentrate

1. In a wok or 12-inch skillet, heat the vegetable oil over medium-high heat. Add the urad dal and chilies and stir-fry for about 1 minute, or until the lentils turn golden brown and the chilies slightly blacken.
2. Add the onion and stir-fry for 8 to 12 minutes, or until they are caramel brown.
3. In a blender, puree the onion mixture with the remaining ingredients until smooth.

Makes about 1 cup

KATARIKAI THUVIYAL
Roasted Eggplant Chutney

- Enjoy this chutney with steamed rice or Rava Pooris (page 194).

- For a more robust flavor, increase the number of chilies and experience that natural euphoria brought on by a surge of endorphins.

I love the flavor and texture of eggplant, especially the ones I grew up with in Mumbai—curvaceously long, sensuously smooth, with a light purple color. This variety is called Asian or Japanese eggplant in the United States and is widely available in supermarkets and ethnic grocery stores. Whenever Amma made this thuviyal, I was enthralled by the way she held each katarikai (eggplant) over the open flames of her kerosene stove—initially with her bare fingers and subsequently with tongs, giving in to its hot, blistered skin, blackened with smoke. As soon as she was done making the thuviyal, I mixed it with a big mound of steamed rice drizzled with warm clarified butter. I especially enjoyed savoring every bite while sitting next to my sister Mathangi, because she could not even bear to look at the eggplant, let alone eat it; the texture reminded her of fish. How lucky for me that I didn't have that problem!

3 medium Asian or 1 medium regular eggplant (1¼ pounds), stems removed

1 tablespoon vegetable oil

1 teaspoon black mustard seed

1 tablespoon urad dal (split and hulled black lentils), sorted

¼ teaspoon hing (asafetida)

1 tablespoon finely chopped fresh cilantro

12 to 15 fresh karhi leaves

2 fresh Thai, cayenne, or serrano chilies, finely chopped

½ teaspoon salt

1. Preheat the broiler or a grill for direct heat.
2. In the broiler pan or a grill rack, cook the eggplant for 10 to 12 minutes, rotating every 3 to 4 minutes, until blackened. Let it sit covered in a medium mixing bowl for 5 to 6 minutes. Remove the blackened skin from the eggplant and mash the pulp with a fork.
3. In a small skillet, heat the oil over medium-high heat; add the mustard seed. When it begins to pop, cover the skillet. As soon as the seed finishes popping, add the urad dal and hing. Stir-fry for 30 seconds, or until the dal is golden brown.
4. Remove the pan from heat and stir in the remaining ingredients. Add to the mashed eggplant and mix well. Serve either chilled or at room temperature. Will keep in the refrigerator for a week or in the freezer for 2 months. Thaw in the refrigerator overnight or microwave on low power.

Makes about 1 cup. Serves 8

MIRCHI CHUTNEY
Roasted Chilies Condiment

I hanker for this chutney with a plateful of Rotlis (page 182). Throw in a bowl of cool plain yogurt and you have a winning combination—the potent, angry Shiva-like chutney mellowed by his beautiful, even-keeled wife Parvati-like yogurt.

6 tablespoons vegetable oil

1 pound banana or Anaheim
  peppers, seeded

1 teaspoon black mustard seed

½ teaspoon hing (asafetida)

1 teaspoon fenugreek seed, roasted
  and ground (see note)

1 teaspoon salt

1. In a wok or 12-inch skillet, heat 2 tablespoons oil over medium-high heat. Add the peppers and stir-fry for 10 minutes or until the skins start to blister. Let cool and finely mince in a food processor or blender.
2. In the same wok, heat the remaining oil over medium-high heat; add the mustard seed. When it begins to pop, cover the skillet. As soon as the seed finishes popping, add the remaining ingredients and the minced chilies. Stir-fry for 2 to 3 minutes to blend the flavors. Cool and refrigerate for up to 2 weeks or freeze for up to a month.

Makes about 1 cup

- I guarantee you a coughing fit when you stir-fry chilies. Please do yourself (and anyone nearby) a favor and ensure proper ventilation when undertaking this task.

- Banana peppers are light green, and about 3 to 4 inches long and 1 inch in diameter. Anaheim peppers are darker green and slightly longer and thicker (and less hot) than banana peppers. Throw in a few Thai, cayenne, or serrano chilies with the milder chilies for an "uplifting" experience. Bell peppers are very sweet but use them if you are so inclined. Thai chilies with bell peppers also provide a good balance.

- To toast fenugreek seed, preheat a small skillet over medium-high heat. Add the seed and roast for 1 to 2 minutes, shaking the pan occasionally, until the seed acquires a nutty aroma and a darker reddish-brown shade. Cool and grind with a mortar and pestle or in a spice grinder.

KISHMISH CHUTNEY
Golden Raisin Relish

It was a treat, growing up in a middle-class home, to eat nuts and raisins on special occasions. My favorite combination was mellow, plump raw cashews with sugary sweet golden raisins. Lali and Amma had to hide them from me for fear of their imminent disappearance, making them unavailable for cooking. My puppy-dog eyes and upside-down smile always curried favor as I sat in my corner not unlike Little Miss Muffet eating cashews and golden raisins. So it was unconscionable to me that Amma made a triple batch of this chutney when I could have appreciated the raisins on their own, in all their dried glory. However, my first bite of this sweet, hot relish nestled in a morsel of Besan Palak Thepla (page 192) replaced my reluctance with downright lusty pleasure.

2 tablespoons vegetable oil
6 whole cloves
2 three-inch cinnamon sticks
1 cup golden raisins
1 cup water
½ cup sugar

½ teaspoon cardamom seed
   (removed from pods), ground
½ teaspoon ground red pepper
   (cayenne)
Juice of 1 medium lime

1. In a 1-quart saucepan, heat the vegetable oil over medium-high heat. Add the cloves and cinnamon sticks and sizzle for about 30 seconds.
2. Add the raisins and stir-fry for 1 to 2 minutes, or until they plump up. Stir in the remaining ingredients and bring to a boil. Lower the heat and simmer, uncovered, stirring occasionally, for 8 to 10 minutes, or until the chutney thickens and turns syrupy.
3. Cool and store in the refrigerator for up to 2 weeks.

Makes about 1 cup

TAMATAR CHUTNEY
Tomato Relish with Coconut

I was amazed how quickly a few ingredients, when used in just the right way, yielded astonishingly complex flavors. I can still vividly imagine Akka, my grandmother, sitting cross-legged on the kitchen's terrazzo floor, crushing the ingredients in the kaloral, a porous gray-stoned mortar and pestle. As she mashed the tomatoes, coconut, herbs, and chilies, the folds of creased skin under her arms shook in harmony to her cyclical motions.

Now, her heavy kaloral has unfortunately been pushed aside to the unused kitchen accoutrement pile to make way for the speedier, noisier, electric blender and food processor. The granite-like stone lies still, collecting dust, but the memory of Akka's vigor remains.

For a simple lunch, I often perk up my Rotlis (page 182) with a few dollops of this tart chutney. You might even try it as a spread on your morning toast to awake those sleeping buds.

❧ Tamarind provides an added acidity to the tomatoes along with an underlying earthy flavor. If unavailable, use 1 tablespoon freshly squeezed lime or lemon juice instead.

❧ This relish will keep for 4 days in the refrigerator or a month in the freezer.

½ pound tomatoes, coarsely chopped
1 tablespoon freshly shredded
   coconut (page 6)
1 tablespoon coarsely chopped fresh
   cilantro
½ teaspoon tamarind concentrate

½ teaspoon salt
1 to 2 fresh Thai, cayenne, or
   serrano chilies
1 tablespoon vegetable oil
½ teaspoon black mustard seed

1. In a food processor or blender, puree all ingredients except the oil and mustard seed until smooth. Transfer to a small bowl.
2. In a small skillet, heat the oil over medium-high heat; add the mustard seed. When it starts to pop, cover until all the seed has popped. Immediately pour the oil-seed mixture into the tomato mixture. Stir well.

Makes about ¾ cup

Thénga Chutney
Coconut Chutney with Garlic

This garlic-spiked chutney is an essential condiment with many of south India's savory dumplings, pancakes, and crepes. This version is reflective of the Telugu- and Malayalam-speaking communities, and I have, over the years, grown to love it. Serve thénga chutney with Idlis (page 128), Masaala Dosai (page 196), or Uru-likazhangu Vadaas (page 54).

1 cup freshly shredded coconut
  (page 6)
½ cup water
1 teaspoon salt
4 medium cloves garlic

2 to 3 fresh Thai, cayenne, or
  serrano chilies
1 tablespoon vegetable oil
1 teaspoon black mustard seed
8 to 10 fresh karhi leaves

1. In a blender or food processor, puree all ingredients except oil, mustard seed, and karhi leaves until the mixture has the texture of a thick pesto. Transfer to a mixing bowl.
2. In a 6-inch skillet, heat the oil over medium-high heat; add the mustard seed. When it begins to pop, cover the skillet. As soon as the seed finishes popping, remove the lid and splutter the karhi leaves in the hot oil. Add the oil-seed mixture to the pureed chutney and mix well. The chutney will keep in the refrigerator, covered, for 4 days or in the freezer for a month.

Makes about 1½ cups

Mithai
Sweets

Anjir Kulfi
Fig Ice Cream

Tayyar Aaphoos Ki Kulfi
Alphonso Mango Ice Cream

Boondi Laadoos
Garbanzo Bean Flour Pearls with Raisins

Pista Kulfi
Pistachio Ice Cream

Kaaju Katri
Cashew Squares

Pal Paysam
Creamy Rice Pudding

Aam Lassi
Sweetened Yogurt with Mangoes

Aam-Papaya Nu Shrikhand
Cardamom-Scented Yogurt Cheese with Mango and Papaya

Maangai Sharbat
Sweetened Unripe Mango Juice with Cardamom

ANJIR KULFI
Fig Ice Cream

Figs offer a wonderfully grainy texture to this ice cream. Their inherent sweetness is cherished by many an Indian and permeates every market after the monsoons. I grew up on the many varieties available in India but favored the purple-black ones the most.

In the United States, fresh figs make their appearance between June and October. They do not need to be reconstituted. Puree them fresh (after stemming them) and add to the chilled reduced milk before freezing the ice cream batter.

Using a wide-rimmed saucepan expedites the milk's evaporation, making for a speedier reduction.

"Anjir khao béta" ("Please eat these figs, son"), coaxed Ameena Aunty, as she adjusted her gold-edged, burgundy churidar around her beautiful gray hair and pushed the silver platter filled with figs toward me. Their color reminded me of the time when my friend Abdul, her son, pinched my arm with vicious glee as I watched the afflicted area turn purple-black. The churidar's silky fabric kept falling back on his Ammi's shoulder but she continued to replace it. Hafeez Uncle, her husband, sat across from her, and she had to show her respect by never exposing her tresses in public. She offered to cut the fruit into slices as she mistook my hesitation for ignorance blended with shyness. Of course I had eaten them before and, yes, I was aware of their juicy flesh and grainy texture. But I appreciated her fuss and was willing to be the object of her caring affection. As she handed me the wedges my mouth began to water. Soon enough, it savored that familiar sweetness.

I had always seen the fruit on its own, never pureed and chilled in creamy suspension, until I visited the newly opened Kwality Ice Cream Boutique by the Gateway of India. One lick of the fig ice cream took me back to Ameena Aunty's warmth, and I wondered if she would have been amused at my total lack of hesitation now.

8 cups whole milk

3 dried figs

½ cup fat-free, cholesterol-free egg product (like Egg Beaters)

½ cup sugar

1. In a large, wide-rimmed saucepan or Dutch oven, bring the milk to a boil over medium-high heat, stirring constantly to prevent scorching. Add the figs and continue cooking the milk down, for 50 minutes to 1 hour, stirring occasionally and scraping the sides of the pan to release collected milk solids, until the milk is reduced to 2 cups. Remove the figs from the milk.

2. Remove the stem end of the figs and puree them in a food processor or blender. Add the fig paste to the reduced milk. Refrigerate for at least 2 hours until well chilled.

3. In a large bowl, with an electric mixer on medium speed, beat together the egg substitute and sugar, scraping the bowl constantly, until the mixture is smooth and creamy yellow.

4. Add the reduced milk-fig mixture and continue beating for 2 to 3 minutes until well blended.
5. Transfer the ice cream batter to an ice cream maker. Freeze per manufacturer's instructions.

Makes about 1 quart

Tayyar Aaphoos Ki Kulfi
Alphonso Mango Ice Cream

❧ Unfortunately, fresh Alphonso mangoes are not exported into the United States. Their pulp is extracted and canned for overseas shipment. I find this tasty enough and not fibrous. Indian grocery stores and other ethnic markets always stock the canned Alphonsoes.

❧ If you are using fresh mangoes, peel them, then score the pulp as close to the pit as possible. Cut the pulp off the pit and process it until smooth before adding it to the reduced milk base.

❧ You will be amazed at this ice cream's richness with only four ingredients.

It was an early June afternoon, and the torrential rains had finally come. In addition to offering relief from the oppressive heat, the rains brought a much-awaited spectacle: vendors carrying wicker and crate baskets balanced adroitly on their heads, sweat and rain pouring down their backs, bellowing into the neighborhood with near-hoarse voices, "Tayyar ratnagiri aaphoos." This was far more alluring to me than the sound of ice cream trucks that made the Little Rascals scurry toward them in the American black-and-white film that I watched on Thursday-at-the-movies at St. Xavier's Boys' Academy. Even though they were extremely pricey at the onset of monsoons, Lali always pampered us with those saffron-hued, orange-red, oval-shaped gifts from heaven—mangoes called Alphonsoes (aaphoos) from the village of Ratnagiri close to Mumbai in the western state of Maharashtra.

The vendor was glad to lower his heavy load and wipe his brow with his stonewashed cotton rag. We helped him open the crate and push aside handfuls of light yellow hay. There were the warm fruits, perfectly colored and sweetly musky when held to our noses. Now started the negotiations, a painful bargaining that we had to endure before the crate was dragged across the threshold into our small kitchen. "Fifty rupees a dozen, memsahib," he purred, twirling his unkempt, bushy black mustache. Lali grabbed the mangoes from our greedy paws and placed them back in the crate. "Arré behenji, what are you doing? Why are you disappointing these poor bucchas?" he questioned, waving his banana-thick fingers toward our disappointed faces. "Highway robbery." Lali's eyes narrowed. "Twenty-five rupees a dozen is all they're worth." He shook his head in disbelief and started packing the crate. "My bucchas will starve with these prices." The door was pulled shut as he sat collecting his thoughts. Seconds later the doorbell rang and Lali opened the door. "Forty rupees, behenji," he pleaded, but the door shut once again.

This went on twice more and then he just gave in. "For you, maaji, and for your sweet bucchas, I give you twenty-five rupees a dozen." I couldn't help notice how Lali had transformed from an English-influenced memsahib to a sisterly bhenji to the hard-nosed maaji in ten minutes. The vendor walked back on to the streets to burden himself with yet another crate and the next haggling customer, bringing his luscious wares to Mumbai's millions.

I, on the other hand rinsed off a warm Alphonso, tearing open its tender flesh with my teeth. I discarded the skin. All that was left now was the juicy pulp, firm around the hard pit. With orange-colored juices dripping down my slippery fingers, hands, and elbows, I inhaled every last bit until all that was left was the bald pit. Well worth the price!

8 cups whole milk
½ cup fat-free, cholesterol-free egg
   product (such as Egg Beaters)

½ cup sugar
1 cup canned Alphonso mango pulp

1. In a large, wide-rimmed saucepan or Dutch oven, bring the milk to a boil over medium-high heat, stirring constantly to prevent scorching. Continue cooking the milk down, for 50 minutes to 1 hour, stirring occasionally and scraping the sides of the pan to release the collected milk solids, until the milk is reduced to 2 cups.
2. Cool the reduced milk and refrigerate for at least 2 hours until well chilled.
3. In large bowl, with an electric mixer on medium speed, beat together the egg substitute and sugar, scraping the bowl constantly, until the mixture is smooth and creamy yellow.
4. Add the reduced milk and mango pulp and continue beating for 2 to 3 minutes until well blended.
5. Transfer the ice cream batter to an ice cream maker. Freeze per manufacturer's instructions.

Makes about 1 quart

BOONDI LAADOOS
Garbanzo Bean Flour Pearls with Raisins

Before south Indian weddings, these candied pearl balls are hand-shaped by the hundreds and placed in plastic bags for the groom's friends and family to take home after the festivities end. They symbolize the union of two people in marital harmony amid great south Indian religiosity and fanfare. I have rarely eaten boondi laadoos outside of weddings, and hence I yearn for invitations to Tamilian nuptials with somewhat alarming frequency.

3 cups water
2 cups sugar
½ teaspoon saffron threads
½ cup milk, slightly warm
3 cups garbanzo bean flour, sifted
1 teaspoon baking powder

Vegetable oil for deep-frying
½ cup raw cashews, coarsely
   chopped
½ cup golden raisins
½ teaspoon cardamom seeds
   (removed from pods), ground

1. In a 1-quart saucepan, bring the water and sugar to a boil over medium-high heat. Lower the heat and simmer, uncovered, for 25 to 30 minutes, or until the syrup reaches a single-thread consistency. Transfer the syrup to large bowl.
2. Steep the saffron threads in warm milk for 1 to 2 minutes until the milk is orange-yellow in color.
3. In a medium bowl, combine the flour and baking powder. Add the saffron milk and stir or whisk well to form lump-free batter the consistency of very thick pancake batter. Let the batter rest for 10 to 15 minutes.
4. In a wok or 3-quart saucepan, heat the vegetable oil (about 2 to 3 inches deep) over medium heat until a thermometer registers 350°.
5. Hold a small-holed colander over the hot oil. Pour in a third of the batter, and let it fall through into the oil in drops. Beads of pearl will float to the surface. Fry for 3 to 4 minutes, turning occasionally, until reddish brown and crispy. With a slotted spoon, remove the pearls and drain completely. Add to the syrup and stir well. Repeat twice with the remaining batter.
6. Add the cashews, raisins, and cardamom to the syrup and stir well. With greased hands, pick up about 3 tablespoons at a time of the pearl-syrup

mixture. Compress it in the palm of one hand, as you would squeeze a stress-reducer handball, to form golf ball–size rounds.

7. Store in an airtight container at room temperature or in the refrigerator. They will keep at room temperature for a week and in the refrigerator for 3 weeks.

Makes about 18 balls

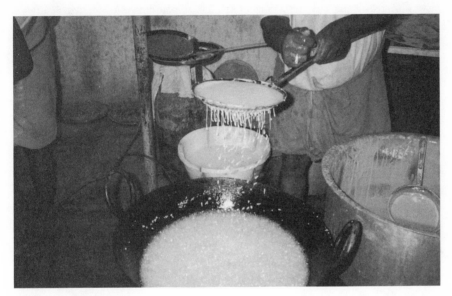

Making Boondi

Pista Kulfi
Pistachio Ice Cream

✂ Grind the pistachio nuts in a blender or food processor until they have the texture of coarsely ground black pepper.

This ice cream is not for the nut-challenged. The grainy texture of the pistachio nuts drives me wild and I indulge in it every chance I get. Although some gourmet stores carry pistachio extract or essence (and some commercial ice creams use them), the real deal in this recipe comes from splurging on raw pistachios nuts. Do yourself a favor and treat yourself to a big bowl of this icy, cream-laden piece of heaven after a hard day's work.

8 cups whole milk
½ cup fat-free, cholesterol-free egg product (like Egg Beaters)
½ cup sugar

½ teaspoon vanilla extract
1 cup raw pistachio nuts, coarsely ground (see note)

1. In a large, wide-rimmed saucepan or Dutch oven, bring the milk to a boil over medium-high heat, stirring constantly to prevent scorching. Continue cooking the milk down, for 50 minutes to 1 hour, stirring occasionally and scraping the sides of the pan to release the collected milk solids, until the milk is reduced to 2 cups.
2. Cool the reduced milk and refrigerate for at least 2 hours until well chilled.
3. In a large bowl, with an electric mixer on medium speed, beat together the egg substitute and sugar, scraping the bowl constantly, until the mixture is smooth and creamy yellow.
4. Add the reduced milk and vanilla and continue beating for 2 to 3 minutes until well blended.
5. Transfer the ice cream batter to an ice cream maker. Freeze per manufacturer's instructions, adding the nuts halfway through the process.

Makes 1 quart

KAAJU KATRI
Cashew Squares

Woohoo! That's my eloquent reaction each time I bite into a fresh batch of these amazingly easy to make cashew squares. Since they're quite rich, I limit myself to two pieces with a cup of Adrak Chai (Page 43) during those long, cold winters in the tundra of Minneapolis.

2 cups raw cashews
1 cup water
½ cup sugar
2 tablespoons Ghee (page 204) or
   unsalted butter

¼ teaspoon cardamom seeds
   (removed from pods), ground
   (optional)

1. Liberally grease an 8-inch round cake pan.
2. In a food processor or blender, pulse the cashews until they have the texture of fine breadcrumbs.
3. In a 1-quart saucepan, bring the water and sugar to a boil over medium-high heat. Lower the heat and simmer, uncovered, for 12 to 15 minutes, or until the syrup reaches a single-thread consistency.
4. Stir in the cashews a few tablespoons at a time, vigorously mixing with wooden spoon to prevent lumps from forming.
5. Add the butter and (optional) cardamom and continue stirring for 1 to 2 minutes until well blended.
6. Immediately transfer the mixture to the greased pan and spread it quickly. Score through with sharp knife into 1-inch squares. Let cool completely.
7. Gently lift out the pieces and refrigerate in an airtight container or zip-lock plastic bag. They will keep for 2 weeks.

Makes approximately 24 squares

❀ For a variation, use 1 cup cashews and 1 cup raw pistachio nuts.

❀ In the sweets shops across India, these delectable cashew squares are displayed and sold with a layer of thinly pounded pure silver (edible, of course) on top.

❀ The cardamom provides a wonderful methol-like flavor, and is often a hallmark of Indian desserts.

Pal Paysam
Creamy Rice Pudding

At least seven times a year pal paysam showed up at our dinner table, one for each of our birthdays. A wedding or a thread ceremony, in which a young boy was inducted as a Brahmin, was another excuse for this delicious symbol of prosperity and well-being. A birth in the family made the reason even sweeter. And so when Babloo came into our home, born to my sister Mathangi, the first male offspring since my birth twenty-three years before, the sweet, creamy rice pudding flowed.

He was beautiful—eyes as wide as the Ganges, skin as satiny soft as rice dumpling wrappers, and an adorable demeanor that would melt away the ire of any sadhu unnecessarily disturbed from an enlightened moment. The paysam's sweetness unfortunately turned bitter by his prognosis of severe microcephalia, a cerebral condition that meant he might survive only three months.

But he pulled through and beat the odds for a year, never being able to hold his large head atop broad shoulders, liquids gingerly forced down his constricting throat that drew choked breaths, tear-filled eyes, and a beatific smile on his wheat-complexioned face. Through it all Mathangi kept her emotions at bay. Her forty-year-old body was directed to have a second child soon to minimize the painful loss from Babloo's imminent departure from his uncomfortable world. As her belly expanded with the growing new baby, Babloo's struggle became more painful to watch. His breathing grew shallower as the nights floated by. The day Sriram was pushed out into the world, his charming, crinkly brow and toothless cry pierced Babloo's tender eardrums as he lay next to the newborn, offering a welcoming, tired smile.

As Sriram's lungs became stronger, Babloo's collapsed now that he had fulfilled his older brother's duties. He lay deathly still, freed from his cumbersome body next to his newly arrived sibling. Mathangi lay in between them, eyes reddened with heart-rending sorrow, feeding Sriram for the first time. A hormonal imbalance surged within her tired body, joyful for new life made possible by the pitiful one-way departure of a kind and gentle soul.

The same day, Babloo was lowered into a tiny coffin. He lay at peace in Mother Earth's ample womb as we all raised our katoris to our lips, filled with sugary paysam for the newborn.

½ gallon whole milk
½ cup uncooked basmati or long-grain rice

1 can (14 ounces) sweetened condensed milk

1. In a large, wide-rimmed saucepan or Dutch oven, bring the milk and rice to a boil over medium-high heat, stirring constantly to prevent scorching. Continue cooking the milk down, for 30 to 35 minutes, stirring occasionally and scraping the sides of the pan to release collected milk solids, until the milk is reduced to 5 cups.
2. Pour in the condensed milk and continue simmering for about 15 minutes. Serve warm or chilled.

Serves 6

AAM LASSI
Sweetened Yogurt with Mangoes

Let's face it, there are two purposes in every individual's life in India: get married and have children. As a child, I longed for the fanfare, the rituals, the hustle, and above all the special meals that were ladled and spooned onto large, lush green banana leaves at Indian weddings. So when my sister Mathangi reached the ripe age of twenty-five, my heart thumped faster with anticipated glee for the process to begin. Appa was no longer alive, so Lali, the family's father figure and eldest daughter, assumed the duties of finding that perfect match for her younger sister. Granted, Lali never conformed to the "traditional" role of a wedded mother, especially as an incredibly independent and successful unmarried physician, but she was the one who would bear Appa's wishes to fruition.

The first advertisement was placed in the matrimonial section of The Hindu, *whose pages were overwhelmed with south Indian men and women waiting for their impending nuptials with bated breath. They were all "fair-skinned" or "wheat-complexioned" individuals, touting their educational background and potential earning power. A caste affiliation was tossed in the ring along with glowing familial lineage and cushioned references to high-quality progeny. Added to the mix was Mathangi's simple ad:* Brahmin girl, very fair complexioned college graduate, seeks matrimonial correspondence from a Brahmin boy of similar stature.

Soon the mail forwarded from The Hindu *to Dr. L. R. Iyer's attention filtered into our home, each letter hoping to make that all-important first impression a great one. Being from the girl's side, we were supposed to be grateful for "further inquiry" from the potential groom. And if one happened to tweak our interests, the enclosed mandatory horoscope, detailing the position of the stars and planets at the time of the boy's birth, was set aside for perusal by our jyotishi, the know-it-all horoscope reader and predictor of the future from historical celestial presence. The stars of both the boy and girl had to match before even a viewing was possible. (The girl's horoscope was also dispatched to the boy's family's jyotishi for his approval.)*

Soon the viewing day arrived. Shivkumar was an engineer from a respectable family. He lived with his parents, a very common situation and a necessity in Mumbai's space-restricted tightness. Mathangi draped a beautiful purple-pink saree that offered a rich contrast to her wheat-colored skin. Her hair was bunched tight and held together by a small wreath of heavenly smelling jasmine flowers that rested against the back of her neck. The pink bindi on her forehead matched her blouse and glistened like morning dew against the pearls of nervous sweat adorning her brow.

Shivkumar was slightly taller than my five-feet-tall sister and his pockmarked face bore a bushy mustache and sallow eyes. After polite conversation, Mathangi entered the room with a tray of tall, sweaty glasses filled to the brim with frothy aam lassis. The mango yogurt shake coated Shivkumar's bristles as he ogled my sister. The eyes said it all and I knew he was bowled over by her reticent charm. After they left, Mathangi gave the okay to go ahead. The engagement took place soon after, and the invitations were printed. It was only then that Mathangi and Shivkumar started meeting in public places to "acquaint themselves." And acquaint Mathangi did.

It was a Sunday evening and we were huddled in front of the television. Mathangi ran into the house sullen and quiet, a reaction we never expected from a newly engaged woman who ought to be basking in the sunny glow of impending marital bliss. Lali cornered Mathangi in the bedroom and she revealed between sobs that she did not want to marry Shivkumar because he was an alcoholic. She was concerned that the "stigma" of being engaged and then not getting married would deter other prospects when the husband game recommenced at the start position. Mathangi was ready to remain single in her maternal home safe and content rather than enter into a marriage destined for misery and pain. Lali, the rock of Gibraltar that she was, broke off the engagement and shouldered every relative's discontent. Years later her fortitude was rewarded when Mathangi married a loving man who respected her for her compassion and love, not her wheat-complexioned Brahmin being.

1½ cups plain yogurt　　　　　　　¼ cup sugar
1½ cups ice cubes
¾ cup milk
¾ cup canned Alphonso mango pulp
　(see note with Tayyar Aaphoos
　Ki Kulfi, page 230)

Place all the ingredients in a blender. Blend on medium speed until well mixed and slightly frothy.

Serves 4

Aam-Papaya Nu Shrikhand
Cardamom-Scented Yogurt Cheese
with Mango and Papaya

❧ You can also use sweet green and red seedless grapes, halved, instead of mango and papaya. Apples offer a delicious crunch but discolor quickly unless you soak them in lime or lemon juice for a few minutes before folding them into the yogurt cheese (although this will impart an unwanted tartness to the finished dish). Use Asian pears and sweet ruby red pomegranate seeds when they are their juiciest best.

Every Gujarati-speaking household serves shrikhand on special occasions like family gatherings during holidays and auspicious religious events like weddings. During the months when mangoes and papayas infiltrate the marketplace, these tropical fruits are a must in this cool, creamy dessert. It is often served with hot-off-the-fryer Rava Pooris (page 194). I have, on many an occasion, shown up at the door of my Gujarati friends at mealtime, hoping to be "invited" in for this sinful combination. Thankfully, they never saw through my transparent ploy!

1 pound plain yogurt
1 cup powdered sugar
¼ teaspoon cardamom seeds
   (removed from pods), ground

1 medium ripe mango, peeled, pitted, and finely chopped
1 medium ripe papaya, peeled, pitted, and finely chopped

1. Line a colander with cheesecloth and place it in a large bowl. Let it drain for 1 hour at room temperature.
2. Refrigerate the lined colander and bowl, loosely covered, for 6 to 8 hours until the texture of the yogurt cheese is smooth and silky.
3. Discard the whey and transfer the cheese to a medium bowl. Fold in the powdered sugar, a few tablespoons at a time, until well incorporated. Stir in the cardamom.
4. Fold in the mango and papaya. Cover and refrigerate for about 2 hours or until chilled. This will keep for a week in the refrigerator or a month in the freezer.

Serves 6

Maangai Sharbat
Sweetened Unripe Mango Juice with Cardamom

This thirst-quenching beverage brings relief during the dog days of summer. Lali introduced me to this delicacy on my seventh birthday and it became an essential ritual every year after that. The cardamom adds a menthol-like perfume to the refreshing taste of cooked and chilled unripe mangoes.

1 large unripe mango (about 1½ pounds), peeled, pitted, and coarsely diced
6 cups water

½ cup sugar
½ teaspoon cardamom seed (removed from pods), ground

1. In a 2-quart saucepan, bring all ingredients to a boil over medium-high heat. Lower the heat and simmer, partially covered, for about 5 to 8 minutes, or until the mango pieces are tender. Let cool.
2. Transfer to a blender in batches and puree each until smooth. Serve chilled in tall iced glasses.

Serves 6

Raghavan Iyer with his Amma (mother) and sister Lali

✢ MAIL-ORDER SOURCES

Here are a few mail-order sources for Indian spices, legumes, and other groceries. Many others exist; check local listings. To locate an Indian grocery store near you, use www.members.tripod.com.

ASIA IMPORTS
1840 Central Avenue NE
Minneapolis, MN 55418
612-788-4571
www.asiaimportsinc.com

KALUSTYAN'S
123 Lexington Avenue
New York, NY 10016
212-685-3451
www.kalustyans.com

PENZEY'S SPICES
Multiple locations
800-741-7787
www.penzeys.com

ETHNIC GROCERS—Web site only
www.ethnicgrocer.com
www.namaste.com

❧ INDEX